W9-CDM-520

Class and Party in American Politics

TRANSFORMING AMERICAN POLITICS

Lawrence C. Dodd, Series Editor

Dramatic changes in political institutions and behavior over the past three decades have underscored the dynamic nature of American politics, confronting political scientists with a new and pressing intellectual agenda. The pioneering work of early postwar scholars, while laying a firm empirical foundation for contemporary scholarship, failed to consider how American politics might change or recognize the forces that would make fundamental change inevitable. In reassessing the static interpretations fostered by these classic studies, political scientists are now examining the underlying dynamics that generate transformational change.

Transforming American Politics brings together texts and monographs that address four closely related aspects of change. A first concern is documenting and explaining recent changes in American politics—in institutions, processes, behavior, and policymaking. A second is reinterpreting classic studies and theories to provide a more accurate perspective on postwar politics. The series looks at historical change to identify recurring patterns of political transformation within and across the distinctive eras of American politics. Last and perhaps most important, the series presents new theories and interpretations that explain the dynamic processes at work and thus clarify the direction of contemporary politics. All of the books focus on the central theme of transformation—transformation in both the conduct of American politics and in the way we study and understand its many aspects.

BOOKS IN THIS SERIES

Class and Party in American Politics

Jeffrey M. Stonecash
Department of Political Science, Maxwell School,

Syracuse University, and Professor-in-Residence,

New York Assembly

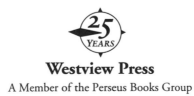

Westview Press

A Member of the Perseus Books Group

Transforming American Politics

All rights reserved. Printed in the United States of America. No part of this publication may be reproduced or transmitted in any form or by any means, electronic or mechanical, including photocopy, recording, or any information storage and retrieval system, without permission in writing from the publisher.

Copyright © 2000 by Westview Press, A Member of the Perseus Books Group

Published in 2000 in the United States of America by Westview Press, 5500 Central Avenue, Boulder, Colorado 80301-2877, and in the United Kingdom by Westview Press, 12 Hid's Copse Road, Cumnor Hill, Oxford OX2 9JJ

Visit us on the World Wide Web at www.westviewpress.com

Library of Congress Cataloging-in-Publication Data
Stonecash, Jeffrey M.
  Class and party in American politics / Jeffrey M. Stonecash.
    p. cm.
  Includes bibliographical references and index.
  ISBN 0-8133-9756-1 (pbk.)
  1. Political parties—United States. 2. Social classes—United States. 3. United States—Politics and government—1945–1989. 4. United States—Politics and government—1989– I. Title. II. Series.

JK2261 .S86 2000
324.273'09'045—dc21

                                                                      00-027528

The paper used in this publication meets the requirements of the American National Standard for Permanence of Paper for Printed Library Materials Z39.48-1984.

10   9   8   7   6   5   4   3   2   1

Contents

Illustrations

Tables

Figures

Boxes

Preface

This book involves an enduring interest of mine: How politics structures a debate about equality of opportunity in society. Do parties organize the electorate to create a party system in which voters with differing interests have means of articulating their concerns? The analysis is also a testimony to the importance of periodically reassessing conventional wisdoms. For some time I read the literature on American politics that argued Democrats had alienated the white working class and that class political divisions were steadily declining. It seemed odd to me that working-class whites would move to a party that has not always expressed great concern for their difficulties in a rapidly changing economy. That led me to borrow the National Election Studies cumulative file from Joe Cammarano, a colleague, and assess the association between class and party voting over time. In the analysis, I presumed that the important matter was the effect of relative income position of respondents. I assumed that people with less income would have different partisan inclinations from those with more income. Although this seemed appropriate to me, I was unaware that most scholars examine class political divisions by asking people to identify their class and then examining how the "middle" or "working" class voted.

The results were clear and very surprising. Since the 1950s less-affluent whites have not deserted the Democratic Party. Indeed, the pattern is opposite to what is often stated. Less-affluent whites did not vote strongly for Democrats in the 1950s. Their political support—voting and party identification—for Democrats has increased over time. The results seem very important to me for understanding post–World War II American politics. What analysts think happened does not appear to have happened; what has happened is important for understanding current partisan political disputes in Washington about public policy.

I do not presume that this book will in any way resolve the issue of how political divisions have evolved in recent decades. I hope it serves to prompt a fresh look at what has happened to electoral divisions in the last four decades. There is much to reexamine and sort, and this analysis is no more than a start. I hope the analysis presented in this book, simple as it is, will accomplish that. I also hope these findings prompt a reconsideration of how the less affluent and their grasp of politics and public policy debates are seen.

Finally, a note about my perspective. In most social science analyses I would not presume that my perspective is a central issue. In this analysis, however, I am assessing class political divisions. I have been impressed by the unease with which many academics react when I use the phrase "class politics." I suspect that they immediately presume that I am an ideological Marxist, more likely to argue for a framework than to present evidence. I am not a Marxist, though I have always thought it is fairly obvious that the less affluent face significant cumulative inequalities and are not treated well within capitalism. I am a moderate—somewhat liberal on some issues, somewhat conservative on others, and a tortured, ambivalent moderate on many issues. I regularly do political polls for Republicans and Democrats.

If I have a primary normative commitment, it is to what I have always found so fundamental to V. O. Key's work: The importance in democracy of diverse views being represented and a full dialogue over what public policy should be. My impetus to conduct this analysis is to explore whether, amid economic change, the electoral conditions prevail for the haves *and the have-nots* to have their concerns expressed. Clearly, our society has diverse needs. We need to provide equality of opportunity and to protect the rewards of achievers. It is my impression that the academic literature has supported the conclusion that the Democrats cannot play the role of raising the issue of equality of opportunity. My hope is that this book will enable us to take another look at the ability of our democracy to have a full and sustained debate about these competing needs.

Pursuing this project was helped enormously by various kinds of support. My colleagues took these results seriously and urged me to pursue the project. Tom Patterson was particularly encouraging about the project's importance in the early stages, which I greatly appreciate. I also thank Suzanne Mettler, Grant Reeher, and Rogan Kersh for encouragement and their willingness to read drafts. Kristi Andersen read an earlier draft, and I greatly appreciate her comments and suggestions. I have been privileged to work for some years with Robert Pecorella of St. John's University as professor-in-residence in the New York Assembly Intern Program, which Jim Murphy presides over with a gentle hand. That experience has provided a remarkable political education that has helped me think about the issues this book addresses. Bob read the manuscript, and his encouragement and comments were of great help. The dean of the Maxwell School, John Palmer, provided invaluable help in the form of a summer grant to hire a graduate student to help me review existing studies in the academic literature about class, race, and cultural issues over the last twenty-five years. Mark Brewer handled that task, and no one could have done a better job. His judgment about what is important in analyses was superb, and his ability to concisely summarize literature was indispensable. His help on this project was invaluable.

Jeffrey M. Stonecash

Class and Party in American Politics

1

Inequality and Political Debate: The Failed Role of Democrats

We live in a capitalistic society. The private market, with minimal constraints, determines the distribution of wealth in society. That process, plus the inheritance of opportunities and wealth from prior generations, invariably creates inequalities in the distribution of income, wealth, and opportunities in society. Many people see the inequalities as natural, unremarkable, even beneficial, rewards for achievements and penalties for not achieving. Further, it is widely argued that inequalities can be overcome through individual effort and that government programs are unnecessary.

Others regard the inequalities of American society as the product of family wealth and background, as fundamentally unfair, and perhaps even illegitimate in a society that professes to believe in equality of opportunity. These critics argue that one's background shapes opportunities and subsequent life chances and that society should adopt policies to increase equality of opportunity.

We also live in a political democracy. The political process is the mechanism for members of society to register their reactions to inequalities. It is through this process that ideas filter about what constitutes fairness and justice. It is also through this process that we debate what actions, if any, should be taken to try to respond to the inequalities that emerge from the private market.

Political debates about whether and how society should respond are crucial in a democracy. They are the means by which groups can argue about the legitimacy of the social order and make their case for whether change is needed. Less-affluent people and their sympathizers use the political process to make their case about the need for policies to create more equality of opportunity for the less-affluent population. Opponents to redistribution use the process to protect their interests. They argue for the importance of incentives and rewards to achievers and the dangers caused by interference in the outcomes of private markets. The debate is crucial. It is the means to decide whether actual conditions have become too divergent from ideals about opportunity and whether society should respond (Hochschild 1995: 15–38).

This debate is more important for the less affluent. Although affluent people need to make their case for the merits of differential rewards, they already possess income and opportunities. Their goal is not redistribution and they do not need to bring about change. If there is to be a challenge to the legitimacy of inequality, the argument for policies to respond must come from the less affluent. The mechanism to carry that debate on a mass scale is a political party. A party acts as a collection of individuals with some rough commonality of interests. That commonality may be tenuous and it may be a struggle to maintain unity, but the party serves to bring together like-minded individuals. Only a party can both carry sustained debate about the broad issue of equality of opportunity and create the unity to enact specific policies to respond to constituents' concerns (Key 1949: 307–312). Academics, think tanks, and government studies may provide the grist for such debates, but only party candidates can command the attention of large numbers of individuals and organize them into a coalition. This sense of commonality and willingness to identify with each other then creates the potential to enact changes to serve the interests of those identifying with the party.

The role of raising the issue of inequality has fallen to the Democratic Party since at least the Great Depression. That does not make Democrats more moral than Republicans, as some might suggest. Rather, Democrats have a constituency that makes them more concerned about such issues, so they are more inclined to carry the argument for policies to increase equality of opportunity.

Conventional Wisdom

Even as inequality has increased over the last three decades, a conventional wisdom has developed that Democrats have stumbled in their ability to address equality of opportunity issues. This analysis challenges that wisdom, but it is important to explain the various strands of research that have come together to form this conclusion. By many accounts, during the 1970s the Democratic Party lost its focus on economic issues. It betrayed the principles that had kept it in power for so long and alienated much of the New Deal coalition. It became too liberal and too identified with a host of cultural issues—civil rights, civil liberties, feminism, abortion, and gay rights (MacInnes 1996; Edsall and Edsall 1991b: 137–214)— and drove southerners away (Black and Black 1987: 232–256). "Like a hapless victim run over by a truck" (Bonafede 1981: 317), the party floundered, burdened with a liberal image on cultural issues. Democratic elites worried more about people who had failed—welfare recipients and criminals from disadvantaged backgrounds—than those who worked hard and "played by the rules" (Greenberg 1996: 36–44). To critics, party elites worried more about the rights of gays and mothers on welfare with illegitimate children than about workers losing jobs (Miller et al. 1988: 15). These preoccupations catered to the civil liberties concerns of affluent white liberals and drove away the party's core constituency—working-class whites—who felt neglected by out-of-touch leaders who didn't care about their values and problems.

The push for the Democratic Party to focus on civil liberties and civil rights issues originated among affluent, well-educated whites beginning in the late 1960s and early 1970s (Ladd and Hadley 1975: 181–221) and continuing into the 1980s (Pierce and Hagstrom 1980; Sundquist 1985: 11–13) and the 1990s. These elites are more supportive of egalitarian cultural tolerance than the middle to lower socioeconomic cohorts. Their support for civil rights, free speech, and gay rights presumably alienated working-class whites and drove them away from the Democratic Party. The result was division among working-class blacks and whites about what role government should play in shaping opportunities.

> The moderately egalitarian New Deal liberalism that produced majorities from the start of the Great Depression through the election of Lyndon Johnson has been undermined by the competition between constituencies and interests that now differ sharply about the meaning of equality. (Edsall 1992: 7)

The result has been alienation of the white working class and the decline of New Deal class political divisions. In this view, affluent whites vote more Democratic than less-affluent whites. That conclusion has become widely stated by academics, who concluded that the adoption of these positions cost the party its most crucial electoral base.

> There has been an inversion of the old New Deal relationship of social class to the vote. In wide sectors of public policy, groups of high socioeconomic status are now more supportive of equalitarian (liberal) change than are the middle to lower socioeconomic cohorts (within white America); and as a result liberal (often, although not always, Democratic) candidates are finding higher measures of electoral sustenance at the top of the socioeconomic ladder than among the middle and lower rungs. (Ladd and Hadley 1975: 27)
>
> Contrary to Key's scenario [of change in the South], however, the Democratic party also became less popular among white working-class southerners. The party's identification with civil rights in particular and social change in general provoked enormous irritation. . . . Although the region's white

workers did not ordinarily convert to Republicanism, they certainly became less Democratic between 1952 and 1984. (Black and Black 1987: 246)

As the Democratic party mobilizes black voters, the party becomes more dependent upon black support, causing many whites to leave the party. When whites defect, the Democratic coalition becomes still more dependent upon black votes, resulting in more white defections, and so it goes (79). Quite simply, the Democratic party was not big enough to accommodate both blacks and whites. Racial hostility, particularly on the part of lower-status whites, meant that race served to splinter the Democratic coalition. (Huckfeldt and Kohfeld 1989: 84)

. . . the Democratic nominating process often produced candidates who were seen as too liberal by much of the general electorate. . . . the association of the national Democratic Party with civil rights and the aspirations of blacks had the effect of alienating millions of white Democrats, including southerners and blue-collar northerners, who felt that black gains came at their expense. (Ginsberg 1996: 9)

Consultants and political commentators have concurred with how the Democratic Party's image evolved.

Whom did the party represent? With whom did it identify itself? There was a widespread sentiment, expressed consistently in the [focus] groups that the Democratic party supported giveaway programs—that is programs aimed primarily at minorities. This was no longer a party of great relevance to the lives of middle-class Americans. (Greenberg 1996: 44)

. . . after 1968, the Democrats stood in the public's eye for a new kind of liberalism, one that spelled permissiveness and moral nihilism, and that ignored and ridiculed the conservative desires of white ethnic working-class Americans who once voted for the Democrats as a matter of ritual. Once the Democrats were seen as supportive of both exotic lifestyles and revolutionary rhetoric, it was only a matter of time before working class Democrats would be driven straight into the waiting arms of conservative Republicans. (Radosh 1996: xi)

Finally, journalists, drawing on existing research and providing their own interpretations, have come to treat the conclusions as accepted wisdom.

The overlapping issues of race and taxes have permitted the Republican party to adapt the principles of conservatism to break the underlying class basis of the Roosevelt coalition . . . (3) . . . race has become a powerful wedge, breaking up what had been the majoritarian economic interests of the poor, working and lower-middle classes in the traditional liberal coalition (4). Working-class whites and corporate CEOs, once adversaries at the bargaining table, found common ideological ground in their shared hostility to expanding government intervention. (Edsall and Edsall 1991b: 154)

... one of the defining traits of American politics over the [last] 25 years has been the defection of working-class, white voters, especially men, from the Democratic Party. (Kohlbert and Clymer 1996: A-23)

The scrambling—in bad years, the reversal—of Lubell's calculus [that Democrats do better among the lower class] is by now a given in American politics: there is no longer a Democratic tilt within the white working class (79). The growing Democratic estrangement from the white working class has been a staple of political analysis and commentary at least as far back as 1970. (Meyerson 1996b)

Many people see the Democrats' situation as part of a broader transformation in the substantive focus of American political debates and in the electorate and the political process. To some, greater general affluence since World War II has reduced the significance of material conflicts (Inglehart 1971; Ladd and Hadley 1975: 195–200). Instead of issues of class and opportunity creating political divisions, new issues are dominating American politics, dividing the electorate along different lines. Some scholars think race has become the great "transforming issue" in American politics (Carmines and Stimson 1989: 14). Many whites have negative attitudes toward blacks and they see welfare and redistribution programs as largely benefiting undeserving blacks (Gilens 1995: 601; Gilens 1996: 1010). The new electoral cleavages in American politics revolve around racial issues (*New York Times* 1988: A-25; Oreskes 1988: 1; McWilliams 1989: 199; Goldfeld 1997). Others see clashes over cultural issues as dominating political conflicts (Edsall and Edsall 1991b; Rae 1992). The new lines of division are between those who differ about affirmative action, abortion, gay rights, school prayer, and family values. As Ben Wattenberg (1995: 13, 75–96) argues, "values matter most." Others stress the role of religious divisions (Petrocik 1998; Layman 1999).

These new issues have displaced the economic issues that were the basis of the New Deal coalition. Class political divisions have steadily declined (Abramson 1974: 102–105; Ladd and Hadley 1975: 73 and 233–239; Ladd 1978a: 98; Ladd 1991: 31–33; Keefe 1994: 214; Abramson, Aldrich, and Rohde 1995: 146 and 152–153), and the inescapable conclusion is that the Democratic coalition is coming apart (Schneider 1984: 2131; Rae 1992: 629). The "New Deal coalition has crumbled" (Stanley and Niemi 1995: 237). The question is no longer if or how change occurred, but what the Democrats might do to recover (Bonafede 1983; Shafer 1985; Radosh 1996; Teixeira 1996: 67–69). The focus of debate becomes how much the party must move to the middle and how much the liberal elements of the party must be stifled to reposition the party in the middle (Penn 1998).

These changes have also affected the electorate and the political process. With economic issues fading in relevance, and without the clarity of political division and debate provided by those issues, the electorate's engagement with parties has declined. Successive generations of voters have become less attached to parties (Abramson 1976), independents have increased (Flanigan and Zingale 1998: 62–64), campaigns are seen as more candidate centered (Salmore and Salmore 1989; Aldrich and Niemi 1996), and the connection of parties to clear sets of constituents has declined (Ladd 1997; Shea 1999).

The arguments that Democrats have alienated the working class and that class divisions have declined have profoundly shaped the American democratic debate. It has become ". . . the new orthodoxy . . . haunting liberal intellectual life, an orthodoxy that waxes nostaligic about the New Deal to blame black political demands for the rightward turn in American politics. . . ." (Reed 1991: 336). The presumption is that it is not possible for a party to address issues of equality of opportunity, or, at least, equality of opportunity with reference to blacks, without losing its core white working-class electoral base.

> The dilemma the Democratic party faces is how to renew its appeal to the country's white middle-class majority—particularly the males—without abandoning its minorities, and therewith its principles. The polarization of the electorate in 1984 raised disturbing questions. Are the divisions in society so deep that a party can no longer champion the rights of blacks without losing whites? Of women without losing men? (Sundquist 1985: 15)

Democrats' inability to effectively raise questions about inequality is important for the party, but also for society in general. Lacking a party to mobilize, organize, and serve as an advocate for the less affluent results in the growth of inequalities, with no inclination to address them. This lack of a sustained debate over the inequality of opportunity for the less affluent has two consequences. First, without a party to serve as an advocate of their concerns, there are fewer policy benefits. As V. O. Key put it years ago, "Politics generally comes down, over the long run, to a conflict between those who have and those who have less. Over the long run, the have-nots lose in a disorganized politics" (Key 1949: 307). Second, there are also dangers for society. A society that experiences increasing inequality, with no means for the electoral expression of grievances about declining equality of opportunity, risks growing and frustrated polarization over the virtues and legitimacy of the system.

The role of the Democrats is essential to call attention to the ideals of equality of opportunity that are central to American society, and to contrast these ideals with the differential rewards that result from capitalism. Republicans, of course, have an equally important role to make an argument about the limits of and disincentives created by redistribution, but the crucial role in a world of extensive inequalities is that Democrats raise these issues. Critics within the Democratic Party base criticisms of their party on that expectation. William Galston has argued:

> American liberalism has always preached equality of opportunity.
>
> For two generations, starting with FDR, the Democratic party presided over the heroic age of American liberalism. Its vision was defined by the twin imperatives of general welfare and equal opportunity. Its historic mission was to mitigate the excesses of raw capitalism and to give excluded groups access to the mainstream of American life.
>
> . . . the decline of the Democratic party is a matter of national concern, because it has the unique capacity to challenge us to diminish the gap between our practices and our principles . . . (Galston 1985: 19–24)

Edsall and Edsall reiterated the argument with a broader focus:

> The fracturing of the Democratic coalition has permitted the moral, social, and economic ascendance of the affluent in a nation with a strong egalitarian tradition, and has also permitted a diminution of economic reward and of social regard for those who simply work for a living, black and white. Democratic liberalism—the political ideology that helped to produce a strong labor movement, that extended basic rights to all citizens, and that has nurtured free political and artistic expression—has lost the capacity to represent effectively the allied interests of a biracial, cross-class coalition. Liberalism, discredited among key segments of the electorate, is no longer a powerful agent of constructive change.
>
> As liberalism fails to provide effective challenge, the country will lack the dynamism that only a sustained and vibrant insurgency of those on the lower rungs can provide. Such an insurgency, legitimately claiming for its supporters an equal opportunity to participate and to compete and to gain a measure of justice, is critical, not only to the politics and the economics of the nation, but also to the vitality of the broader culture and to democracy itself. (Edsall and Edsall 1991a: 86)

For whatever reasons, the conclusion is that it is politically risky to raise issues of equality of opportunity, even at a time when inequality is increasing. The democratic debate must be constrained to cultural issues and middle-income issues. Making an argument for the positive role government can play is politically counterproductive. Class and redistributive issues are dangerous.

Not everyone, of course, has accepted these conclusions. Some argue that the case for the lower class must be made, and that the case must be made within the Democratic Party or advocates for the less affluent must leave the party (Kopkind and Cockburn 1984; Piven and Cloward 1997). Others argue that the evidence about the problems of the Democratic Party in maintaining support has simply been misread. To these critics the problem is that the party has muddled into the middle and has not given the public a legitimate alternative to the Republicans (Ferguson and Rogers 1984; Faux 1996: 91–205). They argue that the party will be successful if only it presents a clearer statement of the need to address inequalities in American society. The party must be more forceful in its critiques of Republican policies, for its own sake and for the American public (Sanders 1992).

Another Look: Reconsidering Political Trends

At the base of all the assessments of the fate of the Democratic Party and the state of American politics is the evidence about whether the Democratic Party alienated the white working class, and what has happened to class political divisions. It is the interpretation of evidence about electoral trends that has led to the conclusions just reviewed. The crucial question is whether the electoral trends of the last several decades support the conventional wisdom that has developed. Briefly stated, the argument to be presented here is that the evidence does not support these conclusions. Indeed, the evidence supports exactly the opposite conclusion. The evidence suggests a growing connection between economic inequality, party positions, and class political divisions.

There are several stories to be told in subsequent chapters about these changes. First, evidence of the demise of the Democratic Party is not so clear. The second is how inequality has increased in American society. The third is how the electoral bases and policy concerns of the parties, particularly with regard to class issues, have evolved over time. Fourth is how a connection between class and party developed over time. Finally, there is the issue of why this connection would be so widely missed and the conventional wisdom so easily accepted. Those stories are presented in separate chapters.

The implications of the evidence to be presented here are significant. If there is a connection between class and party, the conclusions about the plight of the Democratic Party need serious reconsideration. The Democratic Party may be in much better shape than we presume (Dionne 1997). It also suggests that the conclusions about the role of race and cultural issues in shaping electoral reactions and political divisions need reexamination. The issues dominating our democratic dialogues may well be other than many experts have assumed. Finally, the evidence to be presented here has considerable consequence for the argument that politics has become "candidate centered" and less focused on party positions.

Before all those implications can be discussed, however, there is a complex story of change to present. I begin with some evidence suggesting the need for reconsidering the conventional wisdom.

2

The Puzzling Survival of Democrats

It is widely argued that, beginning in the late 1960s, the Democratic Party began a series of missteps. Party leaders focused on issues that alienated their core electoral base, working-class whites. Support for civil rights, in particular, hurt the party. The political transition in the South is perhaps the most frequently cited evidence of the problems faced by Democrats. Within the South Republicans have steadily improved their political fortunes at all levels of government (Black and Black 1987). The erosion of support for Democrats in the South since 1946 in congressional and state legislative seats is shown in Figure 2.1. The percentage of seats held by Democrats has steadily declined since 1946 (Rohde 1991; Stonecash and Agathangelou 1997). The studies assessing this shift are numerous and consistent in their documentation of party decline in this region (Bullock and Rozell 1998: 3–21). The evidence is clear that southern conservative whites are steadily moving to the Republican Party (Black and Black 1987: 248–253).

Although the shift in partisan support in the South is impressive, significant problems arise from citing the party's decline in this region and concluding that the national Democratic Party is in decline. First, although Democrats have less support now in the South than they did fifty years ago, they still win a considerable proportion of seats in the region. The party's percentage of House and Senate seats as of 1998 is only slightly below the level of Democrats in the rest of the nation. Democrats still win many seats in the South (Glaser 1996: 12–13); focusing on their decline neglects people Democrats have retained as supporters in this region.

Long-Term Trends

The more interesting and important question has to do with the national situation of the Democratic Party. Although Democratic Party fortunes were steadily declining in the South, somehow the party was able to

FIGURE 2.1   Percentage of Seats Held by Democrats in South, by
              Legislative Body, 1946–1998

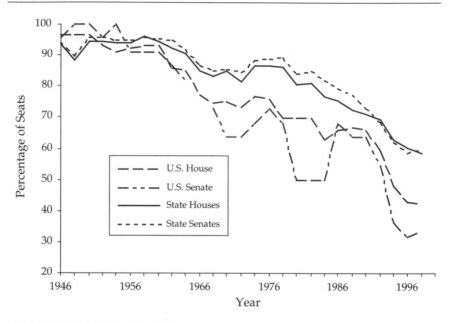

SOURCES: Data collected by author from *Congressional Quarterly* and *U.S. Statistical Abstract*.

maintain roughly the same number of seats in Congress for almost fifty
years. To be sure, the 1994 elections were a serious blow for Democrats
in Congress, but whether that election constitutes an enduring drop in
the party's situation or is more of a short-term change is yet to be seen.
For example, in 1996 and 1998 Democrats have gained seats in the
House. The interesting matter is the long-term trend, and as shown in
Figure 2.2, the overall proportion of seats held by the Democrats in the
House and the Senate remained relatively steady from the 1950s through
1992, even when the party was steadily losing seats in the South.

What changes have allowed the party to lose so badly in its former
stronghold and still survive as the majority party for so long (Petrocik
1981: 87)? Indeed, the organizing questions of this analysis are: Why have
Democrats been able to survive? Who has the party attracted and who
has it lost? What do these trends tell one about the current situation of
the Democratic Party and the possibilities for political debates about
equality of opportunity in American society?

The simple answer to how the Democratic Party has survived is that
the party has done relatively well outside the South, whereas the Republican Party has experienced losses outside the South (Bullock 1988: 569).
In the 1940s, the significant partisan divisions within the nation were

FIGURE 2.2   Percentage of Seats Held by Democrats in U.S. House and Senate, 1946–1998

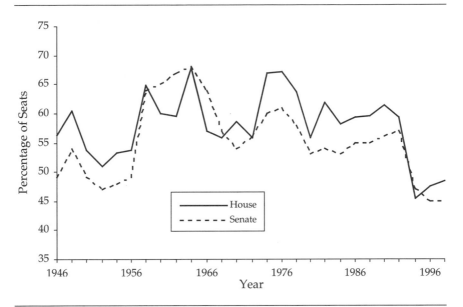

SOURCE: Data collected by author from *Congressional Quarterly.*

largely regional. The South was Democratic and the rest of the country was heavily Republican. Since then, the South and the non-South have moved in opposite directions. Figure 2.3 presents the trends in the percentage of U.S. House seats held by Democrats by region from 1946 to 1998. In 1946 the North[1] was almost 80 percent Republican, but there has been a steady decline in Republican success in that region since then (Speel 1998: 1–18, 24–26). Democrats now hold 57 percent of the seats in the North. The remainder of the country has also experienced movement toward the Democratic Party. In 1946 Democrats held 30 percent of the seats in states outside the South and North, and that percentage increased to 56 percent just before the 1994 elections. As of 1998, Democrats held 41 percent of the seats, a net gain since the 1940s of eleven percentage points. Although Democrats are allegedly experiencing long-term, relentless slippage, it is only in the South that this has occurred. The opposite has occurred elsewhere (Ladd and Hadley 1975: 54–55; Petrocik 1981: 77).

To a lesser degree, a similar pattern has prevailed in the U.S. Senate, as shown in Figure 2.4. The South has moved steadily toward the Republican Party since the 1940s. Outside the South seats held by Democrats was at 40 percent in the 1940s and the early 1950s. By the mid-1950s seats held by the Democrats increased to over 50 percent, and it has stayed at that level.

FIGURE 2.3   Percentage of U.S. House Seats Held by Democrats, by
Region, 1946–1998

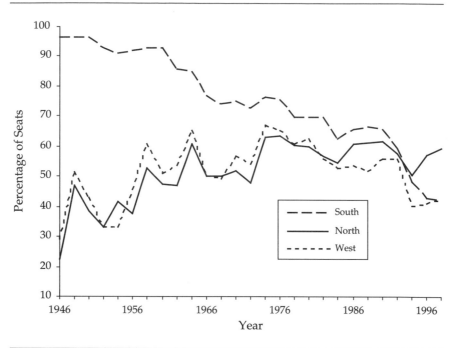

SOURCE: Data collected by author from *Congressional Quarterly.*

These regional trends are not confined to congressional elections alone. Figures 2.5 and 2.6 present the trends in the percent of seats held by Democrats in state houses and senates. The rise in Democratic success outside the South has occurred at both the national and state level. Although there is much to discuss about the erosion of Democratic support in the South, there is also much to inquire about the rise of Democratic support in the rest of the country. What has led to increased success of Democrats (and the decline of Republicans) outside the South at a time when the party is allegedly in decline? If Democrats have gained, what part of the population votes for Democrats who did not in the 1940s and 1950s? The answer may tell us much about whether Democrats have alienated the middle and working classes.

The Argument

Explaining the evolution of support for Democrats and Republicans and who has switched parties are the central concerns of this analysis. My ar-

FIGURE 2.4   Percentage of U.S. Senate Seats Held by Democrats, by
Region, 1946–1998

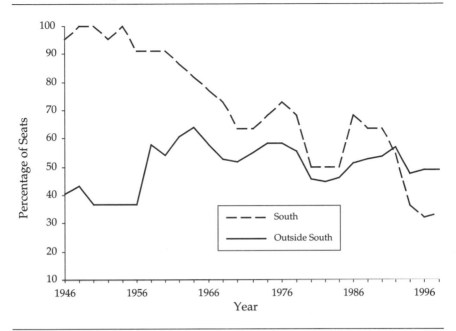

SOURCE: Data collected by author from *Congressional Quarterly.*

gument is that Democrats have not suffered losses, as many scholars have
presumed, among the less-affluent population outside the South. Quite
the contrary; the less affluent outside the South have become *more supportive* of Democrats in recent decades. In the South, despite all the
change, Democrats still win many seats and still do very well among the
less affluent, white and nonwhite. In contrast, more affluent people, particularly in the South, have moved to the Republican Party.

The impetus for these changes has been the interaction between changing social conditions, shifting party electoral bases, and party policy positions. The economic plight of the less affluent has deteriorated in recent
decades, whereas the more affluent have experienced economic gains. At
the same time, the parties have increasingly diverged on issues of class
and concern for equality of opportunity. These changes have produced a
gradual but steady realignment, resulting in increasing class divisions in
the electoral bases of the two parties.

Demographic and economic change have played a significant role in
prompting new political concerns. More blacks have registered in the
South, and created more of a liberal base for Democrats in that region.

FIGURE 2.5   Percentage of Seats Held by Democrats in State Houses,
by Region, 1946–1998

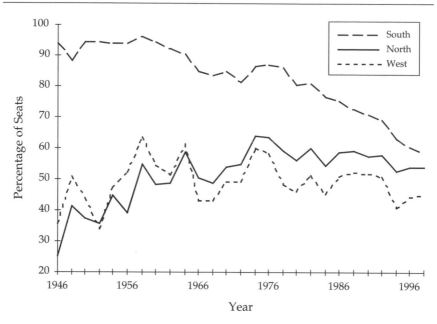

SOURCE: Data collected by author from *Congressional Quarterly.*

Blacks have also migrated outside the South and now provide a substantial electoral base outside the South for Democrats. New minorities, via immigration, now comprise a significant proportion of the electorate, and they have created an additional electoral base for Democrats. The movement of the affluent has also had significant political effects. The South and the Sunbelt have experienced an enormous influx of the affluent, creating new suburbs, and these areas tend to support Republicans.

Economic changes have also been very significant. The economy has undergone continual change, with steady job dislocation and growing inequality in the distribution of income. People in the bottom 40 percent of income distribution have experienced net declines in their real incomes; those in the top 40 percent have experienced net increases. Access to college has become more unequal and access to pension and health care programs continues to be unequal. The issue of inequality has also acquired considerable visibility, with annual announcements of data on increases in inequality.

The parties have responded very differently to these changes. They have adopted very different policy positions, which have in turn attracted

FIGURE 2.6   Percentage of Seats Held by Democrats in State Senates,
by Region, 1946–1998

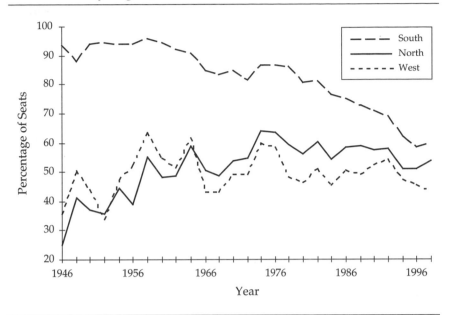

SOURCE: Data collected by author from *Congressional Quarterly*.

very different constituencies. Democrats have taken policy positions that
are more responsive to minority needs and relatively less-affluent people,
whereas Republicans have taken conservative positions that are more responsive to the needs and concerns of the more affluent and to business.
Democrats have been more willing to support progressivity in the tax system, more job training programs, and more aid for college; Republicans
have advocated tax cuts, lower capital gains taxes, and cuts in a broad
array of programs designed to benefit the less affluent. Contrary to other
studies, I argue that the combination of growing inequality and very different party responses to inequality has resulted in growing class political
divisions in American politics.

The implications of these changes are crucial. Although there is widespread commentary that the electorate is less engaged with parties, that
there are more independents, and that class divisions are declining in
American politics, the evidence I present suggests that the electorate has
seen differences between the parties and has sorted out their partisan
support accordingly. Democrats have not alienated the white working
class, and the capacity of the party to play its historical role in the democratic process has not been diminished. Indeed, I argue that the United

States is poised for a more focused debate than it has had in some time. The outcome will be determined by the reactions of the electorate, but the political conditions for a sustained debate about the role of government in shaping equality of opportunity have never been more conducive.

The primary focus of the next several chapters will be on class issues, with class defined by the relative position of individuals in the income distribution. Of course, there has been considerable commentary that race and cultural issues have become significant in recent decades. I do not disclaim the importance of those issues; race issues and racism are clearly important, as well as divisions over abortion, homosexuality, and civil liberties. I argue, however, that attention to these issues has led to sustained neglect of the growth of class divisions in American politics. My intent is to argue for a reassessment of class issues. This book will present evidence for the significance of class in American politics, and will return to the role played by race and cultural issues in Chapter 6.

NOTES

1. North includes Connecticut, Delaware, Illinois, Indiana, Maine, Maryland, Massachusetts, Michigan, Minnesota, New Hampshire, New Jersey, New York, Ohio, Pennsylvania, Rhode Island, Vermont, West Virginia, and Wisconsin. The South includes Alabama, Arkansas, Florida, Georgia, Kentucky, Louisiana, Mississippi, North Carolina, South Carolina, Tennessee, Texas, and Virginia. All others are placed in the "other" category, except Hawaii and Alaska, which are excluded.

3

Social Change and Anticipating Party Fortunes

Discerning the conditions that shape political trends is one of the more demanding challenges facing political commentators. It is also subjective. Analysts often see what they want to see in trends. To many analysts, demography is political destiny (Scammon and Wattenberg 1970: 45). It is presumed that social and economic conditions shape, if not determine, political behavior. For example, people who live in suburbs tend to vote more Republican. Drawing on that relationship, the presumption is that the greater the proportion of people living in suburbs, the greater the support for Republicans. Minorities, on average, have a greater need for government and are more likely to be supportive of government action. So, the higher the percentage of minorities, the better Democrats will do. Although there are always exceptions, enough evidence exists of the connection between social and economic conditions and partisan political behavior to attribute them a significant impact.

Other analysts emphasize the powerful role of ideas and values in shaping political trends. They argue that differences in views about the proper role of government and assessments of its efficacy shape public support for government. Some argue that values and views of which social practices should be endorsed or condemned by government are more important as sources of political views and partisan support than self-interest. Reactions to abortion, crime, and civil rights, for example, are seen by many analysts as important and more divisive than class issues.

Not only do analysts differ about whether demographic or ideological factors are more important in shaping politics, they also differ about whether trends in these areas over the last several decades have created conditions favoring Republicans or Democrats. In general, there are two competing interpretations of how social change has shaped which party and issues have come to dominate American politics. Each interpretation calls attention to particular trends and makes an argument about the impact on political debates and electoral divisions. Not surprisingly, each perspective reaches a different conclusion about whether Republicans or Democrats are best situated to dominate U.S. politics. Before examining political parties and electoral reactions to them, it is first necessary to review the differing views of how the context—social and economic conditions—of American politics has changed in recent decades.

The first set of trends involves changes that are seen as likely to favor Republicans. Over the last thirty years public opinion has become negative about the federal government and "big government," providing sentiment for Republicans to capitalize on. At the same time, more people have become middle class and more people have moved to the Sunbelt and the suburbs, where support for Republicans is likely to be greater (Galston 1985; Reddy 1991). In addition, troubling trends, such as increased crime and illegitimate births, suggest that social decline is occurring. Concern about these trends has given conservative Republicans an opportunity to emphasize personal responsibility and to appeal to voters worried about social decline. The combination of declining support for the national government, population growth in the Sunbelt and the suburbs, and concern about troubling social trends creates a political context conducive to Republicans gaining more support.

Other trends are seen as favoring Democrats. Although support for the national government, in the abstract, has declined, support for specific federal programs has not. Further, in recent decades issues revolving around inequality have become more prominent (Phillips 1991). Issues of equality of opportunity affect large segments of the electorate across their lifespan and provide a set of concerns Democrats can speak about to appeal to voters. As people have moved to the suburbs, the inequality in tax bases within metropolitan areas has increased. That creates schools with very unequal resources, which is a highly visible issue. Access to higher education has become more unequal over the last several decades. There is consistent evidence that there are growing inequalities in access to health care and pensions. Finally, there has been a steady increase in the percentage of the population that is Latino/Hispanic, and this population is likely to be less affluent. If social and economic conditions drive partisan behavior and inequality issues favor the Democrats, then societal trends indicate there is a growing electoral base that Democrats might attract.

These trends, and attempts to interpret them, constitute the political context of American politics that parties must respond to as they seek to build their electoral coalitions. Before examining the policy positions of the parties and reactions of the electorate, these shifting contexts need to be reviewed.

The Presumption of an Emerging Republican Majority

Declining Support for the National Government

Since the 1930s much of the Democrats' success has come from their ability to portray the national government as a means to respond to national problems and to present themselves as the party willing to use that power. In contrast, the Republicans have argued over the last several decades that expansion of the national government results in too much intrusion into citizens' lives and reduces freedom. They also argue that the national government is simply too big and removed from state and local conditions to effectively and efficiently try to shape policy. As Ronald Reagan stated in his 1981 presidential inaugural address, "Government is not the solution to our problems; government is the problem." The evolution of that party position will be reviewed in Chapter 4.

Republicans increasingly argue that their skepticism toward government represents the majority position, as reflected in the declining public trust in the national government. The decline in trust in the national government has been significant. Figure 3.1 presents the responses to an important question that has been asked since the early 1950s in national surveys. The question is: "How much of the time do you think you can trust the government in Washington to do what is right—just about always, most of the time, or only some of the time?" The figure shows the percentage of people who chose "just about always" or "most of the time" (Flanigan and Zingale 1998: 13). There has been a clear decline in trust in the national government since the 1960s (Craig 1996: 46–55).

There is also evidence that the public is less supportive of "big government." Since 1984 several polling organizations have asked the public whether they favor "smaller government with fewer services or larger government with many services." The responses since 1984 are shown in Figure 3.2 (Ladd 1998: 10–11). Although the electorate was divided almost evenly on this issue in the mid-1980s, by the 1990s support had clearly shifted toward a preference for smaller government. These trends have been the basis for the Republican belief that public support is moving to their position that government should play less of a role in our lives, and what power is exercised should be decentralized.

The Movement to the Sunbelt

Amid this decline in support for the national government, there is evidence that the population traditionally most likely to support Republicans is growing as a proportion of the electorate. The South and the states stretching from Texas to California are defined as the Sunbelt (Bernard and Rice 1985: 7). This region of the nation has been viewed for some time

FIGURE 3.1   Trust in the National Government, 1958–1996

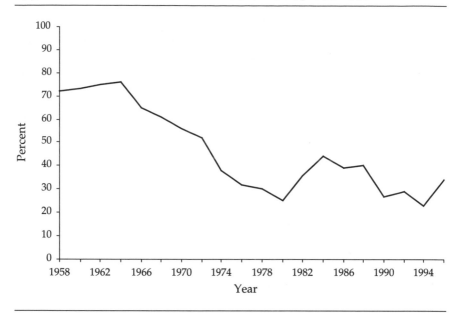

SOURCE: Flanigan and Zingale 1998: 13.

FIGURE 3.2   Support for Smaller or Larger Government, 1984–1996

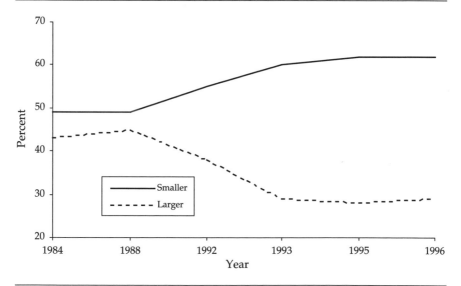

SOURCE: Ladd 1998: 10-11.

as more inclined to vote Republican (Phillips 1969: 7; Sale 1975). Polling data indicate residents in this region are more conservative than the rest of the nation (Erikson, Wright, and McIver 1993: 18). These areas are continually growing and a large base of affluent voters has emerged in these regions that did not exist forty years ago. The population moving to the Sunbelt is presumed to be more affluent, more likely to adhere to the spirit of individualism that has dominated in these states (Elazar 1984: 122–131), and therefore more likely to vote Republican. In addition, organizations such as unions that might facilitate political consciousness among the less affluent have lost membership in the nation, and their strength in the South and Sunbelt is very limited (Curme, Hirsch, and Macpherson 1990: 22–26), leaving individualism to dominate. As the Sunbelt continues to grow, and the Northeast and Midwest do not, a greater proportion of the nation will be in the Sunbelt and presumably more receptive to Republican appeals.

As the population shifts to the Sunbelt, it will also reduce the North's representation in the House of Representatives, which reflects the nation's population distribution, and in the electoral college, which is built around the number of seats a state holds in the House and the Senate. As Table 3.1 indicates, in the 1940s 52 percent of the nation's population lived in the North;[1] by 1990 it had declined to 42 percent. The greatest growth in population occurred in other regions of the nation and this distribution of House seats shifted accordingly. In the 1940s the North had 52 percent of all House seats; after the reapportionment, based on the 1990 census, it had only 41 percent of all seats in the House.

This population shift has also affected the distribution of electoral college votes for the presidency. A larger proportion of electoral votes now come from outside the North, which gives these areas more influence in

TABLE 3.1 The Declining Dominance of the North in Representation

	Percentage Distribution					
	Population			House Seats		
Year	North	South	Other	North	South	Other
1940	52.5	24.8	20.3	52.3	26.3	21.4
1950	51.2	24.8	23.0	51.9	26.4	21.8
1960	50.0	25.0	26.0	50.1	26.0	23.9
1970	48.9	25.3	25.0	48.5	26.4	25.1
1980	44.9	27.7	26.6	45.1	28.3	26.7
1990	42.0	29.0	28.1	41.8	30.1	28.1

SOURCE: Judd and Swanstrom 1998.

presidential elections. In the 1930s the fourteen states encompassing the Frostbelt[2] had approximately 240 electoral votes, and the Sunbelt states had 250 electoral votes. Now the Frostbelt's number of electoral votes is under 200, whereas the Sunbelt has almost 220 (Judd and Swanstrom 1998: 270).

To the extent that the regions outside the North are more conservative and more likely to vote Republican, the Democratic Party faces an eroding electoral base. The presumption is that the electoral base is moving out of the North, and people moving to the Sunbelt are either more affluent or affected by their new environment, and thus vote more conservatively. As the Sunbelt acquires a greater proportion of the population, the presumption is that Republicans will inevitably pick up more House seats. The shift in the South from Democratic dominance to a majority of congressional seats being held by Republicans could easily be seen as verifying this expectation.

The population growth in the West has a particularly unique potential to result in political reactions that are favorable to Republicans. Population growth creates demands for more space and opportunities to pursue economic development. This growth is likely to confront the unique history of the West, where much of the land is not privately owned, and private economic development is limited. Much of the West is owned by the federal government in the form of national parks, land preserves, and military facilities (Conniff 1994), and other portions are owned by Native Americans. Table 3.2 indicates the percentage of western lands owned by the federal government for selected states, and the averages by region of the country.

Most federal lands, designated for federal purposes, are not available for private economic development. Some lands, although owned by the federal government, are leased to private users such as cattle ranchers, who can use the land for grazing but not for projects such as housing developments or new industries. Beginning in the 1970s more federal environmental regulations were imposed on these lands, angering many western residents. That led to outright resentment against the national government, labeled as the Sagebrush Rebellion (Cawley 1993). This confrontation between growing population and federal ownership of land may make many people in the West receptive to Republican criticisms of the federal government and its intrusion into people's lives.

In addition to the affluent's greater movement to the Sunbelt, some analysts argue that there has been a significant exodus from the South by people sympathetic to the Democratic Party. Since the 1950s there has been a major movement of blacks from the South to the North. In 1940, 77 percent of blacks in the United States lived in the South, but by 1970 only one-half of blacks lived in that region (Lemann 1992: 6). In some southern states, such as Florida, the influx of white northerners and the exodus of blacks have reduced the number of blacks from 44 percent of

TABLE 3.2   Percentage of Land Owned by the Federal Government, 1990

State	Percent
Alaska	87.1
Arizona	43.6
California	46.2
Colorado	36.4
Idaho	63.8
Montana	30.3
Nevada	85.1
New Mexico	33.4
Oregon	48.8
Washington	29.2
Utah	63.7
Wyoming	50.4
Region	
North	4.0
South	6.3
Remainder	31.1

SOURCE: U.S. Bureau of the Census, *Statistical Abstract of the United States*, 1991, 111th edition (Washington, D.C.: U.S. Government Printing Office).

the population early in the century to 24 percent in 1980 (Scicchitano and Scher 1998: 229). Such changes have significantly reduced the electoral significance of blacks in many states.

The Movement to the Suburbs

Not only has the population moved between regions, but also within them. Since the 1950s there has been a steady increase in the proportion of the population living in suburbs, as shown in Table 3.3. In 1950, 23 percent of the electorate lived in the suburbs; by 1988, 45.7 percent lived in suburbs. People who live in suburbs are more likely to be white (Hacker 1992: 27), relatively successful economically, sympathetic to the view that individual responsibility is crucial for success, and more likely to support Republicans (Harris 1954: 27–29; Schneider 1992: 35–39). This faith in individualism and its connection to a Republican politician is expressed by a Georgia suburban constituent in a comment about Newt Gingrich, when Gingrich resigned as Speaker of the House of Representatives:

> [Gingrich believed] in giving people the responsibility for living their own lives. People here don't look to the government for their well-being. That's

TABLE 3.3   The Growth of Suburbs

	Percentage of Population in:		
Year	Cities	Rural Areas	Suburbs
1950	32.9	43.9	23.2
1960	32.3	37.0	30.6
1970	31.4	31.4	37.2
1980	30.0	25.2	44.8
1988	31.3	22.8	45.7

SOURCE: *New York Times*, September 11, 1990, A-20.

the way it should be. Gingrich believed that. It works. It really does work. (Bragg 1998: A-8)

As the suburban proportion of the electorate increases, many analysts see this as a part of America more likely to be sympathetic to Republican ideals. The combination of movement to the Sunbelt and the suburbs has led some to presume that the future will be a Republican one (Schneider 1992). It is estimated that in the year 2000, over 50 percent of the electorate will be in the suburbs, giving Republicans a significant advantage (Lemann 1998: 42).

Affluence and Social Decline

Not only has the location of the populace changed, but some analysts argue their concerns have changed. To some scholars, the United States is now in an era of greater affluence, which has reduced the significance of economic conflicts and resulted in a greater focus on quality of life issues. By the 1960s and 1970s, following two decades of sustained increases in income levels, several analysts argued that the real income increases had reduced concerns about economic scarcity and want (Nisbet 1959; Bell 1962; Wilensky 1966; Bell 1973; Lipset 1982: 253). People became less concerned with material issues and more concerned with the quality of life (Inglehart 1972; Ladd and Hadley 1975: 195–200; Rae 1992: 642; Clark, Lipset, and Rempel 1993: 298). Others put the argument more simply, suggesting that "blue collar workers have moved into the same middle-class bracket as white collar workers" (Bonafede 1982: 327), making them less receptive to battles over redistribution issues. In this view, it is the absolute level of income individuals have, not their relative economic situation, that shapes politics. The absolute increases in real income since World War II are seen as having diminished the relevance and power of divisive economic issues.

At the same time that growing affluence might incline voters to have a greater concern with the quality of life, some disturbing social trends might incline the public to be hesitant to support "permissive" Democrats, and more receptive to listening to Republicans stress the importance of families, morality, and an orderly society. The Republicans argue that American society is experiencing social decline and that these trends were brought on, at least in part, by the willingness of Democrats to tolerate any behavior.

The trends have been widely noted and are often grouped together as "social issues" (Scammon and Wattenberg 1970: 40–43). Ben Wattenberg provides a recent summary of the arguments (1995). Relative to the 1960s, crime, such as violent crimes per 100,000, is much higher, but the length of time criminals spend in jail has declined (243–246). Welfare spending has increased, as has the birth of illegitimate children to black and white women (269–270). Conservatives argue that liberals made a fatal mistake in making welfare too accessible, creating a way of life that made it easier to stay on welfare and not work (Murray 1984). A commonly cited statistic in this argument is that currently almost 70 percent of black children are born out of wedlock. The interpretation of that trend has been disputed, but regardless, illegitimate black children have become a regular part of political discourse.[3] Further, there are other trends that society is drifting in directions that are not positive. The divorce rate has increased. The SAT scores of students seeking to attend college have steadily declined since the 1960s, whereas spending on education has steadily risen (187).

Republicans offer a relatively simple explanation of these changes, arguing that Democrats are too sympathetic to the problems of the less affluent, are unwilling to insist on moral standards, and are willing to tolerate almost any behavior. In particular, Democrats are too eager to provide welfare, food stamps, and public housing. A consequence of these programs, from the perspective of conservatives, has been that much of the public has lost the will to work hard, persevere, and practice the discipline necessary to succeed in life (Murray 1984; Magnet 1993). In the view of conservative Republicans, welfare programs created "dependent" recipients who need to have the crutch of federal programs removed to develop self-sufficiency.

Polls indicate that an increasing proportion of the public sees social issues as the most important issue facing the country (Wattenberg 1995: 117).[4] The public wants more money spent combating crime, is not sympathetic to rehabilitating criminals, and wants tougher sentencing (120–121). There is little support for the welfare system (125–127). Relatively affluent whites in the Sunbelt and suburbs, unhappy with trends in crime, welfare caseloads, and illegitimacy, want lower taxes and policies and political stances more in line with their concern for values (Schneider 1987: 42–48).

The emergence of greater affluence and concerns about social issues is particularly significant because of the presumed reaction of the working class. Evidence emerging in the late 1950s and in the 1960s suggested that the working class is prone to intolerance for nonmainstream attitudes and behaviors, and they are more likely than the well educated to react negatively to nontraditional social or cultural behavior (Prothro and Griggs 1960; McClosky 1964; Jackman 1972). As Lipset summarized, building on the work of Stouffer (1955), in commenting on "working-class authoritarianism":

> The gradual realization that extremist and intolerant movements in modern society are more likely to be based on the lower classes than on the middle and upper classes has posed a tragic dilemma for those intellectuals of the democratic left who once believed the proletariat necessarily to be a force for liberty, racial, and social progress. (1981: 87)

Perhaps the racial issue was most revealing of this intolerance, encompassing conflicts over busing, open housing, access to public and private facilities, voting rights, and eventually affirmative action. The power of race issues was confirmed by working-class reactions to George Wallace, who mixed hostility to the national government and its policy experts, populist appeals, and opposition to civil rights for blacks to garner far more votes than anyone expected in his presidential election campaigns (Edsall and Edsall 1991b: 77–80; Kazin 1995a: 221–242; Carter 1995: 324–370). Goldwater and Nixon capitalized on these concerns, and by the late 1960s southern whites and the South began to move to the Republican Party (Black and Black 1992: 141–210).

The combination of greater affluence, troubling social trends, and intolerance among the working class led many analysts to conclude that the working class was being driven more by social and racial issues than class issues (Ladd, Hadley, and King 1971: 56). "Reagan Democrats," for example, were seen as working-class whites who left the Democratic Party, claiming that it had deserted and betrayed them by becoming too focused on social issues. The results were a decline in working-class support for Democrats, a decline of class divisions in American politics, and the expansion of the Republican electoral base. The working-class electoral base that Democrats might have mobilized was not amenable to appeals about growing inequality because they were angry about crime, abortion, affirmative action, and the decline of respect for traditional values.

In summary, there are reasons to see the Republican Party, with themes of less government and more personal responsibility, as well situated owing to recent trends. Support for government and particularly the national government has declined. Movement to the Sunbelt and the suburbs has increased, and these areas appear to be more sympathetic to Republican appeals of self-reliance and less government. The development of greater affluence has diminished concern over economic issues, and, coupled with troubling signs of social disorder, have resulted in more people concerned about quality of life and cultural issues such as crime, illegitimacy, divorce, and abortion. All these trends push people to be Republican.

The Persistence of Potential Democratic Issues

As is often the case, there are also many trends that suggest that conditions are favorable to Democrats. In particular, some very clear trends provide the basis for Democrats to believe there is a substantial electoral base that might be responsive to their concerns with equality of opportunity issues and accompanying programs.

Persisting Support for National Programs

Although there is clear evidence that people have less faith in the federal government, it is not clear that there has been an increase in conservative attitudes or greater support for cutting back specific federal programs. Despite the presumption that the national mood has turned conservative in recent decades, reviews of a wide array of public opinion surveys over time find considerable stability of views, and even many trends toward more liberal attitudes (Mayer 1992: 19–43, 75–110; Page and Shapiro 1992: 67–171). Even when Reagan was popular, public polls about specific programs, regulations, or protections indicate strong support for continuing existing programs, with the exception of welfare (Schneider 1983: 2202–2203; Robinson 1984: 12–15; Ferguson and Rogers 1986). Subsequent polls have continued to show stable support for many national programs. Further, polls indicate growing tolerance for furthering rights for women, homosexuals, and minorities (Sanders 1992: 32–54). It appears that the public endorses the abstract principles of less government and lower taxes, but is fundamentally ambivalent whether to really cut many specific government programs (Free and Cantril 1967). Specific national programs that Democrats support, such as those that protect the environment, regulate the quality of food production, provide Social Security, or monitor how business treats workers, are still deemed worthwhile. The attitude toward government may, in practical terms, be far less negative than presumed.

Not only is the general political climate perhaps less negative toward government than presumed, but there is considerable evidence that many segments of the electorate are experiencing difficulties that may make them support a party willing to provide government help to people who are not faring well amid economic change.

Economic Stagnation

The state of the economy has long been a crucial matter in politics. When the economy is growing, real incomes on average increase, unemployment

declines, and the public is likely to express little dissatisfaction with economic affairs. Prosperity also makes it more difficult for one party to make
an issue of economic problems by appealing to economic frustrations
within the electorate. But not all families have benefited from the economic growth of recent decades. First, the median family income of
American families, which grew significantly from the late 1940s through
the 1960s, ceased to grow much beginning in the early 1970s. Median family income, corrected for inflation and expressed in 1997 dollars, reached
$42,483 by 1979. Since then there has been only modest growth, and by
1997 family income had increased, over a twenty-year time period, to
only $44,568. This stagnation occurred even while, over the twenty-year
period from 1979 to 1999, families at all income levels were working more
hours (Uchitelle 1999: sec. 3:1). The trend in family income is shown in
Figure 3.3.[5]

For many Americans, the sense that the future will bring increases in
real income and greater affluence has declined. Adding to this sense of
pessimism is the widespread belief that a global economy has emerged
and national political interventions to try to alter the workings of private
markets are unlikely to be feasible or efficacious (Kaus 1992; Krugman
1994; Samuelson 1997). This economic stagnation has created real and immediate anxiety and frustration in many U.S. families who worry that
their future prospects for economic security and real income increases are
very limited (Tolchin 1996: 49–70).

FIGURE 3.3   Median Family Income, in 1997 Dollars, 1947–1997

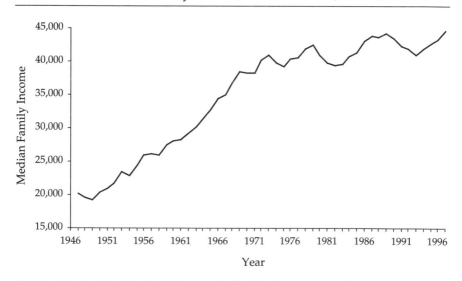

The level of stress stemming from economic pressures has surely been heightened by changes in how family incomes are derived. Since the 1970s average weekly earnings for individual workers have declined (Miringoff and Miringoff 1999: 99–100). Many families have been able to maintain stable *family* incomes only because more and more women have joined the labor force and now provide a growing portion of family income (Danziger and Gottschalk 1995: 76–81). Figure 3.4 indicates the percentage of women in the labor force since 1950. In 1950 that percentage was 23 and by 1960 it was 30 (Kreps and Leaper 1976: 76). It is now almost 60 percent (Hayghe 1997: 42). Although there are many reasons women have joined the labor force, ranging from the enjoyment of a career to economic necessity, having two parents working, with no impact on total family income, is surely a potential source of frustration that could affect political reactions.

Inequalities in the Distribution of Income

The other crucial economic trend that may have partisan consequences is the steady increase in the inequality of the distribution of income in the last several decades. Since the late 1960s and early 1970s there has been a steady increase in the inequality in the distribution of income (Levy 1988:

FIGURE 3.4   Females in the Labor Force, 1950–1996

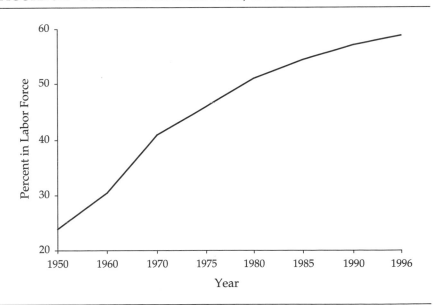

SOURCES: Kreps and Leaper 1976; Hyghe 1997.

13–16; Samuelson 1997: 71). Although this trend is important in and of it-self, it is also crucial to note how different this pattern is from the pattern that prevailed from the late 1940s until the early 1970s. Table 3.4 com-pares the growth in incomes for the earlier era with the most recent one. For this table, family incomes at the beginning of an era (e.g., 1949) are first ranked from lowest to highest. They are then grouped by tenths, from the lowest to the highest. At the end of the era (1969) family incomes are again ranked and grouped. The change from 1949 to 1969 within the groups is then calculated, and the percentage change is determined.

From 1949 to 1969 incomes increased for all income levels. In contrast, from the early 1970s until 1991 increases in income have been experienced primarily by those in the upper income categories. A growth in inequal-ity in American society could come about because all income groups ex-perienced increases, but some groups experienced greater increases than others. Everybody might be enjoying a higher standard of living, but some more than others. That did not happen after 1969. Those in the lowest in-come levels experienced actual declines in real income. The most signifi-cant change occurred during the early 1980s, when the demand for un-skilled labor declined sharply and demand for highly educated workers increased (Levy 1998: 46–49). The same pattern of declining incomes for the less affluent and real increases for the more affluent continued throughout the 1990s (Shapiro and Greenstein 1999; Johnston 1999). The result has been that the last several decades truly embody a case of "the rich get richer and the poor get poorer."

TABLE 3.4   Percentage Change in Income by Income Groups and Era

| | Era and Percentage Change | |
Income Group	1949–1969	1973–1991
Lowest	457.1	−19.0
2	168.4	−8.1
3	130.8	−1.1
4	114.6	4.1
5	106.3	9.6
6	102.2	12.7
7	99.8	15.6
8	94.9	17.8
9	92.8	20.8
Highest	102.2	21.5

SOURCE: Danziger and Gottschalk 1995: 53. Incomes are first grouped from lowest to high-est, and then broken into groups of tenths. The percentage increases in incomes within each category, from the beginning to the end of the era, are then computed. The same differences were reported when the years of 1947–1979 and 1980–1997 were compared (Allen 1999: 57).

Several changes, then, are important. Growth in median family income has stalled. For the last twenty-five years there has been a steady drift toward greater inequality in incomes (Ryscavage 1999: 45–80). More women are entering the labor force to supplement family incomes, but families in the bottom 40 percent of the income distribution are experiencing no growth and even declines. Over the last three decades the percentage of children living in poverty has increased, and the United States now has a higher percentage of such children than most other industrialized nations (Miringoff and Miringoff 1999: 80–85). These trends in equality have become a focus of media commentators and news stories (Edsall 1984; Phillips 1991; DeParle 1991; Nasar 1992a, 1992b). The potential for these changes to become a factor shaping politics is significant.

Inequalities Among Communities

Not only has inequality among individuals increased, but there is also evidence that inequality and segregation among communities has increased. It is largely the affluent and whites who move to the suburbs (Jackson 1985: 231–271; Judd and Swanstrom 1998: 194–205). The movement of the affluent, combined with zoning laws that act to exclude the less affluent (Danielson 1976: 27–106), has led to greater racial (Orfield and Yun 1999) and class segregation within metropolitan areas (Massey and Denton 1993: 24–88; Jargowsky 1996: 989–991). In the last two decades the effort to separate populations has increased even further with the emergence of "gated" communities, which are surrounded by walls, with gates at entrances used to screen people for proper identification. By 1997 it was estimated that 20,000 such communities existed, encompassing over 3 million housing units (Blakely and Snyder 1997: 7).

The steady relocation of the more affluent has resulted in greater differences among communities in the wealth of their populations and tax bases (Rusk 1995: 27–37). The differences in tax bases are particularly important because this in turn creates variations in services and in the quality of schools (Kozol 1991). To the extent that schools differ in their fiscal resources, they are likely to differ in their physical quality, programs, and general resources. Perhaps most important, these variations create a sense of being different and provide another basis for the less affluent to vote differently from the more affluent.

Inequalities among communities are not confined to the Northeast. Although the Sunbelt is often portrayed as prosperous and the Rustbelt as the location of declining communities, the Sunbelt also has its own diversity, with pockets of both affluence and poverty. Less-affluent Sunbelt communities provide a potential electoral base for Democrats. Indeed, an analysis of state legislative elections for 1994 indicates that all of the Sunbelt states have significant diversity in the affluence of legislative districts, and that those variations affect the success of the parties. Democrats do much better as the income level of districts declines (Stonecash 1999d). If less-affluent communities continue to exist, areas will remain where Democrats can win elections.

Shifting Tax Burdens

Not only has the distribution of incomes become more unequal, but the distribution of tax burdens has also become more unequal. The fairness of tax systems is often assessed by how the burdens of taxes vary by the income level of individuals. A regressive tax system is one in which the percentage of income taken in taxes is relatively high for lower-income individuals, and then declines as income levels rise. With a regressive tax, a person making $20,000 a year might pay 15 percent of his income in taxes and a person making $50,000 might pay 10 percent of his income. If the percentage of income paid in taxes increases as income increases, then the tax is regarded as progressive.

In the last decade or so, the entire U.S. tax system has become more regressive. Three significant changes have occurred in recent decades to affect the distribution of tax burdens, or the percentage of income paid in taxes for various income groups. First, there has been a shift in the sources of federal tax revenue. The corporate income tax has become a smaller portion of revenues, and payroll taxes have become a larger portion of revenues. Responding to arguments that the corporate income tax was an unfair burden on companies in an increasingly competitive world, Congress and the president have gradually cut back the corporation income tax. In the 1950s the corporation income tax provided about 27 percent of all federal revenues. By the 1980s it provided approximately 8 percent (Phillips 1993: 111). During the same period, the federal payroll tax (taxes for Social Security and Medicare), which is a flat percentage of earnings, has steadily increased and has become a larger portion of federal revenues. Most of this tax (for Social Security) is regressive because there is a cap on the earnings that are subject to this tax. This cap has steadily increased, and is now at approximately $65,000. People earning income through salary or hourly wages now pay as much as 8 percent of their income, up to $65,000, as the "Social Security" tax (listed as FICA). After $65,000 no tax must be paid. The combination of declining corporate taxes and increasing reliance on a regressive Social Security tax has resulted in a more regressive federal tax system.

Over the last several decades there has also been significant change in the federal income tax. This tax was steeply progressive when it was originally enacted, but few individuals' income was high enough to pay the highest rates. By the late 1970s, with real growth in incomes and inflation pushing up incomes, many more individuals moved into the highest tax brackets (Edsall 1984: 209–214). That led to considerable resentment within the electorate. Beginning in the 1970s, Congress began to lower the highest tax rates from the 70–80 percent level, and by the 1990s the highest rates were in the mid-30s (Phillips 1993: 110). There were particularly significant cuts in federal income taxes during the 1980s that reduced the progressivity of the income tax system (DeParle 1991; Nasar 1992). Tax rates for high-income earners were increased in the early 1990s, but the benefits of the capital gains tax of 1997 went almost entirely to the most affluent (Johnston 1998: 22). Federal taxes are still progressive, but reduced reliance on the corporate income tax, greater reliance on the Social Security tax, and reduced progressivity in personal income taxes have resulted in an increase in the inequality in the distribution of *after* tax income from the 1970s to the 1990s. The conclusion about exactly what happened to inequality depends on whether the focus is on what has happened to the tax burden for the top fifth of incomes or the top 1 percent (Mishel, Bernstein, and Schmitt 1997: 104–121). Critics of inequality tend to focus on the latter, which indicates a greater increase in inequality. Regardless, changes in the tax system have not reduced inequality.

Finally, consider the impact of state and local taxes. States and localities raise revenue primarily from income, sales, and property taxes. The latter two taxes tend to be regressive taxes, though their impact varies from state to state, depending on state exemptions of certain groups, credits for various matters, and so on (Citizens for Tax Justice 1996). In the last decade states have changed the taxes they rely on for revenues. From the 1950s through the 1980s there was a fairly steady increase in the portion of all state-local taxes raised by the state (Stonecash 1983, 1988, 1998), with states relying more and more on sales and income tax to provide tax revenues. During the early 1990s, state governments, increasingly worried about their attracting new businesses, cut state taxes, with most of the cuts coming in the income tax, resulting in greater reliance on the more regressive sales tax (Johnson and Lav 1997). State and local tax systems have never been progressive because of the reliance on the property and sales tax, and the recent changes have resulted in a more regressive state-local tax system. Figure 3.5 indicates the percent of incomes paid in state-local taxes, with all taxes combined, as of 1995 (Citizens for Tax Justice 1996: 1). The relatively affluent pay a much lower percentage of their income in state-local taxes than the less affluent.

Access to Higher Education

Inequalities in access to education are not confined to elementary and secondary education. There are also growing differences in access to higher education by income levels. Study after study indicates that people with

FIGURE 3.5   State-Local Taxes as Percent of Income, by Income
Groups, 1995

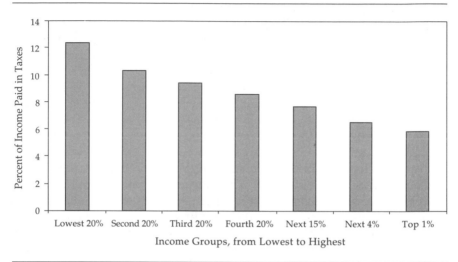

Income Groups, from Lowest to Highest

more education do much better in the job market than people without advanced degrees (Commission on National Investment in Higher Education 1996: 6–8). But not everyone has a chance for further education. The crucial issues are which people have a chance to obtain a higher education degree and how that has changed over time.

The ability to attend college is affected by the costs of attending (tuition, room and board, and books), and the availability of aid to help pay these costs. Over the last thirty years, trends in these costs have had a significant impact on who has access to higher education. Tuition charges have steadily increased at a rate greater than the rate of inflation over the last thirty years, pushing up the real cost of attending college (Commission on National Investment in Higher Education 1996: 10). At the same time, support from government to help defray the costs of higher education has declined. State governments now provide less tax revenue support and devote smaller portions of their budgets to higher education than they did twenty years ago (Mortensen 1995: 1–8). The federal government established the Guaranteed Student Loan program in 1965 and the Pell Grant program in 1972 (Gladieux 1995: 2–3). During the 1970s federal Pell grants, which provide aid to students that does not have to be paid back, covered a substantial portion of the costs of attending public institutions. Since its initial establishment, however, aid in the form of Pell grants has declined, and the federal government has shifted to an emphasis on loans, altering the composition of student aid. Aid provided directly by educational institutions has also declined substantially (The College Board 1998: 12–13).

The policies of the last twenty years have in effect shifted more and more of the burden of higher education from government to the individual (Mortenson 1995: 1–8; Hearn 1998). The trends of the last twenty years have, in effect, resulted in "privatizing" the cost of higher education. From 1985 to 1991 the average cumulative student loan increased from $6,488 to $16,417 (Fossey 1998: 11), and an increasing percentage of students worry about having enough money to finish college (King 1996: 25). The consequence is that the inequalities of the distribution of income have come to play a significant role in affecting who is likely to get a college degree. The less affluent are less capable of participating in a system that emphasizes using family resources or borrowing and assuming significant debts. Figure 3.6 provides an indication of how these changes have affected access to higher education by income quartiles. It indicates the likely success rate in obtaining a college degree for the last thirty years by income quartiles (Mortenson 1995: 1).

The graph indicates the estimated chances of achieving a B.A. by age twenty-four by family income quartile. There are many obstacles to achieving a college degree, but a primary hurdle is lack of financial resources. For the least affluent, these trends indicate little change over

FIGURE 3.6   Probability of a College Degree by Family Income and Year, 1970–1996

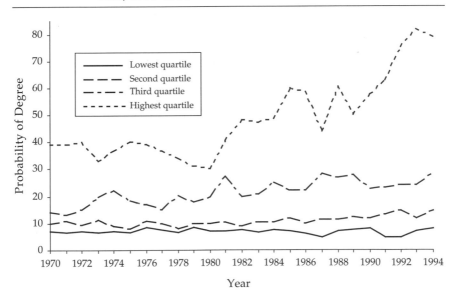

twenty-five years in the chances of achieving a college degree. For students in the top quartile of family income, the percentage has risen from approximately 40 percent to 80 percent, an increase of forty percentage points. For those in the third quartile the gain has been from 15 percent to 29 percent, or a gain of fourteen percentage points. In the lowest income quartile, the change has been from 7 percent to 9 percent, or a gain of two percentage points.

Increasing inequality in incomes has been accompanied by increasing inequality in access to college. Even preparing to apply for college has become affected by class. Students from affluent families have the resources to take SAT preparation courses and obtain assistance in applying to colleges (Schwartz 1999). Students from less-affluent families lack the resources for these services. The inequalities of society are cumulative and growing. To be sure, there have been increases in the chances of obtaining a college degree among all income quartiles, but the differences by income quartile in chances have dramatically increased. These inequalities are surely recognized by the electorate, and provide another possible basis for the less affluent to have different political concerns and to vote differently than the affluent.

Health Care and Pensions

Developments in two other policy areas also have the potential to create considerable stress in individual lives and affect political reactions: access to health care and pension programs. The absence of either health care or a pension may create a sense of vulnerability and shape partisan voting behavior.

Inequalities in access to health insurance, are, of course, not new. In 1954 only 64 percent of the population had hospital insurance, 54 percent had surgical insurance, and 30 percent had general medical insurance (U.S. Statistical Abstract 1956: 571). By 1963, 70 percent had hospital and surgical insurance, but there were still significant variations in coverage by family income. People with medical coverage varied from 34 percent for who made under $2,000 (in 1963 dollars) to 52 percent for those with incomes from $2,000 to $3,999 to 79 percent for people making from $4,000 to $6,999 to 88 percent for those making $7,000 and over (U.S. Statistical Abstract 1965: 571). By 1972 the percent of *workers* with some sort of group coverage had increased to 74 percent, with coverage ranging from 59 percent for the lowest income group (0–$4,999) to 90 percent for the highest income group ($25,000 plus) (U.S. Statistical Abstract 1975: 295). For the unemployed and poor, Medicaid, enacted in 1966 to provide coverage for the poor, surely provided some additional coverage, but there were still significant variations in access to health insurance within the electorate.

Progress in access began to erode during the 1980s. People without health insurance increased from 14 percent to 18 percent from 1987 to 1996. With incomes for most workers declining or stagnant, many have chosen not to enroll in an insurance program because of the costs (Pear 1998: 22). In addition, provision of health insurance is strongly associated with company size and job permanence. Many small businesses do not provide coverage, and the growth of employment in small businesses has left many workers without coverage (Eckholm 1993: A9). Finally, there has been a trend toward hiring more temporary workers; these workers typically do not receive coverage (Mishel, Bernstein, and Schmitt 1997: 267–270). These changes have reversed the trend toward wider health insurance coverage. Workers who make less money remain less likely to be covered (Miringoff and Miringoff 1999: 93), and many with coverage may worry about retaining it. Again, there are grounds for the affluent and less affluent to have different political concerns in this area, and to have different political preferences, depending on how the political parties respond to these issues.

The trend in access to pensions is much the same as that for health care. In general, the percentage of the public with private pensions has increased since the 1940s. In 1940 only 15 percent of private-sector workers were covered by pension plans. That rose to 25 percent by 1955, to 41 percent by 1960, and to 45 percent by 1975. Since then there has been little change (Turner and Beller 1992: 75). As with health care, there are significant variations in who has private pensions (Sass 1997: 113–144). Participation in private pension plans is higher for people in larger companies, full-time workers, and workers who earn higher hourly wages (Turner and Beller 1992: 75). It is difficult to determine the political impact of this situation, but it is clear that broader access to private pension plans has ceased to increase and inequalities in access to these programs persist. In recent years there has been a decline in the percentage of people who have confidence that they will have enough money to live comfortably through retirement. That anxiety is higher among lower income, black, and Latino groups (Employee Benefits Research Institute 1998).

Continuing differences in access to private pensions make the funding of Social Security a crucial matter for many elderly persons. Figure 3.7 indicates how important Social Security funds are for the elderly, by income level. The graph first presents the distribution of the elderly among income categories and then the percentage of income, within each income group, that is derived from Social Security funds (DeParle 1993: A-29). Two matters are important for the emergence of distribution issues in politics. First, despite the evidence that there have been substantial reductions in poverty among the elderly in recent years, a substantial proportion of the elderly still are well below the median family income. Although the

FIGURE 3.7   The Importance of Social Security: Distribution of Elderly
by Income and Percentage of Income from Social Security

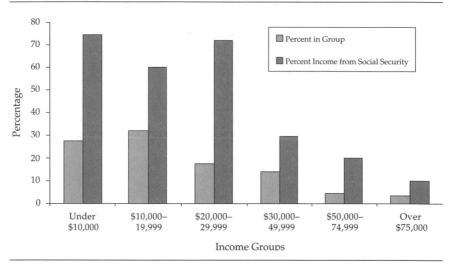

elderly should have fewer expenses for housing and children, the bulk of
the elderly are by no means affluent. In 1993, 78 percent of all the elderly
had incomes below $30,000. For this 78 percent of the elderly population,
Social Security is a crucial source of income. The elderly in the three bottom income groups derive approximately 70 percent of their income from
Social Security. Battles over Social Security, often couched in terms of
maintaining the soundness of the system or restraining its proportion of
the federal budget, are also battles with strong class implications.

In summary, there is considerable evidence that inequality has not declined and there is potential for it to become a significant issue in American
politics. Amid arguments that affluence has increased and economic conflicts have declined, it appears that inequality continues to affect people's
lives. Indeed, inequality might be said to remain with us from "cradle to
grave." Children are born into families and communities that differ significantly in income, and those differences are increasing. They attend local
schools that differ significantly in tax bases and resources, and their access
to higher education is increasingly unequal. As adults, they encounter a job
market that is generating increasing inequalities in family incomes, even
with more and more women joining the labor force. Those unequal incomes
are accompanied by continuing inequality in access to health care and access to private pensions. Inequalities continue into retirement, with Social
Security playing a remarkably different role as a source of income among
the elderly. There is considerable evidence that issues intertwined with inequality have not faded from the political landscape.

This evidence about inequality continues to have a powerful political effect because equality of opportunity is still a crucial part of American beliefs about what is positive about our society (Hochschild 1995; Schwarz 1997). Discrepancies between the ideal and reality create the potential for the issue to become a political issue. Further, although conservatives have mobilized to make the argument that social programs do not work and may even be detrimental, there are counterbalancing attempts to establish the positive effect of government programs (Danziger and Weinberg 1986; Schwarz 1988; Levitan 1990: 36). Even if it is argued that government cannot and should not stop the economic change occurring, there is still a sustained argument that government can help citizens seeking to adapt to a changing economy and thereby preserve equality of opportunity. Government can provide financial aid for local schools with less revenue, and aid to students with less money to go to college (Brint and Karabel 1989). Government can accept shifting employment practices that result in less health care and pension coverage and adopt programs that provide alternative coverage. Although there has been a strong attack on government programs, the ideal of opportunity still exists, efforts to document that government programs work persist, and the argument that government can play a role in responding to the outcomes of private markets persists. Our current national political dialogue continues to contain ideas and language that support both negative and positive views of the role of government.

Immigration, the Shifting Population Composition, and Suburbs

Amid these other changes, the overall composition of the electorate has also steadily and significantly changed in ways that are more likely to benefit Democrats, at least in the near future. In 1950, 10.7 percent of the U.S. population was black, Native American Indian, Alaska native, and Asian or Pacific Islander, with blacks constituting 93 percent of this whole group. Hispanics or Latinos were apparently such a small part of the population that their status was undocumented, so their size cannot be estimated. Although they may have been a growing component of the U.S. population, census reports did not register their significance.

During the last several decades, there have been significant increases in Hispanic and Asian populations, with much of it due to immigration (Hacker 1991: 14; U.S. Immigration and Naturalization Service 1997: 12). In 1980 the black, Hispanic, Asian, and other population had increased to 20.4 percent of the nation's population. In 2000 it is estimated that these groups will constitute 29.4 percent of the population. Blacks and Hispanics, on average, have lower incomes and are inclined to vote for Democrats (Flanigan and Zingale 1998: 92; Abramson, Aldrich, and Rohde 1998: 93). The increase in the size of these groups has the potential to create a significant electoral base for the Democratic Party. Although both of

TABLE 3.5   Blacks and Hispanics, by Region, 1993: Percent of Each
            Region

	Percent of Each Region			
Population Group	North	South	Other	Sunbelt
Black	11.6	17.6	5.4	12.9
Hispanic	5.1	8.1	15.0	13.3
Black or Hispanic	16.7	25.7	20.4	26.2

SOURCE: U.S. Bureau of the Census, *Statistical Abstract of the United States,* 1994. 114th edition (Washington, D.C.: U.S. Government Printing Office) pp. 35–36.

these groups vote at lower rates than the rest of the population (Abramson, Aldrich, and Rhode 1998: 73), their growth as a proportion of the
electorate will make their presence politically influential.

The increase in the Hispanic population, in particular, has come to play
a significant role in Sunbelt states. The percentage of the population in
these states and the "other" region that is Hispanic is shown in Table 3.5.
The table also presents the percentage that is black. Together they indicate the percentage of the population that is a likely electoral base for Democrats.[6] The Sunbelt, often presumed to be a basis for Republican votes,
is 13.3 percent Hispanic and 12.9 percent black, for a combined percentage of 26.2 percent. That is a significant percentage, and suggests the Sunbelt is less of a solid base for Republicans than often presumed.

Further, assumptions about the connections between relocation and
party voting are not so clear as some analysts presume. Movement into
the Sunbelt states is not invariably Republican. An analysis of native residents with migrants into these states since the 1950s indicates that in
some decades they have been more Republican, but in other decades they
have not been so (Gimpel 1999). Finally, although suburbs are often presumed to be largely affluent, white, and political strongholds for Republicans, they are very diverse economically and socially, and there is considerable diversity in suburban voting behavior (Harrigan 1993b:
277–284). As noted some time ago (Hirsch 1968: 514), the suburban partisan vote for presidential candidates fluctuates over time (Nardulli,
Dalanger, and Greco 1996: 488), following national patterns (Harrigan
1993b: 283). The partisanship of the suburban vote also varies by office,
with Democratic state legislators and governors winning majorities in
many suburbs (Schneider 1992: 35–37). The presumption that suburbanization will lead to a Republican advantage is not clear (Mitchell 1999a).

Summary

As noted earlier, political observers often see what they want in political
trends. A wealth of evidence supports the argument that national condi-

tions favor Republicans. Equally significant trends suggest there is an electoral base for the Democrats. The crucial matter is how political parties respond to divergent trends and how the electorate responds to the parties. In Chapter 4 I turn to how parties have changed over time and how their primary policies have evolved.

NOTES

1. As in Chapter 2, North includes Connecticut, Delaware, Illinois, Indiana, Maine, Maryland, Massachusetts, Michigan, Minnesota, New Hampshire, New Jersey, New York, Ohio, Pennsylvania, Rhode Island, Vermont, West Virginia, and Wisconsin. The South includes Alabama, Florida, Georgia, Kentucky, Louisiana, Mississippi, North Carolina, South Carolina, Tennessee, Texas, and Virginia. All others are placed in the "other" category.

2. The states running from Maine to Pennsylvania across to Illinois and up to Wisconsin (Bernard and Bradley 1985: 7).

3. There is clear evidence that what has changed over time is a steady decline in births among married white and black women, and a stable birth rate (number of children born per 100,000 women in the child-bearing years) among unmarried women. Reynonlds Farley, "Recent Trends in Births to Unmarried Women," testimony presented to the U.S. Senate Committee on Finance, Washington, D.C., October 19, 1993.

The consequence is that, of those children being born, an increasing proportion are illegitimate, which leads to the statistic that over 60 percent of all black children born are illegitimate. This does not mean there is no problem of illegitimate children, but it means that it is not a simple case of more and more black women having illegitimate children. The difference is significant in that it is not all black women who are having illegitimate children, as the statistic implies.

The same ambiguity surrounds the divorce rate. It is regularly implied that we have entered an era where a growing proportion of marriages end in divorce, and that was not true in the past. Coontz (1992) argues that it is not that simple. The divorce rates of the 1950s were abnormally low, and the rates since then are perhaps more typical of prior eras than many acknowledge, or are aware of. The presumed decline in SAT scores is also questioned by some, who argue that the proportion of the public taking the tests has increased, and it is not appropriate to compare test scores taken by the best students in the 1960s with test scores taken by a broader cross-section that is less prepared. The point is that the apparent decline is perhaps not as simple and obvious as some commentators regularly imply.

4. Although it is widely asserted that social and cultural issues and values matter, perhaps more than in the past, it is unclear why this is so often presented as if this means that the Democratic Party is in trouble. That is generally the implication, but there are two difficulties with that conclusion. First, surveys that are drawn on to document this rarely include questions about crucial economic issues. Works like Wattenberg's rarely include responses to questions about the importance of equality of opportunity in American society, about perceptions of whether the extent of equality of opportunity has changed over time, or whether

government should address such issues. It is not clear whether such questions are just not asked (for example, the NES data set contains no questions that we could draw on to try to track opinion on these matters) or whether they exist but people choose not to focus on them. Second, the statement that more people care about crime and social disorder is more a consensus that these are areas our society needs to address. It is a statement that implies that we are more prone to be united in concern about these areas. What is missing is any evidence that the parties differ in their concern for the issues, and that the electorate sees a consistent difference in concern between the parties on these issues. What is missing is evidence that there is political division surrounding concern. There may be political division over how to respond to these issues, and a growing public consensus supporting one position (tougher sentencing) may hurt one party (supporting lenient sentencing) if the party sticks with a less-desired position. The crucial matters are that simply asserting that more concern about crime or illegitimate births has some major political consequences without exploring the role of economic issues is inadequate, and presuming that these issues only have the effect of reducing support for one party, without a more careful analysis, does not establish the impact of the issue.

5. These figures are taken from U.S. Bureau of the Census, Current Population Reports, P6-203, *Measuring 50 Years of Economic Change Using the March Current Population Survey*, U.S. Government Printing Office, Washington, D.C., 1998. Table C-10, p. C-19.

6. This population is often characterized as "nonwhite." That characterization is not correct, since the census allows an individual to designate themselves as Latino and white, or Latino and nonwhite.

4

Evolving Party
Constituencies and Concerns

"Stripped of all its rich variation, realignment theory comes down to the notion that something happens and the public responds" (Carmines, Renten, and Stimson 1984: 545). That simple premise is the basis of the following analysis. In this case, the something may be complex and dynamic, involving protracted shifts of party constituencies and policy concerns, but the presumption is that differences between parties eventually register with the public and the electorate changes its political alignment.

Much of the analysis of changes in electoral realignments in American politics has focused on relatively abrupt changes (Key 1955; Shafer 1991). My concern, however, is with gradual, secular changes (Key 1959: 198–199). The argument is that over time Republicans and Democrats have experienced shifts in their electoral bases that have changed the policy concerns and positions of each party.[1] These changing party policy positions have altered electoral perceptions of which party is seen as more conservative or more liberal. Specifically, Republicans have come to be seen as relatively more conservative and Democrats as relatively more liberal. The parties have adopted increasingly divergent positions on class-related issues, with the result that the less and more affluent differ in which party they support.

The dynamics of party differentiation, public perception, and electoral reaction should not be presumed to be precise. The "processes operate inexorably, and almost imperceptibly, election after election to form new party alignments and to build new party groupings" (Key 1959: 198–199). The media often do not treat party differences as meaningful and they are not inclined to convey information about substantive differences between the parties (Patterson 1994). Campaign coverage is often focused more on short-term controversies than debates about evolving policy issues and party differences. Party candidates recognize that and often focus more on some issue that will provide short-term advantages. Further, much of the public does not follow politics closely (Flanigan and Zingale 1998: 143–163). Party positions may change, but much of the electorate may not perceive differences in the parties until well after party concerns have shifted. During any specific election there may be considerable error within the electorate in knowing immediate and long-term party positions.

The process by which the electorate reacts to party positions is likely to be gradual and erratic; voters have limited information and inaccurate perceptions, and acquiring information is costly. The presumption, however, is that the electorate eventually does recognize differences between parties (Popkin 1994: 9–17). Even when differences are recognized, however, abandoning established party attachments and moving to support another party is often difficult for voters. Despite these conditions, the presumption of this analysis is, again, that changes in party positions are eventually recognized and gradually lead to realignment.

Given that it is the long-run connection between party positions and electoral realignments that is important, the focus here is primarily on trends. The content and connections of specific elections—party positions, electoral awareness, and electoral reactions—are of course vitally important (Sears et al. 1980),[2] and occupy much of our attention. Specific campaigns and elections, of course, constitute many of the substantive events that eventually produce trends. But political alignments are also significantly affected by policy debates between elections that trickle down to the public. The concern here is with the cumulative effect of all political events and their perception on electoral alignments.

My focus is on developments since the 1950s. This decade provides a rough baseline for assessing subsequent changes. It is not presumed, however, that this decade represents any sort of ideal type. Although some analysts appear to assume that this was the era in which the New Deal coalition was distinctly present and dominant, in this analysis this decade is simply the first for which we have detailed survey data. The analysis begins with the positions of the parties and the electoral alignments accompanying them in that decade. The movements and events shaping the parties since that time will then be reviewed. In Chapter 5, the trends in electoral reactions to the evolving party positions will be examined.

The 1950s and Early 1960s:
Party Differences with Limits

The 1930s witnessed significant ideological conflicts between the parties over the role of government and resulted in significant class political divisions (Cantril 1951: 589–647, 929–939; Shively 1971). By the 1950s, however, party conflicts were less intense than in the 1930s; Eisenhower appeared to accept much of the New Deal legislation and steady and significant increases occurred in real incomes. The parties differed but they were not polarized, which resulted in diminished divisions in the electoral bases of the parties. The electoral divisions of the 1950s were lesser than divisions in the 1930s for three reasons. First, the elected members of the parties in Congress came from districts with similar constituents, so the parties did not espouse significantly different legislative programs. The major differences in party electoral bases were more regional than class-based. Second, public positions and images of parties were not consistently and significantly different. Third, as might be expected, divisions within the electorate were also limited.

The district electoral bases of the parties in the 1950s and the early 1960s differed, but the differences were primarily a product of regional variations in party loyalties. The House of Representatives provides a good indicator of how party bases differed by region and district conditions. Presidential elections, although the most prominent, produce election results that fluctuate from election to election. House elections, on the other hand, are probably more stable and reflect how party support varies by the constituencies that dominate in a district. Table 4.1 indicates the distribution of party strength for the nation and by region by the economic situation in districts for the 1950s and the 1960s. House districts in the 1950s are characterized by the percentage of deteriorated housing. No information sources provide the median family income of district for the 1950s; this is the only indicator of relative affluence within districts available for this decade. For the 1960s, median family income is available, so that will be used as a more direct indicator of the relative affluence of families within districts. District median family income is presented after adjusting for inflation and is expressed in 1990 dollar values.[3]

The parties in the 1950s did differ in the kinds of districts they represented. Table 4.1 first presents the percentage of housing that was deteriorated, grouped by thirds, and then the percentage of seats won by Democrats during the 1950s in those districts. Democrats did much better in districts with a higher percentage of deteriorated housing, which suggests their base was in less-affluent districts. Although these differences in party success by type of district existed, region played a significant and very confounding role in this, affecting the clarity of the party's concerns and image.

The problem Democrats faced was that much of their base was in less-affluent districts in the South, but these districts were dominated by conservatives. Blacks could not register and vote, and many low-income whites did not register (Key 1949: 529–618). The result was a Democratic Party that, on a national basis, seemingly had a clear base in less-affluent districts, but much of that base was in a region low on support for redistributive policies. The 1956 elections provide a good example of this dilemma. Democrats won

TABLE 4.1   Region, Economics, and Democratic Success, U.S. House of
Representatives Districts and Party Success, 1956 and 1962

1956 Percent Housing Deteriorated	Nation		Region of Nation North		South		Other	
	N	% D	N	% D	N	% D	N	% D
0–12.3	142	41.0	99	39.9	10	60.0	34	37.1
12.4–18.0	140	45.2	90	36.8	21	90.5	34	39.4
18.1 plus	147	82.5	35	64.9	83	96.1	26	62.3
Total	429	56.2	224	42.5	114	92.4	94	44.9

1962 Income Level	Nation		North		South		Other	
	N	% D	N	% D	N	% D	N	% D
0–14,999	25	92.0			23	91.3		
15,000–19,999	83	74.7	13	53.9	56	89.3	16	50.0
20,000–24,999	126	59.5	69	49.3	34	76.5	30	60.0
25,000–29,999	131	51.9	90	51.1			36	55.6
30,000–34,999	57	43.9	46	32.6			22	50.0
35,000 plus	13	15.4						
Total	435	58.6	218	46.8	113	86.8	104	53.9

SOURCES: Data for districts for the 1950s and 1960s are taken from U.S. Bureau of the Census, *Congressional District Data Book* (Districts of the 88th Congress)—A Statistical Abstract Supplement. 1963. (Washington, D.C.: U.S. Government Printing Office).

233 seats in the 1956 elections, but 105 of them were in the South. In the 147 districts with the highest levels of deteriorated housing across the nation, Democrats won 118. Eighty of the 118 were in the South, however, so they provided little basis for the party to serve as a clear advocate of the concerns of the less affluent. Republicans were equally conflicted. Of the 143 districts with low levels of deterioration, Republicans won 90, but 66 were in the North, which was more liberal than the rest of the nation. Although the parties appeared to derive their support from different constituencies, the differences were less than it might appear.

The effect of region on the relationship between district wealth and party continued in the early 1960s. Median family income for districts is available for districts formed after the 1960 census and reapportionment, so differences in party support by the relative affluence of districts can be assessed. On a national basis in 1962 there was still an apparent and significant difference between the parties in the kinds of districts they represented. In districts with the lowest income, Democrats won 92 percent of the seats, whereas in the most affluent districts, Democrats won only 15 percent of the seats. As income declined, the success of Democrats mounted steadily, suggesting the parties represented very different constituents. This national relationship, however, was still largely a product of the distribution of regional loyalties. Most low-income districts were in the South, and it was heavily Democratic. Within each region of the country, there was little relationship between district income levels and the success of Democrats. In general, northern districts were about 50 percent Democratic, and districts in the "other" category were in the mid-50s.

In addition to limited differences between the parties, each party also had considerable internal diversity. In the South Democrats won seats in lower-income, conservative districts. In the North they won districts in lower- to middle-income districts that were liberal. Republicans had their own diversity. Many of their seats were outside the South in northern districts that were relatively liberal. They also won 74 of their 180 seats in less-affluent districts (below $25,000 median family income), which resulted in Republicans with very different constituents than for members from affluent districts.

The result was disagreements within each party, and considerable murkiness as to how different the parties were. Region played as much of a role in structuring divisions as party did. Democrats controlled the House, but the coalitions that passed legislation were often a combination of northern Democrats and Republicans. The 1957 session provides a good example of the nature of the coalitions that often dominated Congress. During the 1957 session there were repeated efforts to reduce budgetary allocations for the Departments of Labor and Health, Education and Welfare. Southern Democrats voted for the reductions and northern Democrats voted against the reductions. Southern Democrats also voted against more public housing units, against a program to provide federal aid for local education construction, and against a new civil rights bill (Congressional Quarterly Almanac 1957: 813).

The policy positions and images of the parties were correspondingly muddled. Many Republicans in the House and Senate had more liberal voting records than many Democrats. The electorate saw almost no difference between Democrats and Republicans on race issues, and on jobs issues Democrats were seen as only modestly more liberal than Republicans (Carmines, Renten, and Stimson 1984: 547–553; Popkin 1994: 60).

These muddled electoral bases and party images affected the divisions within the electorate. By the 1950s the decisive class divisions of the 1930s and 1940s had diminished, and class voting, the difference in the percent voting Democratic between the working and middle class, had declined (Ladd and Hadley 1975: 92–111; Lanouette 1980: 1833; Sundquist 1983: 214–229, 240–262). Table 4.2 indicates the differences in voting for Democratic candidates for the presidency, the House, and the Senate during the 1950s. The data are drawn from the National Election Studies, which have

TABLE 4.2   Class Divisions in the 1950s: Percent Voting Democratic or
Identifying with the Democratic Party Within Low- and
High-Income Groups, and Differences

	President			*House*			*Senate*			*Party ID*		
	Low	*High*	*Diff*	*Low*	*High*	*Diff*	*Low*	*High*	*Diff*	*Low*	*High*	*Diff*
Whites Only												
Nation	42	38	4	56	48	8	53	46	7	55	51	4
South	58	44	14	80	81	−1	76	78	−2	69	74	−6
Other	37	36	1	49	42	7	47	43	4	49	46	3
All Respondents												
Nation	44	38	6	57	47	8	55	47	8	55	52	3
South	58	44	14	80	82	−2	77	79	−2	62	74	−12
Other	39	37	2	51	43	8	49	43	6	51	47	4

NOTE: The percentages are derived by taking the percent voting for Democrats within each
income grouping, in the elections of 1952, 1956, 1958, and 1960, for each office, and averaging the results. Averaging weights all elections equally. The difference is the percentage voting Democratic for the lower third minus the percentage voting Democratic for the top
third. Positive values indicate an expected class division. The results are presented by region because the regions differed so much in their income levels, and because of their political histories. All results are taken from the NES cumulative file for 1948–1998.

been conducted every two years since the 1950s. Respondents were asked
for their family income and the reporting of the data makes it possible to
classify respondents by whether they are in the top third of all family incomes or the bottom third.[4] Respondents are first classified by income and
then the percentage voting for Democrats for those within each group is
determined. The differences in the percentages voting Democratic between the top and bottom third income groups indicate the extent of class
division. In general, the differences are very small, as might be expected,
given the limited differences between the parties (Petrocik 1998).

The parties did differ in the 1950s, but with constraints. The liberal bent
of the Democratic Party was constrained by its heavy reliance on southern Democrats. The conservatism of Republicans was constrained by its
heavy reliance on northeastern, relatively liberal, Republicans. The differences in the images of the parties were correspondingly constrained.
The electorate responded accordingly, and class divisions within American politics were relatively limited. All this was soon to change.

Initiating Change: Chickens and Eggs

The origins of change are difficult to locate precisely. Change can origi-
nate from shifting social conditions that gradually prompt electoral

movements or from events that suddenly emerge on the agenda and force political choices that subsequently prompt voter reactions. Politicians may take the initiative to put issues on the agenda out of conviction or because they believe it will provide short-term political advantages. Sorting out where change originates is difficult (Gerring 1998: 257–275), and is not crucial for the analysis that follows. The presumption is that a number of changes occurred together. New issues emerged as salient, groups mobilized to try to shape their party's positions, the electoral bases of parties shifted, and party positions on policies changed, not necessarily in that order. The precise causal order of changes is not as important as how changes affect party positions and the differences between the parties. The approach here is to review the changes that affected each party and then assess the impact these changes had on the constituencies of each party, the policy positions taken by the parties, and the electoral perceptions of the parties.

Many analyses of political change focus on the Democratic Party. As reviewed in Chapter 1, many analysts see the behavior of Democrats as the driving force affecting the situation of parties. There are also arguments, however, for assigning this role to the Republican Party because of the increasing role conservatives have come to play in the last several decades (Rae 1989: 5).[5] Again, my concern is not to try to resolve the issue of original causes, but to track changes. Despite that, there are signs that tensions and changes within the Republican Party emerged somewhat earlier than among Democrats, so the analysis will begin with the Republican Party.

Republican Tensions and Change

The Republican Party of the 1950s had internal tensions. The party contained two wings, divided by geography and philosophy. The eastern-midwestern wing, which was generally dominant, was positive about business and large business organizations, supportive of a strong international role, and willing to play a role in reforming government. The party had a strong patrician component that was willing to support civil rights legislation and urban social programs to avoid serious conflict within capitalism. At the same time, however, the party also had a western wing that had more of a populist[6] focus. These Republicans were more hostile to large organizations, distrustful of government, more likely to embrace libertarian notions that individual freedom was more important than government assistance, and less supportive of international involvement. These wings had coexisted since early in the twentieth century, with the eastern wing largely dominant (Rae 1989: 29–43; Brennan 1995: 5–7).

During the 1950s, however, the dominance of the eastern wing began to erode in terms of elected officials and intellectual energy. The 1958 elections resulted in significant Republican losses, with most of the losses involving liberal northern Republicans losing to liberal northern Democrats (Carmines and Stimson 1989: 69–72).[7] That election reduced the dominance of the eastern liberal wing within the party.

Just as important, ferment was developing within the Republican Party to challenge the ideas of the eastern wing. The *National Review,* a conservative magazine, was started in 1955 by William F. Buckley. Numerous conservative writers emerged to argue that Republicans should not accept the New Deal and a greater federal role as the new status quo. The John Birch Society was founded in 1958 and the Young Americans for Freedom were founded in 1960. Both espoused conservative views. These and other groups emphasized the importance of faith in individualism and free enterprise and opposition to a significant role for government (Rae 1989: 48–52; Brennan 1995: 8). In the early 1960s the Liberty Lobby and the Americans for Constitutional Action formed. The Conservative Party began in New York in 1962 in opposition to the liberal Republicanism of Nelson Rockefeller, and the American Conservative Union formed in 1965. Perhaps more important, these groups devoted considerable efforts to organizing Republican support. Although the South continued to be seen as the "solid [Democratic] South" by many, conservatives viewed that region as an area where they could make inroads, and they devoted effort to developing the Republican Party there (Brennan 1995: 60–78).

These new groups worked closely with Senator Barry Goldwater from Arizona. Goldwater, frustrated with Eisenhower's acceptance of the New Deal, had emerged as a leader of the conservative wing of the party in the late 1950s. He became head of the Republican Senate Campaign Committee, a position that gave him the opportunity to travel the country. Many of the emerging conservative organizations were based on college campuses and he spoke at campuses across the country to support the conservative movement during the early 1960s (Rae 1989: 53–57; Brennan 1995: 24–38). In the early 1960s he was able to work with many of these organizations to build grassroots support for conservative causes and to gather support for a bid for the presidency. His major defeat for the presidency in 1964, followed by the enactment of a spate of liberal legislation by Lyndon Johnson and the Democratic Congress, led many to assume that his brand of conservatism had no future.

Goldwater's emergence, however, was just the first significant battle between the eastern, relatively liberal, and the southern and western individualistic wings of the party. In his acceptance speech of the Republican nomination, Goldwater had declared, "Extremism in the defense of liberty is no vice." Although liberals in both parties saw the statement as an example of how extreme and out of touch he was, his philosophy was not seen that way by the emerging conservative movement within the party. Conservatives remained in many party positions following the 1964 election, and they worked to recruit and elect more conservatives. In 1966 Ronald Reagan, espousing conservative views, was elected governor of California.

There was still not a sense, however, that there was a significant conservative movement to contend with. Although Republicans gained seventy-seven seats in the 1966 House elections, this gain was seen as a sign that the 1964 disaster was just a short-term result of Goldwater, and that normalcy had been restored. Many moderates and liberals within the party continued to see conservatives as part of a fringe element in American politics, and did not see them as representing a serious threat to the eastern-midwestern dominance of the party.

The differences did not disappear, however, and the 1968 Republican convention brought out the geographical and philosophical differences within the party. Richard Nixon, former vice president and the 1960 presidential candidate, sought the 1968 nomination along with Reagan and Governor Nelson Rockefeller of New York, who had built a reputation as a liberal Republican (Stonecash 1989, 1992). As Table 4.3 indicates, Rockefeller received strong support within the Northeast and the Midwest, whereas Reagan did well in the West and South. Nixon was able to do well enough in all areas to win the 1968 nomination, but the convention revealed the clear split in the party (Rae 1989: 98). The West and the South provided a basis of support for a conservative candidate (Rae 1998: 60–61).

The 1968 and 1972 presidential elections did much to contribute to some ambiguity about the political position of the Republican Party. The apparent position of the parties, particularly the Republicans, was muddled by the presence of George Wallace and the portrayal of George McGovern, the 1972 Democratic candidate. In 1968, Wallace, the governor of Alabama, was a major factor in the election. He was widely seen as someone capitalizing

TABLE 4.3   Support for Nominees Within Republican Party by Region, 1968 Convention

Region	*Percent from Region for:*		
	NAR,[a] others	*Nixon*	*Reagan*
Northeast	67.9	31.8	.3
Midwest	44.6	52.6	2.8
South	7.6	74.2	18.2
West	11.8	47.7	40.4

[a] NAR represents Nelson Rockefeller.

SOURCE: Rae 1989: 98. His regional groupings are used for this presentation.

on racial resentments and opposition to the federal government and appealing to working-class whites (Kazin 1995a: 221–244). His electoral successes in the South and outside the South presented a problem for both parties, and much of the 1968 campaign was seen as strategic efforts to cope with his presence.

Nixon pursued a "southern strategy" in 1968 and 1972 in which he sought to win votes in the South and reduce Wallace's distinctiveness as a candidate who might take conservative votes away from him (Carter 1995: 324–414). He did so by seeking to reassure white southerners that he would not be too aggressive in pushing integration. This caused confusion: Was Nixon really opposed to civil rights, or was he just trying to outmaneuver Wallace? Consequently, it was not entirely clear whether Richard Nixon was a conservative or a moderate. Nixon's presidency also sent some mixed signals: He established the Environmental Protection Agency and proposed a guaranteed income for the poor, but also opposed busing and efforts to help minorities.

The 1972 campaign may have further muddled the sense of whether Republicans were really that conservative, or if Democrats were very liberal. George McGovern was generally presented as a very liberal candidate. Labeling the Democratic candidate a liberal made it less than clear whether Republicans were really conservatives, or if they just appeared to be conservative relative to McGovern. Finally, the events of 1973 and 1974 did not help clarify how the electorate saw the Republican Party. The Watergate scandal involving Richard Nixon led to a significant repudiation of the Republican Party in the 1974 elections, but there was little evidence that the populace rejected any philosophy of the Republican Party. The task of the party after 1974 was to recover, and it was not clear what the party needed to recover from, other than from Nixon. The emergence of Gerald Ford as a moderate Republican president also did not lead to a sense that the party was clearly conservative.

The behavior of the congressional parties also contributed to the lack of clarity of the parties. A common measure of the differences between the parties is the extent to which they oppose each other on votes on legislation. If all Democrats vote together in opposition to Republicans, who all vote together against Democrats, then there is complete party opposition and unity within each party. To the extent that members of opposing parties "cross the aisle" and vote with the other party for legislation, unity in party voting declines. From the 1950s to the 1970s party unity in voting steadily declined, with much of the decline attributable to southern Democrats voting with Republicans on conservative legislation and liberal nonsouthern Republicans often voting with nonsouthern Democrats (Brady, Cooper, and Hurley 1979; Collie and Brady 1985; Rohde 1991:

9–16). Anyone observing party battles in the 1970s might have seen some murkiness in the differences between the parties.

Amid this ambiguity about the concerns and focus of the Republican Party, the party was experiencing change in a conservative direction. After years of support for civil rights similar to the Democrats, after 1964 the Republican Party opposed civil rights legislation (Carmines and Stimson 1989: 102–112). Further, disturbing social trends that emerged in the late 1960s convinced conservatives that American society was headed in the wrong direction and something needed to be done. Crime increased in the mid- to late 1960s. The divorce rate was rising and welfare rolls were increasing, as were illegitimate births. Conservatives saw these changes as even more reason to organize and find conservative candidates to oppose these trends (Gottfried and Fleming 1988: 59–95).

The electoral base of the party also continued to shift. Table 4.4 indicates the percent of the party from the South, the North, and the remainder of the nation for selected years from 1950 through 1974. In 1950, 70 percent of Republican seats were from the North, but the percentage steadily declined through the 1970s. After the 1970 elections 59 percent of northern seats were Republican, but over the next four elections declined to 58 percent to 55 percent to 54 percent to 52 percent. Representation from outside the North was eroding and giving the more conservative representation from other areas more significance within the party.

The 1976 battle over the Republican nomination once again indicated the split occurring in the party. Table 4.5 presents the division of delegate votes by region for Gerald Ford and Ronald Reagan. Ford, the incumbent president, was a moderate from Michigan. Reagan, from California, was conservative. Ford received strong support in the Northeast and the Midwest, whereas Reagan did very well in the South and the West.

TABLE 4.4 Distribution of Republican Seats in House of Representatives, Selected Election Years (percents sum down to 100)

Region	1950	1968	1974
Number of seats	196	191	140
		Percent from Region:	
North	70.9	57.1	55.0
South	2.0	15.2	19.3
Other	27.0	27.8	25.7

SOURCE: Data compiled by author from *Congressional Quarterly*.

TABLE 4.5   Support for Nominees Within Republican Party by Area,
1976 Convention

	Percent from Area for:	
Region	*Ford*	*Reagan*
Northeast	88	12
Midwest	68	32
South	18	82
West	27	73

SOURCE: Rae 1989: 117. His regional groupings are used here and not those used for the other analyses dealing with region.

The Emergence of Conservative Support

While conservatives and moderates were engaging in intraparty battles and the electoral base of the party was shifting, other developments were providing more support for the conservative cause. These developments were not coordinated, and there were considerable disagreements among conservatives and moderates. Despite their differences, these groups provided developed arguments for a conservative approach to government.

The Conservative Intellectuals.   In the midst of the 1960s, there was little in the way of a conservative intellectual alternative to liberalism.

> Since 1933 . . . it was generally assumed that the overwhelming consensus of experts in political science, economics, and the social sciences were of one mind: that the improvement of society could best be achieved by the intervention of government, which would carry out policies supplied by experts and intellectuals, in the main liberal. (Hodgson 1996: 130)

That liberal dominance was challenged beginning in the 1960s. Conservatives formed *The Public Interest* in 1965 to present critiques of liberal views. Conservatives in numerous essays and books began to challenge the presumption that government could solve problems, and argued that individual responsibility and gradual change were crucial in bringing about changes in poverty (Banfield 1970). New think tanks funded by wealthy conservatives emerged to support research and essays by conservatives (Ricci 1993; Stefancic and Delgado 1997; Covington 1998).[8]

Writers began to challenge the wisdom of relying on government programs to improve society. Critics argued that in many cases government programs did more harm than good because they discouraged responsibility and adaptation to private markets. Indeed, by the early 1980s conservatives were arguing that government actions in the area of welfare, despite good intentions, were making things worse. Conservatives did not criticize welfare as if they were selfish and opposed to being generous. Instead, critics argued that creating a system that had no time limits on benefits and provided additional benefits for additional children discouraged a sense of personal responsibility and encouraged recipients to become dependent on welfare (Murray 1984). The crucial matter was that a liberal approach was not just wasteful, but harmful (Hodgson 1996: 130–139). In seeking to help the poor, liberal elites had harmed them (Magnet 1993). These arguments made critiques of liberalism respectable and intellectual, not just arguments to protect the self-interest of the affluent.

Within the field of economics very specific critiques of government action developed. The legacy of the 1930s, the Great Depression, and John Maynard Keynes, a prominent economist, was that government could and should intervene in the economy to increase demands for goods and services and to regulate markets. Conservative economists developed arguments that government intrusion into private markets protected weak companies, artificially inflated prices and profits for certain products, and created expectations that government would intrude, such that pressures to be efficient were reduced (Gilder 1981; Hodgson 1996: 186–215). These criticisms about the negative effects of government intrusion became more plausible as both inflation and unemployment increased in the late 1970s and left many conventional economists unable to explain how these two could occur together.

At the same time conservative economists argued that economic and political freedom were inseparable (Friedman 1962). These conservatives, taking a libertarian perspective, felt that federal government action invariably restricted personal freedom. The argument had powerful implications for the role of the federal government, which grew significantly in the 1960s and intruded into society in many more ways than in the 1950s (Advisory Commission on Intergovernmental Relations 1980, 1981: 35–106). Freedom is a central and highly valued aspect of American society, and conservatives argued that increased federal government involvement in individual lives was detrimental to freedom.

At the same time that an intellectual argument against government was developing, public trust in the national government was declining. In the late 1950s and early 1960s 70 percent of the electorate reported that they trusted the national government to do the right thing "just about always" or "most of the time." By the late 1960s that percentage had declined to 50, and by the late 1970s it was approximately 30 (Flanigan and Zingale, 1998: 13). The effects of the Vietnam War, Watergate, perceptions of failed federal programs enacted in the 1960s, and the growing inflation and unemployment of the late 1970s provided proof to many that the federal government was not to be trusted. Action by the federal government was increasingly suspect. National government intrusion was presented as not only detrimental to freedom, but as harmful to the performance of the economy.

The Conservative Christian Movement.   The social changes of the 1960s— increases in crime, divorce, and illegitimate births—also prompted concern among conservative Christians, who were worried about the moral direction of the nation. Conservative Christians had traditionally not been heavily engaged in politics.[9] The emphasis among fundamentalists was on their personal relationship with Jesus and personal salvation. The presumption of conservative Christians that they could stay out of politics and their way of life would still be safe was challenged by a number of decisions and events.

In the early 1960s the Supreme Court ruled that prayer in public schools was not constitutional. In 1974 the Supreme Court ruled that abortions were legal. As the 1970s evolved, claims of gay rights became more prominent. Perhaps the most important matter, however, was the attempt by the Internal Revenue Service in 1978 to revoke the tax-exempt status of Christian schools. The IRS argued that many of these schools were formed to avoid desegregation, and they did not deserve tax-exempt status as a religious institution. The IRS eventually dropped the issue, but this attempt by the federal government to intervene in religious schools was seen as a significant threat by conservative Christians. This was an intrusion into their one safe haven of school and family (Hodgson 1996: 166–178).

These events prompted conservative Christians to reconsider their sense of how much political involvement was necessary. The Moral Majority formed in 1979 as an organization to raise money for conservative causes and to mobilize conservative Christians to try to have some political impact. These groups found the Republican Party far more conducive to their interests than the Democratic Party, particularly in the South (Green et al. 1998). These groups developed a mutually beneficial relationship with Republicans. They were able to provide votes, financial organization, and funding to conservative Republican candidates. This prompted Republicans to listen more to the concerns of conservative Christians and to seek to represent their concerns. Each side benefited from the relationship.

Uniting Conflicting Groups.   Despite these developments, the emergence of a conservative intellectual movement, public dissatisfaction with the federal government, and the mobilization of conservative Christians, there was still an enormous problem in creating a unified conservative movement. The difficulty was, and still is, that these groups differ fundamentally in their support for government intervention in society. The libertarians and the free-market economists are strongly committed to removing the federal government from society and the economy. Using government to direct society is seen as a fundamental threat to the crucial condition of liberty. They feel that removing government from families and stressing moral values will help restore the traditions of the past. The conservative Christians, on the other hand, have come to see the federal government, captured by liberal elites, scornful of their values, as a clear danger to Christian values. They want to elect people sympathetic to their concerns and then use the power of the federal government to reshape the moral rules of society. They want to reestablish school prayer, curtail abortion rights and gay rights, and protect Christian schools. The clash between these groups involves a fundamental principle. One group wants to reduce all government intrusion, and the other thinks it is crucial to use government power to preserve moral order. One wants to allow, even encourage, change in society, particularly the economy, because that will modernize the economy (Dionne 1997: 199–299), whereas the other wants to protect and preserve a more traditional order. To build a conservative coalition, the challenge is to unify these groups.

The conceptual unifier emerged from the populist tradition. Although populism has meant many things to different groups, one enduring theme of populism has been the argument that larger forces are destroying society. In earlier eras, such as the late 1800s, those larger forces were banks, railroads, monopolies, and industrial elites (Wiebe 1967: 44–110). In the current political world, the larger force was interpreted as the federal government and its liberal, out-of-touch elites who dictated unwanted, intrusive, and destructive policies to states, localities, local organizations, and families (Greenberg 1986: 44–46). George Wallace first articulated this interpretation, though many thought he was railing only against racial integration (Carter 1995: 264–293). Richard Nixon, Ronald Reagan, and others adopted the theme and promoted the notion that the federal government was the enemy. They were able to make the argument that the conflicting conservative groups shared a common enemy (Kazin 1995a: 254–268). These groups could be mobilized to pursue the mission of capturing the federal government so they could reverse its practices. Conflicts in goals might persist, with one wanting to diminish federal power, and the other wanting to use power to intervene, but that conflict could be minimized because each group focused on different policy concerns. The libertarian, market camp wanted cuts in taxes and regulations, whereas the conservative Christians wanted interventions in social policy, so they focused on different aspects of society. That conflict has persisted and creates tensions within the party.

Regardless of these tensions, the concerns and image of the Republican Party began to shift as conservative groups became more closely identified with the party. The party, its electoral bases shifting to the South and the Sunbelt and with conservatives continuing to organize to acquire more power within the party, became more concerned with tax cuts, opposition to the federal government, and a conservative social agenda.

Pursuing a Conservative Agenda

The election of Ronald Reagan symbolized the trends occurring within the Republican Party. Reagan, seen in earlier years as too conservative for the party, now seemed to embody the party's new direction. He always argued that he became acceptable to the party, not because he changed but because the party moved in his direction. Reagan pursued a clear agenda in his first two years. He thought government was too big, too intrusive, and took too much of people's money. He proposed cuts in federal regulations, and wanted to ease environmental regulations. He supported cuts in the federal income tax and supported the idea that as government cut its tax revenues, the economy would flourish. He proposed that the federal government turn many functions over to the states, along with transition funds to help states eventually assume full costs. He wanted to cut back on federal welfare and endorsed the idea that welfare created dependency and that government should cut welfare and return people to independence. He demonstrated his stance regarding labor when the air traffic controllers, who manage the landing of airplanes at airports, went on strike. He fired all of them and refused to reconsider the issue. He supported significant increases in military spending, but cuts in social programs. He made it clear that his objective was less government in the broad area of social programs, but a stronger defense (Palmer and Sawhill 1982, 1984).

Republicans were subject to relentless criticism during this period, but Reagan communicated great faith in his ideas. There was continual concern that the party would be seen as favoring the rich and uncaring about others. That fear was allayed by numerous analyses that concluded Reagan had attracted many blue-collar workers (known as Reagan Democrats) to the party in the 1980 election (Pierce and Hagstrom 1980; Bonafede 1981; Sundquist 1983–1984: 583; Galston 1985). The combination of Reagan's victory, his rising popularity in his first few years, and commentary that he had bolstered the party and ushered in a more conservative era provided enough reinforcement for many Republicans to become convinced that conservatism had a strong future. Moderate Republicans thought Reagan's approach was too conservative, but they were fighting a losing battle, much like the mid-1970s transitions. Reagan won reelection in 1984 by a large margin against the Democratic candidate, Walter Mondale, who said he would raise taxes and pursue national planning. The clearly contrasting approaches and the large margin of victory for Republicans encouraged a conservative approach.

While Reagan was establishing a conservative policy image for the party, the party's electoral base continued to shift. Table 4.6 presents the success of the Republican Party by region and by the median family income of House districts for 1966 and for 1984. Again, the House is of interest because it is possible to indicate how the party fares in relatively smaller geographical units that vary in income levels. There are several changes worth noting. First, the overall distribution of seats by region shifted, with the North losing 22 seats, the South gaining 10, and the remainder of the country gaining 12. Second, the Republican Party also shifted its source of seats over two decades, losing 21 in the North and gaining 20 in the South and 2 in the remainder of the country. Third, and perhaps most important, was the change in which seats they won. In 1966 the Republican party won 109 of its 187 seats in the North and did just as

TABLE 4.6   Region, District Income, and Republican Success, U.S. House of Representatives, 1966 and 1984

| | | | Region of Nation | | | | | |
| Income Level | Nation | | North | | South | | Other | |
1966	N	%	N	%	N	%	N	%
0–19,999	108	32.4	13	61.5	79	21.5	16	62.5
20,000–24,999	126	42.9	69	47.8	27	22.2	30	50.0
25,000–29,999	131	47.3	90	48.9	5	40.0	36	44.4
30,000–34,999	57	47.4	37	47.7	1	0	19	47.4
35,000 plus	13	69.2	9	66.7	1	100.0	3	66.7
Total	435	43.0	218	50.0	113	23.0	104	50.0
Rep Seats	187		109		26		52	
Income Level	Nation		North		South		Other	
1984	N	%	N	%	N	%	N	%
0–19,999	6	33.3	3	0	3	66.7	0	0
20,000–24,999	50	14.0	10	0	33	12.1	7	42.9
25,000–29,999	130	40.0	37	40.5	58	37.9	35	42.9
30,000–34,999	138	47.1	76	44.2	18	55.6	43	48.8
35,000–39,999	62	45.2	41	51.2	5	40.0	16	31.3
40,000 plus	49	73.5	28	67.9	6	100.0	15	73.3
Total	435	43.7	195	45.4	123	37.4	116	47.4
Rep Seats	190		89		46		55	

SOURCE: Data compiled by author from *Congressional Quarterly.*

well in the lower-income districts as it did in the more affluent districts. By 1984, in the North, the party won only in middle income to affluent districts, and its success increased as the income level rose. The transition in the South was somewhat parallel. In 1966 the party's success in the South, limited as it was, did not vary as income increased. By 1984 the South had developed many more relatively affluent districts, and the party found its success increasing (except for the oddity of winning two of three of the poorest districts) as income levels increased. By 1984 the Republican Party had more seats in the South, and in the North and the South its success was greater as income increased. It was acquiring more of a base in the more conservative South and it was developing an electoral base comprised of a greater proportion of affluent districts.

The party was also attracting more conservatives. From the early 1970s to the mid-1980s conservative whites opposed to government efforts to guarantee jobs and to freedom of choice on abortion steadily moved to the Republican Party (Carmines and Stanley 1990: 28–29). In the South, conservatives were steadily leaving the Democratic Party and moving to the Republican Party (Black and Black 1987: 249–254).

The concerns of the party remained conservative after the mid-1980s. The Reagan administration proposed and secured a significant cut in the federal income tax in 1986, despite persistent criticisms of many Democrats that the cut was of more benefit to the affluent (DeParle 1991). The election of George Bush as president in 1988 suggested a somewhat less conservative Republican approach, but his administration still continued to push cuts in the capital gains tax (or taxes on increases in the value of assets, stocks, or investments), which largely benefits the affluent. He also continued to attack affirmative action as a betrayal of the American commitment to individualism and equality of opportunity. The party's platforms, developed during presidential elections, and presidential speeches were used to express support for individualism, decentralization of responsibilities from the federal government, the importance of the family, and concern for social decline (Gerring 1998: 129–158). Republicans consistently articulated the theme that government should stay out of the economy and let the private sector develop as it might (Dionne 1997: 151–230). A crucial part of the Republican message from 1980 to 1992 was that government was bad and that the federal government was particularly bad. As Lee Atwater, a key strategist and campaign manager during this era put it:

> In the 1980 campaign we were able to make the establishment, insofar as it is bad, the government. In other words, big government was the enemy, not big business. If the people are thinking that the problem is that taxes are too high and government interferes too much, then we are doing our job. But if

they get to the point where they say the real problem is that rich people aren't paying taxes, that Republicans are protecting the realtors and so forth, then I think the Democrats are going to be in pretty good shape. (cited in Edsall and Edsall, 1991a: 73–74)

During the late 1980s and early 1990s Republicans in the House and the Senate continued to advocate tax cuts, less regulation, and more government activism to enforce conservative social norms.

The 1994 Election and After

The two years leading up to the 1994 elections were particularly important in establishing the concerns of the Republican Party. The loss of the presidency prompted the party to reassess its image and positions. To many conservatives, the challenge to the party was clear.

To most Americans Republicans were still the party of the rich, fat, white guys not connected to the people. What we are trying to do is become the populist party. The challenge for the party was to blame government for the nation's cultural and economic dilemmas and to identify itself as the anti-government, anti-Washington party. (cited in Balz and Brownstein 1996: 14, 22)

The Clinton administration's actions in 1993 and 1994 provided a remarkable opportunity for Republicans. Clinton, responding to the increasing number of individuals without health care and the growing cost of health care in America, proposed an elaborate national health care program. Much of the expanded coverage would be paid for with a "tax" on existing premium payers, which meant people who were better off would be paying to support people less well off. Republicans were able to use Clinton's positions in 1993 and 1994 to create a continuing contrast between their resistance to more government and the Democratic preference for more government, bureaucrats, and regulations. Republicans planned carefully for 1994, raising money and creating a clear message to communicate nationally to voters (Jacobson 1996; Polsky 1997).

Their major innovation was the Contract with America. The contract was based on five principles: individual liberty, economic opportunity, limited government, personal responsibility, and security at home and abroad. The contract presented specific proposals that Republicans pledged to vote on within the first 100 days of the session, if they were in the majority. They pledged to make Congress live by the same personnel rules as the rest of the country, balance the budget, cut the capital gains tax, and provide a tax cut for families (Gingrich and Armey 1994). Although the contract was not widely known, it was very well known among the more affluent, and this segment of the electorate was very positive about it (Moore et al. 1994: 20–21). Republicans also made attacks on welfare a major theme in campaigns (Katz 1994). Overall, little in their agenda communicated concern for the less affluent, but appealed to people who did not need government and found taxes and regulations a burden and irritant in their lives.

The election produced the first majority for the Republicans since the 1950s. It also changed their electoral base even further. Table 4.7 presents the base of the Republican Party in 1962, the year before Barry Goldwater ran, and for 1994, following the November elections. In 1962 over half (116 of 180, or 64 percent) of Republican seats were from the North. The party won roughly the same percentage of seats in most districts, except for the 9 most affluent districts, where they did very well. They had only 16 seats in the South. The 1994 election produced a very different electoral base. Only 89 of 230 Republican House seats came from the North, or 39 percent of the party's seats. In the North, party success increased as

TABLE 4.7   Region, District Income, and Republican Success, U.S. House of Representatives, 1962 and 1994

Income Level	Nation		North		South		Other	
				Region of Nation				
1962	N	%	N	%	N	%	N	%
0–19,999	108	21.3	13	46.2	79	10.1	16	56.3
20,000–24,999	126	40.5	69	50.7	27	14.8	30	40.0
25,000–29,999	131	48.1	90	48.9	5	60.0	36	44.4
30,000–34,999	57	56.1	37	62.1	1	0	19	47.4
35,000 plus	13	84.6	9	88.9	1	100.0	3	66.7
Total	435	41.4	218	53.2	113	24.2	104	46.2
Rep Seats	180		116		16		48	
Income Level	*Nation*		*North*		*South*		*Other*	
1994	N	%	N	%	N	%	N	%
0–19,999	19	21.1	4	0	13	23.1	2	50.0
20,000–24,999	91	33.0	21	19.1	46	30.4	24	50.0
25,000–29,999	129	56.6	50	44.0	43	65.1	36	63.9
30,000–34,999	88	61.4	44	52.3	17	76.5	27	66.7
35,000 plus	108	63.9	63	63.5	12	83.1	33	57.6
Total	435	52.9	182	48.9	131	51.9	122	59.8
Rep Seats	230		89		68		73	

SOURCE: Data compiled by author from *Congressional Quarterly*.

the income of districts increased. In the South, the party now had 69 seats, compared to 16 in 1962. There were far more affluent districts in 1984 than in 1962, and the party did very well in those districts. The party now had a House membership that was based heavily, but not exclusively, in more affluent districts. That greater success among the more affluent at the district level also occurred among individuals in 1994. That election produced a significant increase in the party's success among more affluent voters (Stonecash and Mariani 2000).

Having won control of Congress, the Republicans wasted no time in staking out their positions. The election produced a class of over seventy freshman Republican members, many of them conservative, who demanded that the party pursue conservative principles. Republicans proposed cuts in the general federal income tax and in the capital gains tax. They sought to give states more freedom in how they managed nutrition programs for the less affluent. They sought to cut back federal inspection programs that protect worker safety. They sought to cut welfare and turn it over to the states (Maraniss and Weisskopf 1996). They wanted a smaller federal government and less government intrusion into private lives. The party, emboldened by its new majority, sought to cut the federal budget, and was so convinced of the support for their positions and so committed to them that the impasse evolved into a shutdown of the federal government in late 1995 (Balz and Brownstein 1996; Drew 1996). The party had won power, established a clear set of priorities, and taken a very prominent stance in favor of them. In 1998 and 1999 the party continued to push for restraint of government programs and tax cuts.

In summary, since the early 1960s the Republican Party has changed significantly. The conservative movement became much more organized and moved from being a group contending for power to a dominant force within the party. The electoral base shifted from a majority of seats in the North to a majority coming from the South and the West. To be sure, there are still many moderates within the Republican Party and they continue to argue for moderation in party positions (Rae 1998: 63–64). It is clear, however, that conservatives have dominated the formation of policy positions in recent years. The party, whether represented by the presidential or the congressional wing, has adopted more conservative views, with opposition to the national government, taxes, and social programs central to their positions. By the 1990s there was little in their rhetoric that communicated concern for the less affluent. The focus was on an "opportunity society" and individualism (Dionne 1997: 159–230), which is much more likely to appeal to the affluent. Little in their policy presentations addressed issues of growing inequality or problems of people lacking health care or pensions. There was less concern for the growing costs of attending college.

Attracting Conservatives

It is often asserted that America began a conservative drift somewhere in the late 1970s or the early 1980s. As noted in Chapter 3, however, the evidence for that assertion is very mixed. Support for conservative positions has increased for some issues, whereas support for liberal positions has increased for other issues (Mayer 1992: 111–134). Clearly, however, conservative opinions have been forcefully presented and have played a significant, if not dominant, role in political discussions in the last two decades.

Although the percentage of the electorate with conservative views may not have increased, it is perhaps more likely that conservatives have been mobilized to become a more organized political force. A constituency with specific concerns is more likely to have an impact in political debates if they are concentrated in one party and constitute a significant part of the party. The most important change in the Republican Party over the last three decades has probably been their ability to attract many conservatives who were previously in the Democratic Party. As the Republican Party came to be seen as more conservative, it attracted more conservatives, who then became a larger part of their electoral base. Their concentration within the Republican Party has given them relatively greater dominance within the party and provided them with a vehicle for making a forceful argument for the conservative perspective.

The NES surveys provide a means to assess the extent of this change. In NES surveys, respondents are asked whether they identify themselves as liberals, moderates, or conservatives. Respondents are also asked about whether government should guarantee jobs or let people get ahead on their own, whether government should provide health insurance or let people arrange their own private insurance, whether government should help minorities or if minorities should help themselves. Table 4.8 focuses on people who regard themselves as conservatives or who prefer solutions without government involvement. The table reports the percentage either identifying themselves as conservatives or holding conservative opinions who also identify with the Republican Party, for the 1970s, the 1980s, and the 1990s. It also reports the percentage of Republican Party identifiers who hold conservative positions. That is, the table indicates the tendency for conservatives to identify with the Republican Party, and then how much the Republican Party consists of conservatives.

For all four questions, the percentage of conservative respondents identifying with the Republican Party increased from the 1970s to the 1990s, with the increases ranging from ten to sixteen percentage points. For example, among self-identified conservatives, 57 percent identified with the Republican Party in the 1970s, and by the 1990s, 67 percent did. In addition, the dominance of conservatives within the Republican Party increased from the 1970s to the 1990s. For three of the four indicators,

TABLE 4.8   Mobilizing Conservatives: The Movement of Conservatives to the Republican Party and the Gradual Increase in Their Dominance of the Party

| | *Those Holding Conservative Positions in the Republican Party, and as a Percentage of the Republican Party* | | | | | | | |
| | *Self-Defined Conservatives* | | *Government Not Provide Jobs* | | *Government Not Provide Insurance* | | *Minorities Should Help Themselves* | |
Decades	*In Rs*	*Of Rs*	*In Rs*	*Of Rs*	*In Rs*	*Of Rs*	*In Rs*	*Of Rs*
1970s	57	47	43	62	45	55	39	52
1980s	62	49	50	64	55	52	46	56
1990s	67	57	55	65	61	55	49	65
Δ 1970s–1990s	10	10	12	3	16	0	10	13

SOURCE: NES Cumulative File, 1948–1996. The actual questions and the years asked follow. The table presents the percentage of those with the conservative position (indicated following each question) who are in (identify with) the Republican Party, and the percentage of Republican Party identifiers who hold the conservative position. Responses within each decade are treated as one group.

Self-Defined Conservatives: "We hear a lot of talk these days about liberals and conservatives. Here is a 7-point scale on which the political views that people might hold are arranged from extremely liberal to extremely conservative. Where would you place yourself on this scale, or haven't you thought much about this?" 1–3 are then collapsed into liberal, 5–7 into conservative. Years: 1972–1996.

Government Guarantee of a Job: "Some people feel that the government in Washington should see to it that every person has a job and a good standard of living. Suppose these people are at 1. Others think the government should just let each person get ahead on his / her own. Suppose these people are at 7. Where would you place yourself on this scale, or haven't you thought much about this?" 1–3 are then collapsed into liberal, 5–7 into conservative. Years: 1972–1996.

Government Provision of Insurance: "There is much concern about the rapid rise in medical and hospital costs. Some feel there should be a government insurance plan which would cover all medical and hospital expenses. Suppose these people are at 1. Other feel that medical expenses should be paid by individuals, and through private insurance programs. Suppose these people are at 7. Where would you place yourself on this scale, or haven't you thought much about this?" 1–3 are then collapsed into liberal, 5–7 into conservative. Years: 1970, 1972, 1976, 1978, 1984, 1988, 1992, 1994, and 1996.

Help Minorities: "Some people feel that the government in Washington should make every possible effort to improve the social and economic position of blacks. Others feel the government should not make any special effort to help minorities because they should help themselves. Where would you place yourself on a 7-point scale?" 1–3 are then collapsed into liberal, 5–7 into conservative. Years: 1970–1996.

there was an increase from three to thirteen percentage points. For the other there was no decline. By the 1990s, depending on which question is used as an indicator, from 55 to 65 percent of Republican Party identifiers were people holding conservative positions (Beck 1997: 7–8). The shift in concerns of the Republican Party attracted more conservatives into the party. Having a constituency that is increasingly conservative, of course, is likely to reinforce the concerns of the party. From the early 1960s to the 1990s the Republican Party had moved from a relatively moderate and mixed-constituency party to one in which conservatives were of increasing importance.

The Democrats

The important matter for voters is the alternatives presented to them in an election. Do the parties differ, and in what ways? Much as with the Republican Party, the Democratic Party has undergone significant change since the early 1960s in its electoral bases and concerns. Their story has been told more, so the review can be somewhat shorter. Although the Democratic Party's recent history has been widely written about, it is unclear whether the portrayals have been accurate and what the dominant policy positions within the party are now. Nevertheless, the party has clearly changed since the early 1960s. Before moving to the ambiguity of the present situation, the broad changes of recent decades are important to review.

To simplify, the Democratic Party has gone through roughly three phases since the 1950s. It has moved from a party conflicted by disagreements between its conservative and liberal wings during the 1950s and 1960s to a party seen as very liberal in the late 1960s and 1970s to a party, beginning in the 1980s, struggling with whether to be moderate or liberal. Just what defines the Democratic Party now is a matter of considerable dispute. That ambiguity is of considerable importance for comparing the party with Republicans.

The 1950s and Early 1960s

The Democratic Party in the 1950s and early 1960s was a party with significant internal divisions. Its majority in Congress came from having a substantial bloc of seats in the South, which was more conservative than the rest of the country. Table 4.9 indicates the number of seats that the Democrats in the House of Representatives had from each region of the country from 1958 through 1962.

The party needed 218 votes in the House to pass legislation and their seats from votes outside the South did not provide that majority. The composition of the party and the importance of the South resulted in a party with a very mixed agenda and image. Many of the Democrats from northern districts wanted to provide more federal aid for local schools, adopt some sort of civil rights legislation, and provide more funding for social programs. The southern wing, however, was unwilling to support

TABLE 4.9   Distribution of Democratic Seats in House of
            Representatives, 1958–1962

	Number from Region		
Region	*1958*	*1960*	*1962*
Total	280	259	255
North	118	106	102
South	106	106	97
Other	56	47	56

SOURCE: Data compiled by author from *Congressional Quarterly.*

this agenda, and the resulting image of the party was not clearly liberal
or conservative. If Democrats wanted to take action in many areas, they
had to form a coalition with northern Republicans (Deckard and Stanley
1974; Brady and Bullock 1981), which they often did.

The Emergence of a Liberal Agenda

The mid- to late 1960s significantly changed the image of the Democratic
Party. Lyndon Johnson won the presidency in 1964 in a landslide over
Barry Goldwater and carried a large number of congressional Democrats
with him. The party had a large majority in both houses of Congress as
it began the 1965 session. Johnson, responding to an extensive public debate about issues of inequality, and a large majority based on rejecting a
conservative Republican Party candidate, moved the party into its second
phase with an extensive and clear agenda of liberal legislation. Congress
enacted legislation expanding civil rights, providing more federal aid to
local education, establishing and strengthening environmental regulations, providing loans to college students, providing more equality of access to housing, establishing Medicaid, and enacting programs to try to
reduce poverty (Mayhew 1991: 57–63). Although the Democrats still
drew on support from northern Republicans to enact much of this legislation, there was no doubt that it was the Democratic Party that initiated
change and advocated a more activist agenda for the federal government.

The perception that the Democratic Party was very liberal was accentu-
ated by the events of 1968 through the early 1970s. The party, facing challenges from southern blacks about representation, opened up its process of
selecting delegates for the national presidential candidate to minorities and
reduced the influence of party leaders who may have wanted to slow
change. The new rules enabled liberal activists with diverse concerns to influence the process of selecting a party candidate (Polsby 1983). The ultimate impact was the selection of George McGovern as the 1972 Democratic

nominee for president. McGovern was widely portrayed as very liberal and the party was portrayed as preoccupied with minority rights and liberal causes; the party suffered a resounding loss in the presidential election of 1972.[10]

Some Democrats saw the loss as a reason to seriously reconsider the policy directions of the party and its image. Democrats were continuing to lose seats in the South and critics argued that changes in the process of selecting delegates had given extreme liberal activists too much influence over the party platform, choosing candidates, and establishing the party's image (MacInnes 1996: 73–88). This party debate was temporarily avoided as Watergate and Republican president Nixon's demise unfolded in 1973. By November 1974, the Republican Party was in serious trouble and Democrats benefited with enormous gains in Congress and across the nation. That was followed in 1976 with the presidential victory of Democrat Jimmy Carter. In a very short period of time, the party moved from anguished introspection in 1972 to unified control of both branches after 1976.

Political Defections and Debating the Party's Focus

The next several years, however, were unpleasant for the Democratic Party. Jimmy Carter did not seem to know how to handle larger symbolic issues and he was particularly berated for his inability to project an image of competence. He did not seem to know what to do about the energy crisis as Middle Eastern countries cut oil supplies to the United States (Hodgson 1996: 239–242). Unemployment increased to the highest levels in years, and inflation reached levels (over 10 percent) that shocked many people. The Iranians seized the American embassy and Carter could not devise a solution. America seemed humbled at home and abroad under Carter.

This negative image of the Democrats helped to elect Ronald Reagan. His election was the beginning of a widespread discussion about whether America had turned conservative. Reagan had always proclaimed his conservative inclinations. The crucial question was what his election meant about the political drift of the country (Kopkind 1984; Ferguson and Rogers 1984). To some, the election of Reagan was really only the product of the terrible condition of the economy in 1980. Carter, as the incumbent president, was blamed and the loss was seen by many as a product of short-term events that would recede in the public's mind (Gans 1980). The party had had an unfortunate candidate and events had simply turned against the party.

Others, however, were much more negative and alarmist about the future of the party. Reagan had criticized Democrats as hopelessly liberal, and many accepted the criticism because of what they found in election returns. The essential argument was that the party had become "too concerned about fringe issues" of abortion, civil liberties, feminism, gay rights, civil rights, and affirmative action, rather than bread-and-butter economic issues. The party could not reconcile the concerns of its divergent constituencies (Samuelson 1980). Democratic Party stances on social issues had alienated its core constituency, white working-class ethnics (Radosh 1996: 134, 181–184, 199). The conclusion was that the party had to move away from strong support for these social issues and move back to economic issues and less concern with the fringe issues (Edsall and Edsall 1991b: 163–166).

Interpreting the Democratic Situation

The arguments about who the Democrats had alienated were based on fundamental assumptions about the image of the Democratic Party, the nature of the working class, and what shaped American politics. These assumptions, while more a part of the world of academics, consultants, and Washington commentators than the general public, had been emerging for some time and were crucial in shaping the debate following the late 1970s about what direction the party should take. The evidence about electoral behavior is particularly important because of its influence in shaping debates. The conclusions derived from analyses are very questionable, but as Curtis Gans said in reviewing the 1980 election, ". . . instant political analysis is often politically self-serving and wrong . . . [but] it produces lasting political myth which, in turn, tends to color the conduct of American politics" (1980: 630).

The basis for the conclusion that the working class might desert the Democratic Party over race and cultural issues began in the 1950s. Studies of that era found that people with less education (the working class) were least likely to be tolerant about free speech and civil liberties (Stouffer 1955; Prothro and Griggs 1960; McClosky 1964; Jackman 1972). This intolerance created potential for lower-class voters to be preoccupied more with issues of race, gay rights, and abortion than with issues of class. Preoccupation with social issues would pull them away from voting on the basis of their economic position, resulting in a decline in class divisions as the less affluent left a Democratic Party taking liberal positions. The conclusion, as expressed by Lipset, had powerful implications:

> The gradual realization that extremist and intolerant movements in modern society are more likely to be based on the lower classes than on the middle and upper classes has posed a tragic dilemma for those intellectuals of the democratic left who once believed the proletariat necessarily to be a force for liberty, racial, and social progress. (1981: 87)

The possible role of intolerance became a clear reality in the 1960s. The "cultural" issues of free speech, civil rights, feminism, and gay rights all became part of the political debate (Edsall and Edsall 1991b). Perhaps the most explosive issue was race, involving busing, open housing, access to public and private facilities, voting rights, affirmative action, and concerns about crime (Rieder 1989: 248–258). Whatever doubt existed about the power of race issues was dispelled by the political support George Wallace received. He mixed hostility to the national government and its experts, populist appeals, and resistance to black concerns to garner far more votes in presidential primaries than anyone expected (Edsall and Edsall 1991b: 77–80; Carter 1995: 324–370). Although Wallace's appeal may have been more than racial in nature (Kazin 1995a: 221–242), many voters saw him as essentially appealing to racist anger. Commentators then tended to focus on the movement of white southerners out of the Democratic Party, though many neglected to identify which whites were leaving the party (Ladd and Hadley 1975: 227–231; Brown 1991: 75–150; Black and Black 1992: 141–175; Gillon 1992: 288–289; Sanders 1992: 99; MacInnes 1996: 53; Carmines and Layman 1997: 92). The presumption was that race was driving all whites out of the Democratic Party and that race was the "transforming issue" of American politics (Carmines and Stimson 1989: 14; Edsall and Edsall 1991a: 53–54). Given the prior analyses of the greater intolerance of the working class, the conclusion that race issues would lead to defections of working-class whites from the Democratic Party was plausible, resulting in a decline in class political divisions in U.S. politics.

At the same time another body of research concluded that since the 1940s the working class declined as a percentage of society. Long-term economic development raises incomes and education levels, which moves more of the population into the middle class. At the simplest level, the argument was that increasing general affluence in the society would result in a population with a smaller percentage of poor and working-class people. The working class would then constitute a smaller part of the electoral base of the Democratic Party (Axelrod 1972: 14; Axelrod 1978: 623; Axelrod 1986: 282). Increasing affluence would mean fewer class conflicts and less concern with such issues (Nisbet 1959; Bell 1962; Bell 1973; Lipset 1981: 253; Wilensky 1966). From this perspective, the problem facing the Democrats was that a constituency crucial to the party, the working class, was moving into the middle class and becoming more concerned with preserving their newfound status than supporting redistributive policies.

Other analysts argued that the more important impact of increasing affluence is altered values. As income and education increase, concerns about scarcity and materialism slip away, people become more concerned about the quality of life and postindustrial values, and class conflict declines (Inglehart 1971; Huntington 1974: 189; Ladd and Hadley 1975: 195–200).

All these analyses had their limits. There were criticisms that the evidence of working-class intolerance was not as persuasive as suggested and that the questions used in analyses were less than credible as indicators of tolerance (Hamilton 1972: 399–467; Erikson, Luttbeg, and Tedin 1989: 172–173). Although race and reactions to race issues were presumed to be the transforming and driving force of American politics, it sometimes appeared to be more a matter of assertion than documentation. For example, as shall be reviewed later, the percentage of whites voting for Democratic presidential candidates changed very little from 1952 to 1996. In addition, to assume that the lower class was fading away ignored mounting evidence about inequality of incomes and that the less affluent were steadily losing ground economically (see Chapter 3). Further, there are reasons to be very skeptical of this research because the questions used to measure postindustrialism had little, if anything, to do with economic conflicts (Davis 1996). There are also reasons to be skeptical about the notion that class is defined by the absolute level of income of families, rather than their relative level. If working-class families experience a real increase of $10,000, but others experience gains of $20,000, there are surely reasons to doubt that people ignore their status relative to the more affluent.[11] Further, the arguments that the working class was intolerant, becoming middle class, and less concerned with material conflicts were not always compatible. If the working class was becoming middle class it follows that the intolerance of the working class is less relevant.

Despite these problems, the conclusion that class was less relevant to American politics became widespread. The conclusion that class divisions were declining became a regular conclusion in academic analyses (Nisbet 1959: 11–14; Alford 1963: 103; Ladd, Hadley, and King 1971: 47; Glenn 1972; Abramson 1974: 102–105; Knoke and Hout 1974: 704; Glenn 1975 120–121; Ladd and Hadley 1975: 73, 233–239; Trilling 1976: 95–130; Ladd 1978a: 98), and they remain with us (Ladd 1991: 31–33; Beck and Sorauf 1992: 166; Carmines and Stanley 1992: 221–222; Keefe 1994: 214; Flanigan and Zingale 1998: 101–102; Abramson, Aldrich, and Rohde 1995: 146, 152–153; Ladd 1996: 204–206; Lawrence 1997: 40).

Given these accumulated studies, the conclusion that by the early 1980s there had been a significant defection of the working class to Reagan and the Republicans seemed very plausible. The actual evidence of this shift, however, is not so clear. That evidence deserves a brief review because of its importance for subsequent interpretations of the Democratic Party's situation and for which divisions dominate American politics. The presumption was that the Democratic Party had become too liberal and had alienated its electoral base. There is no doubt that Reagan moved voters to the Republican column in presidential elections. The crucial question is whether it involved a greater movement to him primarily among the working class, such that class divisions declined, or whether it was more of a general movement of all groups to Reagan.

The ways in which class divisions have been measured are important. An overview of the development of that analysis is also presented in the Appendix for readers with more interest in that subject. Diverse approaches have been taken to define the class of individuals (Knoke 1976: 59–68; Jackman and Jackman 1983: 1–41). Class has been measured using income, occupation, education, or combining the three into an index of socioeconomic position. Other scholars who emphasize the importance of class consciousness and argue that individuals should be allowed to classify themselves by class simply ask people to define their class.

Although these various approaches continue to be used, each has its limits. The occupation-based measures are surely difficult to rely on over time because it is unclear, as the occupation structure of the society changes from manufacturing to service, how to classify many service or white-collar jobs. These jobs may have status but not pay well, or have low status but pay well.

The self-identification approach has several limitations. The presentation of only two alternatives collapses differences in ways that may significantly affect results. Very affluent individuals are given little choice but to define themselves as middle class. Perhaps most important, responses to how people see their social status is likely to be affected by people's desires about how they would like to be seen. How they like to see themselves may have little to do with what drives their vote, particularly in a society experiencing increasing inequality. Further, many of the analyses using this measure focused only on votes in the presidential election. The conclusion was that class divisions were declining (Abramson, Aldrich, and Rohde 1986: 150–151). The difficulty was that the same decline did not occur in House or Senate races, and it did not occur for party identification (Stonecash 1999c). As the Appendix indicates, decline in class divisions, using this measure, occurred only in presidential races.

Perhaps most important are the actual studies that became the basis for the conclusion that the working class was deserting the Democratic Party. The evidence was not as clear as many analysts implied. Analysts appeared to presume what had happened, and then saw that in the results. Others chose not to see some results. Box 4.1 presents some examples of the results used to conclude that Democrats had lost the working class. The first, taken from a 1978 publication, compares the 1964 and the 1974 elections. The first election, 1964, was one of the larger landslides for Democrats in recent history. The second, driven by the Republican's problems with Watergate, also was a landslide for Democrats. The results were used to argue that Democrats by 1974 were gaining support among high-status whites (a nine-point gain relative to 1964) and alienating low-status whites (a seven-point loss relative to 1964). The difficulties with this analysis are numerous; it was accompanied by comments about an "inversion" of class relations, but no inversion occurred. Lower-status whites in 1974 were voting for Democrats at a higher rate than higher-status whites. Further, these were two very unusual elections, and more years and elections should be analyzed before reaching that conclusion. There appears to be a rush to judgment in this conclusion.[12]

The second set of data was presented by Pierce and Hagstrom to analyze the 1980 election. The conclusion was that Carter had lost the middle class and had suffered "massive attrition" among blue-collar workers. Carter clearly lost support among both groups, but his losses were about the same among all groups. It is a significant overreach to turn general losses in one election for one office into an argument about selective losses and the drift of the entire party. It is also interesting that the authors do not see the difference in 1980 of twenty-five percentage points between people making less than $10,000 (50 percent voting for Carter) and those making more than $50,000 (25 percent for Carter) as indicating anything important.

Finally, the last data are from an analysis published in 1984. Ladd, responding to the arguments of William Schneider (1983) and David Broder (1984) that class divisions had reemerged as significant, countered with an argument that there was no evidence of the revival of class divisions. He presented the trend for 1974–1984 of the percentage of low- and high-income voters indicating they are supporters of the president, without averaging them for each presidential era. The averages of his data are presented here, along with his assessments of them. The average difference between low- and high-income voters doubles for Reagan compared to Ford and Carter, but Ladd prefers to characterize this as "somewhat greater" and generally argues that "shifts in the extent of class voting have on the whole been strikingly small" (41). What electoral patterns actually occurred will be examined in the next chapter, but the analyses just reviewed were common during this era. Taken together, the analyses about working-class intolerance, the eruption of race issues, and the presumed decline in the working class made it plausible that class divisions had declined in American politics.

It soon became widely stated, as noted in Chapter 1 and above, that the Democrats had alienated their core constituency (Ladd 1985: 5; Barnes and Weicher 1985: 49; Smith 1996: 260) and had to rethink their policies and concerns (Bonafede 1983: 2053; Galston 1985: 17; Bonafede 1985: 216). The defeats of liberal Democratic presidential candidate Walter Mondale in 1984 and moderate Michael Dukakis in 1988 reinforced that conviction that the party was too liberal (Schneider 1988: 31–35 and 56).

BOX 4.1   Class Divisions

" . . . the contemporary realignment comprises an inversion of the old class relationship in voting, an inversion first evident at the presidential level but likely to penetrate the entire range of electoral contests. . . ." (240)

Democratic Percentage of the Congressional Ballots, White Voters by Socioeconomic Position, 1964 and 1974

Status	1964	1974	Change
High	48	57	+9
Middle	65	62	−3
Low	74	67	−7

SOURCE: Ladd and Hadley, *Transformation of the American Party System* (1975: 239).

"Carter suffered his biggest losses since 1976 among the big middle-income group of persons. . . . Among occupational groups, the worst news for Carter was the massive attrition among blue collar workers." (1877)

Family Income	Carter 1980	Change
Under $10,000	50	−11
$10,000–15,000	47	−9
$15,000–25,000	38	−12
$25,000–50,000	32	na
$50,000 plus	25	na
Job Head of Household		
Professional/Manager	33	−8
Clerical/White Collar	42	−13
Blue Collar	46	−12

SOURCE: Pierce and Hagstrom, "The Voters Send Carter a Message" (1980).

"The income spread under Reagan is somewhat greater than it had been in prior years. It is also clear, however, that the split is not accurately described as a new "class chasm." (43)

Average Percent Saying They Are a Supporter of the Current President

Income	Ford	Carter	Reagan
Low	46.4	58.6	35.6
High	60.1	46.7	60.1
Difference	13.9	11.9	24.5

SOURCE: Ladd, "Is Election '84 Really a Class Struggle?" (1984).

These electoral problems prompted an extensive debate within the Democratic Party about what positions it should adopt to revive its fortunes (Galston 1985; Kuttner 1988; Galston and Kamarck 1989; Barnes 1990; *Harper's Magazine* 1990; Rothenberg 1991; Wills 1997). Many moderate to conservative Democrats sought to push the party to adopt more moderate positions (Hale 1995) or to focus less on ideology and redistribution and more on problem solving and general growth in the economy (Schneider 1989). The Democratic Leadership Council, comprised of moderates, was created in 1985 to serve as a vehicle for the expression of these concerns.

The moderates argued that the party was too liberal, too concerned about civil liberties and rights issues, and was alienating whites with its concern for minorities. Studies indicated that the party had lost its claim as the party of prosperity, and the Republican Party was now seen as more effective at managing the economy (Lawrence 1991: 808). It was widely noted that "No Democrat except Lyndon Johnson in 1964 has won a majority of the white middle class vote since Truman's squeaker" (Clark 1985: 443). The moderate recommendation was that the party move to the middle and communicate to middle-class voters that they understand their concerns. Central to their argument was that the Democratic Party did not demand that the beneficiaries of government programs have some responsibility for their behavior. The party found itself in the position of apologizing for men deserting wives, for illegitimate births, for crime, and for lengthy stays on welfare, all because it was presumed that these behaviors were the product of society (Edsall and Edsall 1991a: 62–69).[13] Beneficiaries became victims, and not responsible for their behavior (Wattenberg 1995: 19–26). This position did not sit well with a middle class that was working harder and not making any progress, and provided a basis for Republicans to critique the party and attract converts. Critics within the Democratic Party argued that the party had to create an image of a new Democrat, who would reform entitlement programs and curtail spending programs (Galston and Kamarck 1989; MacInne, 1996; Greenberg, 1996; Ladd 1998; Penn 1998). The concern that Democrats focus more on "values" issues has been persistent. The party went so far as to hire a consultant to travel the country prior to the 2000 elections to conduct seminars about how to use the language of "values" in their political discussions (Mitchell 1999b).

These arguments did not go without a response from liberals. Critics argue that the party's real problem is that it lacks a clear identity of fighting for lower- to working-class interests and that it should make those concerns central to its message (Ferguson 1986; Kuttner 1987; Sanders 1992; Miller and Ferroggiaro 1995; Meyerson 1996a; 1996b). These critics believe that the ambiguity about the party's primary concerns has made it difficult for the party to mobilize the less affluent to vote, and this has cost the party support at the polls (Kazin 1995b).

Amid this debate about policy positions, the debates about whether Democrats are losing the working class continues. Following the 1994 elections, when Republicans won fifty-two House seats to take the House and also won the Senate, it was common to read statements such as "Non-college educated voters deserted the Democrats in droves" (Teixeira and Rogers 1996: 13–14). The authors note that the decline in support for Democrats was ten percentage points for high school dropouts, eleven points for high school graduates, twelve points for those with some college, and zero points for those with a college degree or more (14). The differences in decline as education varies are by no means systematic, but this evidence is seen by many as the Democratic Party has alienated its core constituency. On the other hand, other studies have concluded that the evidence about the party alienating the working class (Teixeira 1997) or losing "angry white males" (Reeher and Cammarano 1996) is very weak.

As these arguments about the future of the party unfolded, the constituency base of the party continued to shift. Much as with the Republicans, shifts in the electoral base of the party created new tensions within the party. There were significant changes both in the South and outside the South for Democrats. In the South and Sunbelt, there was a significant increase in black registration and in the size of the Latino population. Those additions to the South electorate resulted in districts with very different constituencies in terms of income and the percent nonwhite. Although Republicans were winning more seats, there continued to be House districts very amenable to a Democratic Party concerned about the less affluent.

Outside the South, something very different was happening. Whereas Republicans began to experience success in the South in the 1950s, Democrats were gaining seats outside the South. Many of the seats the Democrats won outside the South were in lower-income districts, and many of these had a high percentage of minorities. These new members were relatively liberal, and they resented the Republican language of personal responsibility as a direct attack on their constituencies (Balz and Brownstein 1996: 87–94). These new liberal members also had conflicts with the more moderate members of the Democratic Party.

Table 4.10 indicates how the source of Democratic seats in the House changed for the party from 1962 to 1992 in the South and outside the South. Again, if the success rates of the party by district income are examined for 1962 for the nation, it appears that the party did very well in lower-income districts and not as well in affluent districts. The difficulty was that this result was largely due to the party's success in the less affluent South. The nation's lowest income districts were in the South, and Democrats held almost all those districts. Outside the South the party had no clear pattern of great success in lower-income districts. In terms of raw

TABLE 4.10   Region, District Income, and Democratic Success, U.S.
House of Representatives, 1962 and 1992

			Region of Nation					
Income Level	*Nation*		*North*		*South*		*Other*	
1962	N	%	N	%	N	%	N	%
0–19,999	108	78.7	13	53.9	79	89.9	16	43.8
20,000–24,999	126	59.5	69	49.3	27	85.2	30	60.0
25,000–29,999	131	51.9	90	51.1	5	40.0	36	55.6
30,000–34,999	57	43.9	37	37.8	1	100.0	19	52.6
35,000 plus	13	15.4	9	11.1	1	0	3	33.3
Total	435	58.6	218	46.8	113	85.8	104	53.9
Dem Seats	255		102		97		56	
Income Level	*Nation*		*North*		*South*		*Other*	
1992	N	%	N	%	N	%	N	%
0–19,999	19	79.0	4	100.0	13	76.9	2	50.0
20,000–24,999	91	75.8	21	85.7	46	80.4	24	58.3
25,000–29,999	129	58.9	50	60.0	43	53.5	36	63.9
30,000–34,999	88	52.3	44	59.1	17	29.4	27	55.6
35,000 plus	108	41.7	63	42.9	12	25.0	33	45.5
Total	435	57.7	182	57.7	131	59.5	122	55.7
Dem Seats	251		105		78		68	

SOURCE: Data compiled by author from *Congressional Quarterly.*

numbers, the party had 97 of its 255 seats in the South, with its other seats drawn from a diverse set of districts.

By 1992 significant changes had occurred. Within the South and the North the party did much better in lower-income districts (Stonecash and Lindstrom 1999). The party, to be sure, also won seats in relatively affluent districts, but it did much better in lower-income districts. Those seats in lower-income districts became the basis for much of the liberal wing that did not want taxes or programs cut. Although the "New Democrats" were arguing that the party should move to the middle, the liberal wing of the party was unwilling to relent on the need for programs for their constituents. By the 1990s the party was no longer a fountain of liberal programs, as it was during the 1960s, but there was still a vocal liberal wing to the party that competed with the moderates to define the party image. The result was clearly a somewhat muddled image of what defined the Democratic Party.

Liberal Dominance Within the Democratic Party

The story of the evolution of the Democratic Party is not as clear as that of the Republican Party. Some changes are clear and others are less clear. The Democratic Party did experience a shift in its electoral base, at least as measured by geography and the characteristics of House districts. As noted in Chapter 2, since the 1950s the party steadily lost seats in the South, a more conservative region, and gained seats outside the South. As Table 4.10 indicates, by 1992 the party had a clear base in lower-income House districts. It has been widely noted that after 1964 black voters moved strongly away from the Republican Party and to the Democratic Party, becoming a larger part of their electoral base. Given those trends, it would seem clear that many critics were right that the party had become more, and perhaps, too liberal.

It is not clear, however, that the party was as dominated by liberals as many suggested. Table 4.11 presents the percentage of liberals identifying with the Democratic Party and their relative dominance within the party by decade. The questions used are the same ones used for assessing the significance of conservatives within the Republican Party. In this case the focus is on those holding the liberal position—identifying themselves as liberals, supporting a position that government should intervene to provide jobs or health insurance, or to help minorities. The patterns are very different from those found for the Republican Party. First, there was little change in the party identification of liberals. Most of those who identified themselves as liberal or who held liberal views, at least on these questions, were already in the Democratic Party by the 1970s. There may well have been significant shifts in the party identification of liberals during the 1950s and the 1960s, but it is not possible to assess that using these data, since these questions were not asked prior to the 1970s. Although the Republican Party was acquiring conservatives, the Democratic Party already had attracted most liberals. Second, liberals generally have not constituted a significant portion of the party, either in the 1970s or in the 1990s.

Although conservatives became more dominant and constituted more than 50 percent of the Republican Party from the 1970s to the 1990s, and the party leadership became more conservative, liberals were not a large part of the electoral base of the Democratic Party in the 1970s and their predominance within the party did not grow over time.

The trend, if any, in the primary concerns of the Democratic Party is not entirely clear, therefore. On one hand, there was a shift away from the South, more House representatives in low-income districts outside the South, greater reliance on a black constituency, and enough dominance of liberals such that moderates mobilized against liberals. On the other

TABLE 4.11   Liberal Dominance in the Democratic Party

| | *Those Holding Liberal Positions on the Following Issues* | | | | | | | |
| | *Self-Defined Liberals* | | *Government Provide Jobs* | | *Government Provide Insurance* | | *Government Help Minorities* | |
Decades	*In Ds*	*Of Ds*	*In Ds*	*Of Ds*	*In Ds*	*Of Ds*	*In Ds*	*Of Ds*
1970s	73	26	68	36	63	54	65	38
1980s	75	25	66	39	56	49	67	34
1990s	80	29	66	40	66	56	71	31
Δ1970s–1990s	7	3	−2	4	3	2	6	7

SOURCE: NES Cumulative File, 1948–1996. The actual questions and the years asked are the same as those presented in Table 4.8. The table presents the percentage of those with the liberal position (indicated following each question) who are in (identify with) the Democratic Party, and the percentage of Democratic Party identifiers who hold the liberal position. Responses are merged within decades.

Self-Defined Liberals: "We hear a lot of talk these days about liberals and conservatives. Here is a 7-point scale on which the political views that people might hold are arranged from extremely liberal to extremely conservative. Where would you place yourself on this scale, or haven't you though much about this?" 1–3 are then collapsed into liberal. Years: 1972–1996.

Government Guarantee of a Job: "Some people feel that the government in Washington should see to it that every person has a job and a good standard of living. Suppose these people are at 1. Others think the government should just let each person get ahead on his/her own. Suppose these people are at 7. Where would you place yourself on this scale, or haven't you thought much about this?" 1–3 are then collapsed into liberal. Years: 1972–1996.

Government Provision of Insurance: "There is much concern about the rapid rise in medical and hospital costs. Some feel there should be a government insurance plan which would cover all medical and hospital expenses. Suppose these people are at 1. Other feel that medical expenses should be paid by individuals, and through private insurance programs. Suppose these people are at 7. Where would you place yourself on this scale, or haven't you thought much about this?" 1–3 are then collapsed into liberal. Years: 1970, 1972, 1976, 1978, 1984, 1988, 1992, 1994, and 1996.

Help Minorities: "Some people feel that the government in Washington should make every possible effort to improve the social and economic position of blacks. Others feel the government should not make any special effort to help minorities because they should help themselves. Where would you place yourself on a 7-point scale?" 1–3 are then collapsed into liberal. Years: 1970–1996.

hand, by the 1990s moderate "New Democrats" like Bill Clinton had significant influence on the party, and liberals remained less than a majority of the party. The media widely discussed the problem of the liberal Democratic Party during the 1980s, but by the 1990s that topic received far less attention, perhaps reflecting the moderation of the party image. Although the question of whether the party had an image that was liberal or moderate cannot be easily settled, it is clear that the Democratic Party had maintained a set of policy preferences different than that of the Republican Party. It is the contrast of the party images that are important when we try to explain how the electorate reacts.

Summarizing Evolving Party Differences

Since the 1950s the political parties have changed in their constituencies and concerns. The positions of the parties on major issues have changed. Is there specific evidence of these changes? Party "positions" and their evolution cannot be summarized in any simple way. Parties are collections of diverse views, and which views dominate within a party varies from issue to issue and from time to time. Some party members receive more coverage than others, so some messages get more attention than others. Further, how the media portray party messages and what information the electorate receives are another issue. With those cautions noted, it appears that the Republican Party has *become* more conservative, with a segment of the party arguing that the party should be more moderate. The Democratic Party has *remained* a relatively liberal party, compared to the Republican Party, but with many party members seeking to moderate the image of the party, and some party members arguing that it should remain liberal.

Perhaps the most important matter is that the policy concerns of the parties now differ more than in the 1950s and the 1960s. The differences show up in several ways. The electoral bases of the parties in Congress have become more distinct. In the House Republicans are more likely to win seats in higher income districts and Democrats are more likely to win seats in lower income districts. The party candidates who run for congressional seats now differ in their policy stances. Democratic candidates are now much more likely than Republicans to support public spending on public education, health care, jobs retraining, increasing taxes on higher incomes, and concern about poverty and inequality (Erikson and Wright 1997: 137–138). The party platforms are different, with Republicans more likely to stress individualism, the family, and liberty (Gerring 1998: 125–158) whereas Democrats are more likely to mention social welfare and the problems of minorities, poverty, and support for redistribution (Gerring 1998: 205–253).

The votes of the parties in Congress provide further indications of their differences. After the civil rights confrontations of 1964, Democrats became much more supportive of civil rights laws (Carmines, Renten, and Stimson 1984; Carmines and Stimson 1989). Democratic officeholders and activists generally take much more liberal positions than Republicans on using government to support welfare spending, raising the minimum wage, providing tax credits for the working poor, and supporting job training programs (Pomper 1972; Wilson 1985: 300–307; Aldrich 1995: 169–173). Democrats in Congress increasingly vote for liberal positions, and Republicans vote for more conservative positions (Taylor 1996: 279–281). During the 1980s when Democrats were in the majority in the House they made a concerted effort to call attention to the issue of the increasing inequality in the distribution of income (DeParle 1991: A-12). During the 1980s and 1990s the parties have continually presented different positions on the role government should play in society. Republicans emphasize the importance of cutting taxes, reducing the role of government, and allowing free markets to determine outcomes, whereas Democrats emphasize the importance of government trying to help those experiencing job loss as the economy changes (Dionne 1997: 151–230).

The growing division between the parties has become evident in Congressional votes. A standard way to assess party divisions is to calculate the extent to which members of one party vote with each other and against the other party. This can be represented by calculating an index of party unity, which is the average for all members, of the percentage of votes on which a party member supports his or her party (Rohde 1991: 8–9). The trends in party unity follow a pattern that would be expected for parties experiencing changing electoral bases. From the 1940s through the 1960s party unity scores steadily declined, with southern Democrats in particular defecting from their party. Since the early 1970s, however, there has been an increase in the percentage of votes in the House in which the parties vote against each other (Rohde 1991: 15; Fleisher and Bond 1996). In recent years the newer members of each party have tended to vote strongly with their party against the other (DeSart 1998: 6–9) and each party has experienced a decline in members who have moderate voting record (Saunders 1998). As might be expected, the House and Senate have experienced a steady increase in party unity voting levels, or in the extent to which party members vote together and in opposition to the other party (Strahan 1998: 28–29).

Finally, the differences emerge in the ratings given to each party by interest groups. The Americans for Democratic Action, a liberal group, gives high scores to those who vote for liberal policies and low scores to those who vote against them. The scores are then scaled with 100 complete agreement with ADA and 0 complete disagreement. In the 1960s Democrats received an average rating of approximately 55 from ADA and Republicans averaged approximately 20. By 1996 the average Democratic score had increased to 75 and Republicans were at 10. The difference increased from 35 points in the 1960s to 65 points in 1996 (King 1998: 1; Grosclose, Levitt, and Snyder 1999: 41–42).

Current Party Differences

Each party has internal differences and tensions about what policies should be adopted. The images of each party are less than precise. The Democratic Party has debated and struggled with how liberal they wish to be and has vacillated somewhere between liberal and moderate in the last decade or so. The Republicans also have dissenters, with moderates arguing that the party should tone down its conservative wing (Sack 1999).

Despite these tensions, the parties now differ significantly. The Republicans have taken decidedly more conservative positions since the early 1980s. In particular, the party has regularly adopted positions that indicate less concern for the less affluent and for nonwhites. Republicans led the initiative in 1996 to limit welfare. They have continually proposed cuts in the capital gains tax and in taxes in general (Mitchell 1997a: A-1; Mitchell 1997b: A-1; Rosenbaum 1998: A-18; Mitchell 1998: A-20). They have led efforts to reduce the power of unions by eliminating the automatic deduction of union dues that provide funds for political contributions for unions (Greenhouse 1998: A-10). Republicans have opposed providing welfare and food stamps to illegal immigrants or granting legal status to illegal immigrants (Purdum 1997: A-1). The party has consistently opposed affirmative action. The party has sought to cut federal housing assistance for the poor (Dao 1998: B-3). Republicans sought to cut regulatory efforts by agencies such as OSHA, which inspects working conditions to make sure they are safe. They sought to reduce subsidies for student loans for college (Wells 1995: 3740). They have opposed allowing the Census Bureau seek to find "missing" low income and minority transients in the 2000 census through sampling (Holmes 1998a: A-11; Holmes 1998b: A-13). In 1999, with budget projections suggesting that there would be a surplus in coming years, the Republicans proposed a tax cut of $792 billion, with 80 percent of the cuts going to those 20 percent with the highest incomes (Brinkley 1999; Stevenson 1999). In all these efforts, Democrats opposed the Republicans, either wanting no changes or wanting to make much less significant cuts in federal programs or taxes.

The most fundamental difference between the parties involves the issue of government and its relationship to society, and it is perhaps best illustrated by the language party leaders use in describing society and government. To Democrats there are problems that people have and government can help these people. To Republicans there are valued principles of opportunity, liberty, and freedom, and government is more than likely to hinder the achievement of these principles.

In Bill Clinton's 1998 state of the union address he was careful to use the language of personal responsibility that Republicans had seized on and used to mobilize conservatives and moderates (Clinton 1998: A-19–20). He referred to opportunity, responsibility, and hard work. But he also presented a speech systematically focused on an array of people's problems and how government could be of help. He mentioned the difficulty parents have paying for college and proposed a Hope Scholarship. He spoke of workers displaced by economic change and proposed more job retraining funding. He suggested classrooms were too crowded and proposed government funding for more teachers. He referred to workers having trouble with health care programs and proposed a Consumer Bill of Rights. His list of problems and proposals was lengthy. Although he emphasized the language of individual responsibility that Republicans had skillfully used to argue that Democratic did not hold people responsible, Clinton implicitly articulated a notion that people's problems were recognized and could be addressed by a positive government.

The contrast with Republican language is important. Senator Trent Lott, the majority leader of the Republican-held Senate, responded to Clinton. His identification of problems and solutions was very different. He immediately called attention to differences between the parties. He articulated notions of how problems would be solved and how they would not be solved.

> [our plans] highlight some real differences between the Republican Party and the President concerning what government should do and how much of your money government should take.
>
> Big Government or families? More taxes or more freedom?
>
> Americans are overtaxed, overregulated, and overgoverned.
>
> . . . the only way to limit government and expand individual freedom is to eliminate the I.R.S. as we know it.
>
> The President seems to think that Big Government can solve all your children's problems if you will just give Government more of your money—and more control of your lives. Nonsense. We think the best things for safe, healthy children are healthy stable families—not more government programs that require parents to work longer, take home less, spend less time with kids (Lott 1998: A-21).

The solution to difficulties would come from individuals and families, and government was a hindrance, an interference, and a threat to liberty. Drawing on the populist perspective discussed earlier, government was by no means a positive force in lives, but a threat to lives. Bob Dole, the 1996 Republican presidential candidate, had articulated the same perspective in accepting the Republican nomination at the party's convention.

We have surrendered too much of our economic liberty. The freedom of the market is not merely the best guarantor of our prosperity, it is the chief guarantor of our rights. A government that seizes control of the economy for the good of the people ends up seizing control of the people for the good of the economy. When [our opponents, the Democrats] gather to themselves the authority to take the earnings and direct the activities of the people, they are fighting not for our sake, but for the power to tell us what to do. Are they taking care of you, or are they taking care of themselves? (Bob Dole 1996 acceptance speech at Republican convention)

The party differences have become unmistakable. The issue is whether the electorate sees these differences, and, if so, how voters react to them.

NOTES

1. It should be noted that the concern here is not with party organizations. There is an extensive body of research that has developed that focuses on whether parties as organizations have declined or reemerged as significant actors with diverse resources valuable to candidates. Although that concern is clearly important to tell us about one aspect of parties, it is not clear what the connection is between a decline or rise in organized activity and party positions and electoral reactions. For a review of this literature and a valuable commentary on the issue of the political consequences of change, see Coleman 1994.

2. Works such as Sears et al. (1980), for example, focus on the role of self-interest versus "symbolic" politics, such as party identification and self-defined ideology. Are demographic traits in a particular election related to supporting specific policy positions, and are those relationships greater than those for party identification and ideological self-placement? Although such studies are valuable, the presumption here is that, if social conditions, party responses, and electoral response are associated, the concern should be with how demographic traits are associated with identification with and support for parties over time.

3. For all of the following analyses, all median family income figures for House districts are adjusted for inflation and expressed in 1990 dollar values. The Consumer Price Index for various years since 1960 was first found. The CPI index was then divided by the value for 1990, making 1990 the base of 1.00. This results in index values for prior years median that are less than 1.00. The median family income for districts for prior years was then divided by this new index. Since the index is less than 1.0, it converts nominal dollar amounts for earlier years to real dollar values, with values expressed in 1990 dollar values. Thus for all the following tables, the distributions are of district values expressed in real, 1990, values. This is significant because from the 1960s to the 1990s many districts did experience real increases in median family incomes, although many did not. Overall, the diversity of median family incomes among all districts decreased from 1960 though 1980 and then increased again to a level greater than in 1960.

4. The top third and bottom third classification is done for all respondents. Since regions may have fewer or more respondents in a category than the national

distribution, the distribution for a region may not end up one-third in each income category. For example, since the South was poorer in the 1950s, it has a higher percentage of respondents in the lowest category.

5. Rae argues that "the major change has come from within the Republican party, where a conservative movement, ideological and purist, has emerged" (1989: 5).

6. Populism is used here as a movement opposed to large organizations and social change that destroy a way of life and threaten the liberty of the common man (Kazin 1995a: 12–17).

7. To be accurate, Carmines and Stimson measured only liberalism on race issues, so the general liberalism of these northern Republicans was not covered in their analysis.

8. There are numerous such think tanks, with the most prominent being the American Enterprise Institute, the Cato Institute, the Heritage Foundation, and the Hoover Institute. For reviews of other think tanks, see the items just cited, plus Democratic Party, U.S. House of Representatives, 1998.

9. The current consensus appears to be that the emergence of fundamentalist political activity is a relatively recent phenomenon. Although it is clear that fundamentalists became more active politically in the 1970s and 1980s than in the 1950s and 1960s, it is not clear that this activism is entirely new. Larson, discussing the background of the Scopes trial in Tennessee, argues that political activity by fundamentalists also increased significantly during the decade prior to the 1925 trial (1997: 11–39). That may be the case, although it still appears that there was a significant increase in mobilization of the conservative Christian community beginning in the 1970s.

10. The turmoil of the Vietnam War, urban riots, and extended protests within the country, all these events linked to the Democratic Party, also hurt the party in 1968 and 1972, but the primary concern is the extent to which the party was seen as liberal. The acceptance of minorities and liberal activists increased the perception that the Democratic Party was liberal.

11. A fuller review of these arguments is in the Appendix.

12. In the same vein, some analysts have also argued that the conclusion that Catholics are conservative and prone to move away from the Democratic Party because of this is also not supported by the evidence (Greeley 1977: 199–203).

13. As an aside, it is difficult to avoid the impression that many people writing about the Democratic Party, usually critical but supportive party members, were so profoundly influenced by the experiences of 1968–1972 that their sense of the party's situation was fixed by those years, and they found it difficult to integrate subsequent years into their sense of the party. Many overviews of the party focus on specific encounters in 1968–1972, often with a sense of anger or betrayal. To some people, it appears there is a sense that those the party was seeking to help turned on them, demanding more, showing no gratitude, and even accusing them and blaming them for problems. The analysis of Edsall and Edsall communicates a clear sense that someone should have had enough common sense to see the pitfalls of moving away from individual responsibility (1991b). Racial tensions also are significant in these reactions. Wattenberg, writing about individual responsibility, refers to "Lawrence O'Brien, [being] hounded out of a public meeting by

black welfare mothers, hooting loudly" (1995: 19). Further, there also seems to be a sense that Democratic elites are to blame for not having enough common sense or courage to challenge civil rights leaders seen as radical and intransigent. Radosh, commenting on the civil rights movement, says ". . . it is the civil rights movement that launched the Democratic Party on a trajectory that ended in disaster. [After dealing with issues of representation of Mississippi at the 1964 national convention] Democrats would move on to a disastrous overreaction and takeover by guilty white liberals and race-conscious black militants (1996: 2). MacInnes makes repeated reference to the inability of white leadership to stand up to black militants during the late 1960s and early 1970s (1996).

5

Electoral Response and Realignment

Political parties, at least in theory, serve as a crucial mechanism of representation in American politics. To the extent that broad collections of groups in American society have common interests, a party can serve to articulate their concerns in the political process. Whether the interests of people identifying with a party are ultimately responded to depends on the complex process of reaching political decisions. A fundamental premise of a democratic society, however, is that differing views should be considered in the process. Parties can organize the interests of one broad collection of interests and argue for their concerns versus the interests of others. They can create a dialogue about fundamental differences in interests and views. Parties, despite negative contemporary commentary, can be valuable and very relevant.

Despite the simplicity of that statement, several conditions must prevail to achieve this representation, and each does not occur easily. First, a broad collection of groups must have some identifiable commonality of interests, and those interests must be distinguishable from another set of interests. People who lack but want health care insurance differ from those who have insurance, and the former can be appealed to and organized as a constituency. Students who cannot afford college differ from those who can and the former can also be appealed to and organized as a constituency. If there are no such differences within the public about an issue, then there are no differing group interests that a party could choose to represent. Second, parties must adopt policy positions that respond more to one set of interests than to another; parties must espouse different policy positions. Third, the electorate must perceive a relevant difference between the parties, form reactions to them, and respond by identifying with or voting for one party versus the other.

Change complicates this process. As social conditions change, it may take a while for voters to perceive and accept that their personal situation has clearly changed and that this change may persist. It may take parties a while to recognize the changing problems and needs of the electorate and to form policies to respond to problems. If the policies parties support and seek to enact change over time, it may then take the electorate a while to recognize the changes and to discard existing attachments to respond to the evolving party positions (Fiorina 1981: 95–105). The electorate does not follow politics closely and generally has low levels of information about specific party policies (Glynn et al. 1999: 249–298). Acquiring information about where parties stand is costly (Popkin 1994). Given these conditions, the response to changing political conditions is erratic and slower than if party positions were clear and information was not costly. In addition, during the last thirty years the national media have become more negative about political parties, less inclined to report substantive policy differences between the parties, and more inclined to treat party policy proposals as strategic maneuvers (Patterson 1994: 53–175). This change in the content and tone of media coverage of politics will make it even more difficult for citizens to acquire and sort information about party differences.

The prior chapters have presented information on some important social and economic changes that could serve as the basis for the emergence of parties with different policy agendas. The changes in inequality are of prime interest for the analysis that follows. A society that values equality of opportunity is experiencing steadily increasing inequality of opportunity and outcomes. Access to education, health care, and pensions have become more unequal, as has the distribution of income. These trends have been developing for some time, and are now recognized as not just temporary phenomena.

Chapter 4 indicates that the parties have increasingly taken divergent policy positions in response to these developments. Both parties have ongoing internal disagreements about what policies to adopt, to be sure, but the differences between the parties on policy issues have clearly increased. Compared to the 1960s the parties are now elected from very different districts and take different positions. Democrats have remained more concerned about programs to help people facing economic difficulties. They have been much more willing to use the national government to address issues of inequality and what they see as the limitations of private markets. Republicans have been much more inclined to seek to limit the size of government and accept the outcomes of private markets. In addition, the parties differ on how government should be used to intervene in people's lives on cultural issues such as abortion, civil rights, civil liberties, and gay rights. Republicans have been more inclined to use government to prohibit and limit abortion, whereas Democrats have been more willing to use government to protect gay rights, civil rights, and free speech.

These evolving party positions, particularly on issues of equality of opportunity, create the possibility for a growing class political division in

American politics. Whether that division has developed depends on the reaction of the electorate. In particular, do economic issues, broadly defined, still matter to voters? Do voters see differences between the parties and have these perceived differences increased? What is the reaction to the perceived differences? How have voters responded in terms of party identification and voting behavior? The trends that have evolved in these areas will indicate whether parties play the role of representing different interests and creating a dialogue—an exchange of views—about what public policies should be pursued in U.S. politics. The results will also provide information about the questions raised in Chapters 1 and 2: Did Democrats alienate the working class? How have they survived while losing large portions of the South?

Issue Concerns and Perception of Party Differences

Much contemporary political commentary suggests that economic issues have declined in significance (Wattenberg 1995) and ideological differences have declined (Weisberg, Haynes, and Krosnick 1995: 251). Despite those claims, when voters are asked what they like and dislike about political parties over the last thirty years, 75 percent regularly include economic issues as a significant component in their primary concerns (attitudes about big government, states' rights, planning, government action to improve social conditions, control of or interference in private enterprise) as a basis for their reactions to the parties (Kelley 1988: 190; Geer 1991: 224; 1992: 52). Economic issues still appear to matter to the electorate.

The electorate also sees differences between the parties, with some change over time. Studies in the 1960s found the public saw broad differences in party positions on the role of the federal government and those perceptions affected voting. People who voted for Democratic presidential candidate Lyndon Johnson in 1964 were much more supportive of a strong federal role (Kirkpatrick 1968: 90), as were people who voted for Democratic candidate Hubert Humphrey in 1968 (Kirkpatrick and Jones 1970: 701). Economic issues continue to be a source of partisan divisions. Voters who are supportive of New Deal economic policy positions continue to strongly identify with the Democratic Party, whereas people opposed to these positions continue to strongly identify with the Republican Party (Kelley 1988: 192–193). A study of the years 1976–1992 found that "Democrats are seen as the party of inclusion and government spending, whereas Republicans are viewed as allies of the wealthy and opponents of government spending and intervention" (Baumer and Gold 1995: 33). Democrats are seen as the party of the people and the poor, as supporters of welfare, and this image has been relatively stable over time. Republicans have an enduring profile as the party of big business and conservatism (Baumer and Gold 1995: 37–39; Sanders 1988: 586).

As policy differences between the parties have continued, an increasing proportion of the electorate has come to recognize these differences. From the 1950s to 1968 the percentage of the electorate seeing a difference between the parties on aid to education, providing medical care, and guaranteeing jobs steadily increased (Pomper 1971; 1972). In the 1960s about 50 percent of the electorate saw a difference between the parties, and by the 1980s that percentage had increased to over 60 percent (Mayer 1998: 205). The Republican Party is now seen as the more conservative party. In the 1960s about 60 percent saw the Republican Party as more conservative, and by 1992 it had increased to about 80 percent (Aldrich 1995: 174). The shifts in policy concerns of the Republican Party appear to have registered with the electorate.

This shift in the perception of the Republican Party has been pushed along by particular actions. Ronald Reagan's proposals in his first two years in office contributed to the image of the Republican Party. As noted in Chapter 4, Reagan sought to lower inflation by contracting the economy. He also sought to cut numerous social programs. The combination of a recession and cuts in social programs produced negative reactions about his concern for the less affluent.

> The proportion of Americans who felt that Reagan "cares most about serving upper-income people" shot up from 29 percent in April, 1981, to a majority in September, 1981, where it remained throughout the recession. In the latest poll [June 1983] that majority reached a peak of 58 percent.
>
> In February and March [1983] majorities of about 2 to 1 told the ABC-Post poll that they viewed Reagan as "a rich man's President" who is "unfair to the poor" and "has no idea what people who aren't wealthy are going through." (Schneider 1983: 2203)

Although Reagan was able to mobilize and represent conservatives, and win two terms as president, he also contributed to a sense of a significant difference between the parties and he polarized the electorate more than any president since Kennedy (Schneider 1983: 2200, 2205–2206; Sundquist 1983: 418–424, 444–446; Stone, Rapoport, and Abramowitz 1990). The perception of differences in the policy concerns of the parties continued to increase through the early 1990s (Abramowitz 1994: 644).

Reactions to the Parties

Although the electorate may see differences between the parties, do these differences elicit positive or negative reactions? Specifically, do the less and more affluent differ in how they react to the parties over time? It would be ideal to have a time series question that asks something like: "Which party best represents your concerns?" The National Election Study, conducted every two years, is the national political survey with the most continuity, but it does not use such a question. The practice has not been to ask directly about the representation connection between voters and the public. Perhaps the best questions that can be used involve asking people about their likes and dislikes about the parties. These responses are by no means the ideal way to assess how voters react to the parties. Voters can offer whatever responses they wish, and the reasons offered by voters for their reactions may vary considerably. Although the responses do not involve reactions to a constant issue, they do indicate whether the electorate sees either party generally positively or negatively.

To assess these reactions, respondents were first asked things they like about each party and then things they dislike about each party. The net reaction to each party is indicated by the number of likes minus the number of dislikes. Crude as the indicator is, it does provide a rough indicator of the reaction of voters to each party. As reported here, the indicator is the net number of likes minus the number of dislikes.

Presenting Results

In reporting changes in this indicator and others that follow, several decisions about the presentation of results are important to explain. First, as indicated in Chapter 2, the regions of the country have moved in very different directions over time. The South has steadily moved to the Republican Party, whereas the remainder of the nation has moved to the Democratic Party over time. As will be seen, the changes in party reactions within these two regions have been very different over time. For that reason, the results that follow will be presented by these two regional groupings. The South, widely seen as the area experiencing the greatest change, will be presented first, followed by an analysis of the rest of the nation. The entire nation will then be examined.

The second important matter involves how to use income in presenting results. The argument of this analysis is that the opportunities and economic situations of voters of different income levels have evolved very differently in recent decades. The political parties have responded with positions and messages of very different relevance to lower- and higher-income voters. The important matters to assess, then, are how low- and high-income voters respond to those messages. Electoral reactions, therefore, will be presented primarily for low- and high-income voters, though the middle class will be briefly reviewed.

To capture economic situation, family income is used. As noted earlier, other measures of class have been used, each with merits and problems, as discussed in the Appendix. Family income is used as a measure because this directly captures the resources that individuals have at their disposal, and indicates the opportunities and general quality of life people experience. Income, for example, is strongly associated with whether people have experienced increases or decreases in their economic situation in recent years (Danziger and Gottschalk 1995: 39–92). Income is associated with the quality of local schools (Orfield 1991) and with the chance to attend college (Mortensen 1995). It is associated with whether people have health insurance and pensions (Mishel, Bernstein, and Schmitt 1997: 41–271). Because of these associations, the presumption is that income provides a valid indicator of the limits and opportunities people face. It is also a meaningful way to group individuals to track political responses as social conditions and party positions evolve.

More precisely, the presumption is that the important political matter is the *relative* economic position of individuals over time, not the absolute level of income (Easterlin 1974). The absolute level of income is inappropriate because individuals may experience increases in real income over time but still lose ground to others, such that their opportunities remain much less than the more affluent. Family income directly measures the total economic situation within which an individual lives, so it is used instead of personal income. Although sources of family income (types of jobs held, proportion from two income earners, and so on) clearly have changed over time, it is a family's total available resources that are likely to reflect an individual's relative economic situation.

This focus on relative position is also compatible with the way income is recorded in the NES studies. In the NES surveys, respondents are presented with many categories, with small increments between categories, and asked to choose a category. In the 1948–1998 cumulative file, the actual family incomes of respondents are not presented, but incomes are grouped by percentile position and the situation of respondents is reported by their relative position in that year's income distribution. This approach is more appropriate given the concern for relative economic situation. The percentile groupings used by NES are reasonable divisions, given the theoretical concerns of this analysis. NES groups income into five groups, using the same percentile groupings for each year. The percentile groupings are 0–16, 17–34, 35–62, 63–95, and 95–100. Using individuals grouped by the same percentile groups within each year also eliminates the need for dealing with inflation and changes in real income. People in a particular percentile grouping may make more or less in absolute dollars over time, but the important matter is their relative situation. To reduce the number of categories involved and to make the top and bottom groups roughly equal in terms of the percentages of the electorate involved, individuals in the first two categories are grouped together, whereas those in the highest two categories are grouped together.[1] This allows comparing the voting behavior over time of those in the bottom third (0–34 percent) of the income distribution, with those in the top third (64–100 percent).

Third, there is the issue of how to handle time. Elections are invariably unique, in that different issues dominate in any given election. It is very common and appropriate to focus on specific elections, but my concern is with long-term trends, not the impact of each presidential and congressional election. To increase the focus on trends, data in the following presentations are often grouped by decade. This reduces the number of data points that must be compared and makes it easier to see trends. To weight each election equally, results for each year within a decade are averaged.[2] This counts each election, regardless of sample size, as the same.

Finally, much of the commentary about the plight of the Democratic Party (see Chapter 1) and many of the analyses have focused on the behavior of whites (for example, see Abramson, Aldrich, and Rohde 1995: 146, 152–153). To provide some comparability with previous analyses, results will first be presented for just whites, as identified by respondents in the NES surveys. Focusing just on whites, however, excludes an increasing proportion of the American public (approximately 30 percent now), so the results for all respondents will also be presented.

Structuring the Analysis

The concern here is group political behavior over time. There are two equally valid traditions of analysis in this area: class analysis and determinants of voting choice. Each approach asks a different question, employs a different kind of analysis, and regards different kinds of information as appropriate to answer the question. In the tradition that focuses on class cleavages, class is treated as a variable of fundamental and primary interest (Campbell et al. 1960: 340–350; Alford 1963; Lipset 1981: 230–278; Abramson, Aldrich, and Rohde 1995: 152–155). With this approach the focus is on the absolute levels of party voting by a group (class) and then the differences between the levels. The absolute levels of party voting are important because if a majority of the less affluent do not vote for the liberal party, it is difficult to argue that the liberal party acts to mobilize or organize the less affluent (Alford1963: 81). The same logic applies to how the more affluent behave with regard to the Republican Party. When a majority of each group votes for different parties, then the difference between the two in party voting becomes an important indicator of cleavage.

The analysis of the determinants of vote choice, on the other hand, is concerned with the relative impact of various traits on vote choice (Axelrod 1972; Declercq, Hurley, and Luttbeg 1975; Erikson, Luttbeg, and

Tedin 1989; Lawrence 1991; Stanley and Niemi 1991; Kenski and Sigelman 1993; Nadeau and Stanley 1993; Levine, Carmines, and Huckfeldt
1997; Lawrence 1997). This tradition treats class and other variables (self-
identified class, occupation, education, self-defined ideology, positions
on various issues) as potentially competing and spurious sources of vote
choice. That is, one may be interested in the impact of income and occupation on how people vote. These two tend to be positively associated,
since people with higher incomes tend to have more prestigious jobs.
Since the two overlap in real life, it is often difficult to establish which
trait really affects voting. An association between occupation and voting
may be owing in large part to the income of an individual and it is difficult to separate the relative impact of income and occupation. Issues of
specification, or which variables are included or excluded in the analysis,
become very important. Multivariate analyses (usually regression) are
used and the size and statistical significance of coefficients are the information of interest.

The approach used here falls into the first tradition of analysis. The
questions of importance are whether Democrats have alienated the white
working class—the absolute level of voting for Democrats—and how voting within the group compares to the partisan voting of the more affluent. A regression analysis, although valuable for sorting out relative impacts, does not address the issue of the absolute levels of partisan voting
by groups. A relationship between income and party voting might become more positive or more negative over time, but slopes do not indicate the *level* of voting for Democrats as income varies, since that depends
on the other variables included in the analysis. The concern is not
whether income matters more or less, after controlling for other variables,
but how different income groups are voting. For these reasons, the focus
is on levels of voting by income groupings over time.

Middle-Class Political Behavior

Most political commentaries and analyses about trends in American politics focus on the less affluent and the middle class. The more affluent have
received less attention, for reasons that are unclear. The primary concern
here is with comparing the reactions of the less and more affluent, or those
in the bottom and top thirds of income distribution. The reactions of these
two groups indicate whether class divisions are increasing over time. If issues of class, equality of opportunity, and opposition to redistribution are
increasingly important and the parties diverge in their positions on these
issues, then the reactions of the less and more affluent are the most important indicators of whether class divisions are increasing.

This is not to argue for a moment that the middle class is not important politically. Their swing from one party to the other over time is crucial in determining electoral outcomes. The middle class may also systematically tend not to support one party, fundamentally shifting the balance of power in the political process and altering the focus of political debates. Before moving to examine differences between the less and more affluent, it is first important to assess whether the middle class has drifted over time to one party or another. Figure 5.1 presents the percentage of whites in the middle third of the income distribution voting for Democratic candidates for president, the House, and the Senate, since 1952.

Despite concern with the alienation of the middle class from the Democratic Party, the evidence does not indicate any systematic movement of the middle class away from the Democratic Party. This is the case if an analysis focuses only on whites or all voters. As Figure 5.1 indicates, there is no clear trend in their support. There has been, to be sure, considerable fluctuation from election to election. In 1964 white middle-class voters moved heavily to Democratic presidential candidate Lyndon Johnson, and in 1968 and 1972 they moved heavily away from Democratic presidential candidates Hubert Humphrey and George McGovern. The white middle class supported Democrats in 1976 but supported Ronald Reagan

FIGURE 5.1   Percent of Middle-Income Whites Voting for Democrats, 1952–1998

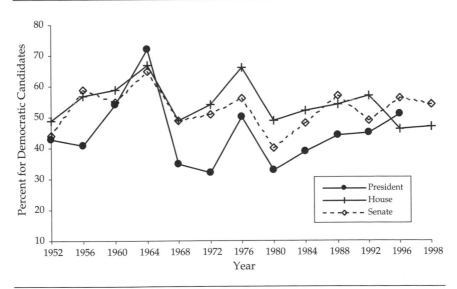

SOURCE: NES Cumulative File 1948–1998.

in 1980. The votes for congressional candidates for the House and the Senate generally followed these fluctuations, though the range of the fluctuations is more limited, to be expected when multiple candidates are involved. In presidential and Senate elections, following the fluctuations from 1960 to 1980, the white middle class has drifted toward Democratic candidates. In House elections the same pattern occurred until 1994 and 1996. In the 1994 (not shown) and 1996 House elections the white middle-class vote for Democrats decreased relative to 1992 (Stonecash and Mariani 2000).

To provide a more precise assessment of trends in support for Democratic candidates, Table 5.1 presents the results of a linear regression of Democratic support for each office on time, or the year of the election. All years for which results exist are used. If the slope is negative, it means there is a trend of declining support for the Democratic Party. A slope of zero indicates no trend over the time period 1952–1998, whereas a positive slope indicates increasing support. The table also presents the level of support by decade, with results within a decade averaged.

For presidential and Senate elections, there is only a very slight negative slope, and time explains only 1 percent of the variance in the dependent variable. Elections to these offices have almost no discernible trend. House elections show a larger negative slope, and the variance explained is 10 percent. For House elections, the average vote for Democrats declines from 56.0 in the 1950s to 52.2 in the 1990s, a decline of 3.8 percentage points. It is difficult to see a significant and sustained movement of the white middle class away from Democrats in the time series data and

TABLE 5.1   Trends in Middle-Income Voting for Democrats, Whites, 1952–1998

			Decade Averages				
	Slope	R^2	*1950s*	*1960s*	*1970s*	*1980s*	*1990s*
President	−.09	.01	42.0	53.7	41.0	38.7	48.0
House	−.12	.10	56.0	57.8	57.2	53.8	52.2
Senate	−.04	.01	54.3	54.8	56.8	49.0	50.6

NOTE: For the presidential elections, the percentage of votes received by the Democratic candidate (the three-code variable vcf0705 is used, so as to work with the actual percentage of the vote received by Democratic candidates) by income categories are used. A simple average was computed, thus, weighting each election equally. For House and Senate elections, the percentages voting for the Democratic candidates (vcf0707 and vcf0708, respectively), are used. The House and Senate averages and regressions are computed using all election years in NES, and not just presidential election years.

SOURCE: Analyses run by author, using data from the NES Cumulative File 1948–1998.

in these decade averages. Democrats have lost some support in the House, but stability with fluctuations seems to be more the case than any sort of trend. Given this relative, if erratic, stability of partisan voting of the white middle class, the crucial matters are, again, the reactions of the less and more affluent. The South, which has experienced the greatest change, will be analyzed first.

The South: Net Party Reactions

The South began moving toward the Republicans in the 1950s (Converse 1966a) and it has continued that movement. Although that is widely recognized, the important issue for understanding parties and political divisions is to know who has come to see the party positively. Table 5.2 presents the net reaction (likes minus dislikes) for the two parties for those

TABLE 5.2 Net Reaction to Two Parties, in the South, Low- and High-Income Respondents, by Decade, 1952–1996 (positive numbers are pro-Democratic, negative are pro-Republican)

	Low-Income			High-Income			Net Diff by Class
	Dems	*Reps*	*Diff*	*Dems*	*Reps*	*Diff*	
White Respondents Only							
1950s	.59	−.21	.80	.22	−.17	.39	.41
1960s	.16	−.05	.21	−.18	.09	−.27	.48
1970s	.07	.02	.05	−.11	−.02	−.09	.14
1980s	.34	−.09	.43	−.17	.49	−.66	1.09
1990s	.20	−.19	.39	−.63	.38	−1.01	1.40
All Respondents							
1950s	.68	−.17	.85	.22	−.16	.38	.47
1960s	.44	−.18	.62	−.11	.05	−.16	.78
1970s	.36	−20	.56	−.05	−.11	.06	.50
1980s	.50	−.19	.69	−.06	.42	−.48	1.17
1990s	.42	−.24	.66	−.43	.20	−.63	1.29

NOTE: Results from NES cumulative file, 1948–1998. All years are not included, because some years the questions were not asked. These questions were not asked in 1998. In each decade there were the following number of years that the questions were asked: 1950s (3), 1960s (3), 1970s (3), 1980s (5), 1990s (4). The variables used are vcf0316 and vcf0320. The results within each decade were then averaged, giving each election within a decade the same weight. The difference score is the Democratic net likes minus the Republican net dislikes. A positive difference means the Democratic Party has a net positive assessment. A negative difference means the net reaction to the Democratic Party is negative, or the Republican Party is seen more positively than the Democratic Party.

SOURCE: NES Cumulative File 1948–1998.

in the bottom and top thirds of income distribution. The difference in net reactions to the two parties for each income group are also presented. If a party has a positive score it means that group has more likes than dislikes for the party. To the far right is the difference in those differences, which indicates how far apart less and more affluent groups are in their net reactions. The greater the difference, the more divergent the two income groups are in how they see the parties. As discussed above, the results within each decade are averaged, and the concern is how net reactions have varied over time.

For low-income whites in the South a distinct pattern emerges. The South was overwhelmingly Democratic in the 1950s. The net reaction to the Democratic Party among the less affluent was relatively positive (.59) while the net reaction to the Republican party was negative (−.21). As the issues of civil rights and other cultural issues emerged in the 1960s and early 1970s, the stances of the Democratic Party became less appealing to lower-income southerners and the Republican Party became more appealing. In the 1980s and 1990s, with the Republican Party more concerned with tax cuts and less government, the Republican Party again was seen more negatively, whereas the assessment of the Democratic Party was more positive. The net effect was that by the 1990s lower-income respondents saw the Democratic Party as more positive than the Republican Party. In the 1990s, lower-income whites saw the Democratic Party *less positively than in the 1950s,* but their reaction to the Republican Party *was negative,* such that, relatively speaking, *they still saw the Democratic Party more positively than the Republican Party.* Political choices involve *comparing* two parties, not just whether a party comfortably represents all of an individual's concerns. The same pattern prevails when all respondents, whites, and nonwhites are considered together.

For high-income whites, the pattern is very different. In the 1950s the Democratic Party was seen positively, and the Republican Party was seen negatively. Beginning in the 1960s the Democratic Party acquired a negative assessment among high-income whites and by the 1990s the assessment of Democrats was more negative than in any other decade. The reactions to the Republican Party, on the other hand, were very different. After a period of ambivalence in the 1960s and 1970s, the reaction became very positive in the 1980s and 1990s. By the 1990s the combination of a negative view of Democrats and a positive view of Republicans resulted in the more affluent being relatively very positive about the Republican Party. A negative sign indicates a net positive view of Republicans compared to Democrats.

Since the 1950s, then, the relative reactions by class to the parties have shifted considerably. Low-income whites, after a period of vacillation in the 1960s and 1970s, have evolved to a net positive assessment of the Democratic Party and a net negative reaction to the Republican Party. High-income whites in the South have moved decisively to see the Republican Party positively, and the Democratic Party negatively. The pattern is the same when all respondents are considered. The evidence suggests that class reactions to party images have evolved in very different directions (Stanley 1988; Stanley and Castle 1988; Nadeau and Stanley 1993).

Finally, the last column of Table 5.2 indicates the net difference in reactions to the parties between low- and high-income respondents. Among lower-income white respondents in the 1950s, the net difference was .80, or relatively positive toward the Democratic Party. High-income whites were less positive to the Democratic Party, .39, but they were still positive, so the difference between the two groups was somewhat limited, or .41. By the 1990s low income residents were a net positive of .39, whereas the high-income respondents were a net negative to Democrats of −1.01, for a net difference between classes of 1.40. This divergence in class reactions has grown steadily since the 1970s. Again, the likes-dislikes indicator is crude and clearly imperfect, but it does suggest that general reactions follow the pattern one might expect, given the policy positions the parties have taken over time.

Net Party Reactions Outside the South

The changes in the rest of the nation, presented in Table 5.3, are very different from those in the South. Although in the South the major change was in the reactions of the more affluent, outside the South the major changes have been among the less affluent (Stonecash et al. 2000). More affluent whites outside the South show no clear pattern. Their differences in reactions to the Democratic and Republican Parties are fairly limited and reveal no trend across the five decades.

Less-affluent whites, however, have a very distinct trend. In the 1950s the reaction to the Democratic Party was positive, but the reaction to the Republican Party was also positive. The reaction to the Democratic Party, after experiencing a dip in the 1970s, continued to be positive and even increased slightly in the 1990s. The reaction to the Republican Party, however, turned steadily negative over time. The net differences by class in reactions to the parties steadily increased from the 1950s to the 1990s. As the last column indicates, the net differences in the 1950s were modest, but the net difference by class in reactions to the two parties has steadily diverged. High-income respondents display no clear pattern of reactions to the parties, though they do move negative toward Democrats in the 1990s. The major change, however, is in the reactions of people with low income. They remain somewhat stable in their reactions to the Democratic Party, but they become steadily more negative toward the Repub-

TABLE 5.3   Net Reaction to Two Parties, Outside the South, Low- and
High-Income Respondents, by Decade, 1952–1996 (positive
numbers are pro-Democratic, negative are pro-Republican)

	Low-Income			High-Income			Net Diff to Dems
	Dems	*Reps*	*Diff*	*Dems*	*Reps*	*Diff*	
White Respondents							
1950s	.33	.07	.26	.00	.20	−.20	.46
1960s	.30	−.05	.35	−.07	.07	−.14	.49
1970s	.16	−.20	.36	−.11	−.07	−.04	.40
1980s	.36	−.17	.53	.02	.14	−.12	.65
1990s	.41	−.46	.87	−.23	−.15	−.08	.91
All Respondents							
1950s	.43	−.01	.44	.02	.17	−.15	.59
1960s	.42	−.14	.56	−.01	.02	−.03	.59
1970s	.26	−.26	.52	−.07	−.10	.03	.49
1980s	.47	−.27	.74	.08	.07	.01	.73
1990s	.47	−.49	.96	−.15	−.18	.03	.93

NOTE: Results from NES cumulative file, 1948–1998. All years are not included, because some years the questions were not asked. In each decade there were the following number of years that the questions were asked: 1950s (3), 1960s (3), 1970s (3), 1980s (5), 1990s (4). The variables used are vcf0316 and vcf0320. The results within each decade were then averaged, giving each election within a decade the same weight. The difference score is the Democratic net likes minus the Republican net dislikes. A positive difference means the Democratic Party has a net positive assessment. A negative difference means the net reaction to the Democratic Party is negative, or the Republican Party is seen more positively than the Democratic Party.

SOURCE: NES Cumulative File 1948–1998.

lican Party. The result is that net reactions to the Democrats become more positive, and the result is an overall growing difference between low- and high-income respondents.

Two matters are important to note about these trends outside the South. As noted in Chapter 1, numerous analysts of political change have concluded that the Democratic Party alienated the white working class. Although definitions of working class can justifiably vary from one study to another, the results presented here, using a plausible grouping of the bottom one-third of whites, do not indicate a pattern of alienation of the white working class. To be sure, there was a drop in the positive reaction to the Democratic Party in the 1970s, while the party was experiencing considerable turmoil and identification with liberal causes, but that negative reaction did not persist. Perhaps most important is that a negative reaction to the Republican Party developed among the less affluent.

Net Party Reactions: The Nation

Table 5.4 presents the results for the entire nation, and they reinforce the prior results. The less affluent were positive about the Democratic Party in the 1950s. Their assessment declined in the 1970s, and then returned to near the 1950s level in the 1990s. Their reaction to the Republican Party has become steadily more negative. The more affluent (with respondents from different regions combined) have not followed a pattern of developing a strong reaction to either party. Even with that, though, they have been relatively positive toward the Republican Party in the 1980s and 1990s. The combination of the less affluent becoming positive about Democrats and negative about Republicans, and the more affluent becoming relatively favorable to Republicans, is that class differences in reactions to

TABLE 5.4   Net Reaction to Two Parties, the Nation, Low- and High-Income Respondents, by Decade, 1952–1996 (positive numbers are pro-Democratic, negative are pro-Republican)

	Low-Income			*High-Income*			*Net Diff to Dems*
	Dems	*Reps*	*Diff*	*Dems*	*Reps*	*Diff*	
White Respondents							
1950s	.41	−.01	.40	.04	.13	−.09	.49
1960s	.26	−.05	.31	−.09	.08	−.17	.48
1970s	.14	−.13	.27	−.11	−.06	−.05	.32
1980s	.36	−.14	.50	−.01	.21	−.22	.72
1990s	.35	−.37	.72	−.30	−.06	−.24	.96
All Respondents							
1950s	.52	−.07	.59	.06	.11	−.05	.64
1960s	.42	−.16	.58	−.02	.03	−.05	.63
1970s	.29	−.24	.53	−.06	−.10	.04	.49
1980s	.48	−.24	.72	.05	.14	−.09	.81
1990s	.45	−.39	.84	−.21	−.11	−.10	.94

NOTE: Results from NES cumulative file, 1948–1998. All years are not included, because some years the questions were not asked. In each decade there were the following number of years that the questions were asked: 1950s (3), 1960s (3), 1970s (3), 1980s (5), 1990s (4). The variables used are vcf0316 and vcf0320. The results within each decade were then averaged, giving each election within a decade the same weight. The difference score is the Democratic net likes minus the Republican net dislikes. A positive difference means the Democratic Party has a net positive assessment. A negative difference means the net reaction to the Democratic Party is negative, or the Republican Party is seen more positively than the Democratic Party.

SOURCE: NES Cumulative File 1948–1998.

the parties have steadily diverged over time. Political choices, again, always involve comparing two parties, and class differences have steadily increased. The less affluent do not see the Republican Party as an attractive alternative to the Democratic Party, even though less-affluent whites may have problems with the party's positions on civil rights or civil liberties issues.

To be sure, there is much to be learned about why these reactions developed. What issues were most important in prompting these reactions? What dynamics of party interaction played a role? This analysis by no means answers those questions. Despite these limitations, the parties clearly have drawn different reactions from the less and more affluent over time.

To provide an indication of the specific trends in these reactions, Figures 5.2 and 5.3 present the year-by-year net likes minus dislikes for two of the most significant groups. Figure 5.2 presents net reactions for people in the South to the two parties for high-income whites. High-income whites increasingly see the Republican Party positively, whereas the Democratic Party is seen negatively. Figure 5.3 presents the net reaction to the two parties outside the South for low-income whites. Low-income whites have become steadily more negative about the Republican Party,

FIGURE 5.2   Affect Toward Parties, 1952–1996, for High-Income
             Southern Whites Only

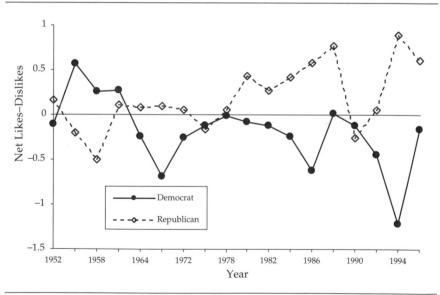

SOURCE: NES Cumulative File 1948–1998.

FIGURE 5.3   Affect Toward the Parties, 1952–1996, for Lower-Income
Groups, Non-South Whites Only

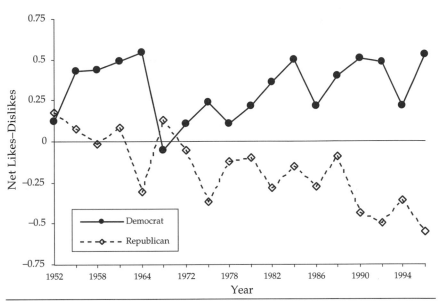

SOURCE: NES Cumulative File 1948–1998.

and after a decline in the late 1960s and 1970s, have become more positive about the Democratic Party.

Although the primary concern here is with electoral reactions by class,
the overall images and reactions to the parties are also important. For
much of the 1980s and the 1990s political commentary has focused on
image problems the Democrats have faced. The image of the Republican
Party received less attention, at least until the late 1990s and the disputes
over budgets and impeachment became important. Figure 5.4 presents
the net likes for each party since 1952. It is clear that the Democratic Party
has had times when its image turned negative, such as the late 1960s and
the early 1970s, and 1994, when reactions to the party plummeted. But
overall the reaction to the party has been fairly positive. Perhaps the most
interesting matter is that Republicans have struggled with developing a
positive reaction within the electorate. Indeed, since 1980 the party has
had more years with a negative reaction than years with a positive one.
Aside from the remarkable year of 1994, Republicans have struggled to
create an overall positive image with the electorate (Wills 1996).

The pattern of likes and dislikes results from the NES surveys are cor-
roborated by the pattern of reactions to congressional candidates.[3] Survey

FIGURE 5.4   Affect Toward the Parties, 1952–1996, All Respondents
                   Within the Nation

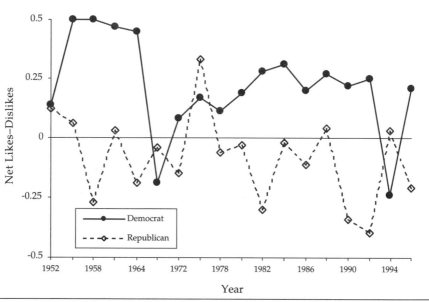

SOURCE: NES Cumulative File 1948–1998.

results from the CBS/*New York Times* polls also confirm the trend in reactions to the Republican Party. Beginning in 1984 this survey asked respondents if they had a favorable or unfavorable opinion of each party. From 1984 through 1991 the Republican Party generally received a 60 percent favorable and a 40 percent unfavorable rating. Beginning in 1992 their favorable rating dropped to around 50 percent and the unfavorable rating rose to 50 percent. By the 1996–1998 time period, when the federal government was shut down by a dispute over the budget and Republicans voted to impeach President Clinton, their ratings had dropped to 40 percent favorable, and their unfavorable rating remained at 50 percent (Stevenson and Kagay 1998: B-5). Again, the crucial matter in politics is the comparative assessment of the two parties, and although Democrats clearly have had times when they drew negative reactions from the electorate, there is considerable evidence that Republicans have struggled just as much, if not more, with generating positive electoral reactions.

Party Voting Patterns

The final and clearly most important matter in politics is how people vote. There have been long-term changes in the constituencies and concerns of the parties. Shifting party concerns have drawn somewhat expected reactions from the public. The antitax, antigovernment stance of the Republican Party has drawn a positive reaction from the more affluent in the South, whereas that stance has drawn a steadily more negative reaction from the less-affluent outside the South. Democrats have also had their difficulties, but there has been no systematic trend of positive or negative reactions to the party. For the nation, the net effect is that the less affluent have become more negative about the Republican Party, and the more affluent have continued to be ambivalent.

Do these party differences and reactions carry over to partisan voting behavior? For there to be such a connection, a relationship needs to exist between issue concerns, voter ideology, and which party voters support. The evidence indicates that although ideology and issue positions within the electorate may not have been closely connected in the 1950s,[4] these connections grew in subsequent decades (Pierce 1970: 31–39; Nie and Anderson 1974: 583; Schulman and Pomper 1975: 10–15; Hartwig, Jenkins, and Temchin 1980: 553; Pierce and Hagner 1982). There has been a connection between issues and the policy images of the parties for some time (Jackson 1975: 176; Conover and Feldman 1982: 234–235), and the relationship between ideology and party identification has also grown over time. Voters who are liberal are now more likely to identify with the Democratic Party and conservatives are more likely to identify with the Republican Party (Abramowitz 1994: 644; Abramowitz and Saunders 1998: 636–637). The crucial matter is whether voting patterns have also changed.

The South

As before, it is important to assess change by region because of how change has evolved in each region. Table 5.5 presents the levels of Democratic voting within the South for president and members of Congress (the House and the Senate) for whites, by income groups, by decade, and by region. Table 5.6 presents the results for all respondents by decade and region. Figures 5.5 and 5.6, respectively, present the year-by-year levels of voting for the president and members of the House in the South. These results parallel those found for likes and dislikes in the South. As Figure 5.5 indicates, in presidential elections among less and more affluent white voters, there was a significant drop in support for Democratic candidates in the late 1960s and early 1970s. Beginning in 1980 a pronounced class separation in support for Democrats emerged, with low-income white voters going back to the Democratic Party, and high-income white voters moving strongly to support Republicans. The pattern in House elections, shown in Figure 5.6, is somewhat different in timing, but the result is similar. Support for Democratic candidates dropped from 1952 until 1964,

FIGURE 5.5   Percent Voting Democratic for President, by Income
Groupings, Southern Whites Only, 1952–1996

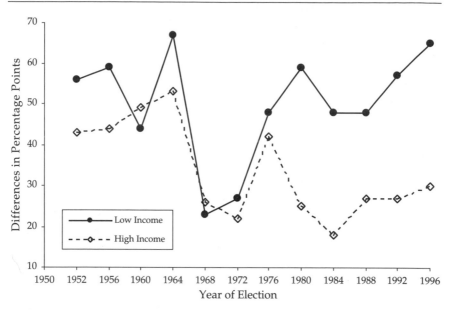

SOURCE: NES Cumulative File 1948–1998.

when a distinct class separation occurred. This separation did not occur
in 1966, but returned in 1968 and persisted from then until 1982, when
there was no difference. Since then, amid a general and noticeable drop
in support for the Democratic Party, a larger difference has developed
and continued (Petrocik and Steeper 1987: 43; Petrocik 1998: 17–20). Although it has been widely noted that the Democratic Party has had problems in the South in recent years, as this trend confirms, it is also clear
that a significant class division has developed.

The trend in the political division by class in the South in support for
Democrats is shown in Figure 5.7, which presents the difference in percentage points between low- and high-income voters in voting for Democratic candidates for the presidency and the House. The difference has
steadily increased since the 1970s for both offices. A primary source of
this growing division has been the relatively greater decline in support
for Democrats among more affluent voters.

This growing political division by class has enormous significance for
understanding political debates in the South and in the rest of the nation.
There has been considerable argument that the primary factors reshaping
southern politics are race issues (Ladd, Hadley, and King 1971: 56) and

FIGURE 5.6   Percent Voting for Democratic House Candidates, by
Income Groupings, Southern Whites Only, 1952–1998

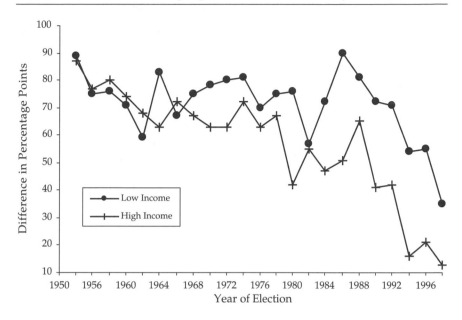

SOURCE: NES Cumulative File 1948–1998.

cultural issues (Edsall and Edsall 1991b; Rae 1992: 641; Aistrup 1996: 19).
Many of the 1950s gubernatorial races in the South had revolved around
race issues (Black 1976). The success of Republican presidential candidate
Barry Goldwater in the South in 1964 was widely attributed to his stance
opposing federal intrusion into "state issues" (Ladd and Hadley 1975:
162–166; Black and Black 1992: 270). George Wallace's run for president
in 1968 and his success in the South suggested that the primary issue in
campaigns revolved around "appeals calculated to solidify white opposition to racial change" (Black and Black 1973: 280). As Carmines and
Stimson argue with regard to the entire nation, race was "the issue transforming American political parties" (1989: 14). "Issues of race . . . soon
moved to the center of political belief systems" (Carmines and Stimson
1982: 6). The negative reactions of whites to race issues were most pronounced in areas with higher concentrations of blacks (Schoenberger and
Segal 1971: 585; Black 1973: 84; Wright 1976: 215; Knoke and Kyriazis
1977: 905; Glaser 1994: 33–34). The evidence that southerners have higher
levels of racial prejudice than other regions of the country (Kuklinski,
Cobb, and Gilens 1997: 323) makes the conclusion that race is fundamental in driving change in the South very plausible.

FIGURE 5.7   Percent Difference Between Low- and High-Income
Voting for Democratic Candidates for President and
House, Southern Whites Only, 1952–1998

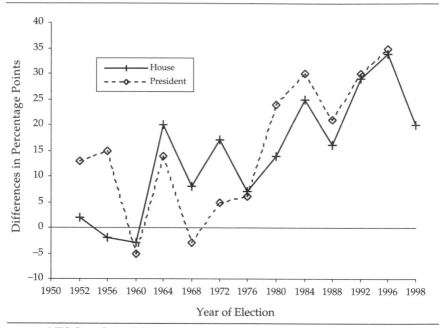

SOURCE: NES Cumulative File 1948–1998.

Racial issues are presumed to be so important in part because of their
effect on other political divisions. It is often argued that one of the most
significant impacts of race issues is their effect on class divisions. As Key
stated it, the crucial matter was the "... willingness to subordinate to the
race question all great social and economic issues that tend to divide people into opposing parties" (1949: 315–316). Black and Black restated the
theme almost a quarter of a century later. "Efforts to divide the white
electorate on the basis of class economic differences became secondary"
to race appeals (Black and Black 1973: 280). Numerous studies have concluded that class divisions are not relevant to explaining change in the
South (Gatlin 1975: 49; Campbell 1977: 51). Cassel went so far as to argue
that "continued preoccupation with explaining party choice and presidential voting in terms of social class or status polarization would seem
to inhibit development of better explanatory models" (1978: 706–707).
Class divisions do not exist in this view, because racial changes are seen
as most threatening to lower-class whites. The presumption is that voting
is largely driven by opposition to blacks, which means that "the class

TABLE 5.5 The Rise of Class Divisions: Percent Voting Democratic for Low- and High-Income Groups, and Differences, by Decade, Whites Only

	President			House			Senate		
Decade	Low	High	Diff	Low	High	Diff	Low	High	Diff
Entire Nation									
1950s	42	38	4	56	48	8	53	46	7
1960s	49	47	2	56	52	4	53	50	3
1970s	42	33	9	61	49	11	58	49	9
1980s	46	30	15	62	48	14	59	47	12
1990s	61	39	22	61	45	16	59	44	15
Non-South									
1950s	37	36	1	49	42	7	47	43	4
1960s	51	48	3	50	48	2	50	45	5
1970s	44	33	12	55	47	8	56	47	9
1980s	43	31	12	57	47	10	56	46	10
1990s	55	40	15	62	44	18	59	45	14
South									
1950s	58	44	14	80	81	−1	76	78	−2
1960s	45	43	2	71	69	2	58	66	−8
1970s	38	32	6	77	66	11	62	57	5
1980s	52	23	29	75	52	23	64	53	11
1990s	61	29	33	59	27	32	55	36	19

SOURCE: NES Cumulative File 1948–1998.

cleavage between the Democratic and Republican parties is diminished" (Giles and Hertz 1994: 324). Many analysts apparently presume that race issues are so powerful and general in their effects on whites that they find it appropriate to explain change in the South by generally referring to white movement away from the Democratic Party (Brown 1991: 75–150; Black and Black 1992: 141–175; Gillon 1992: 288–289; Sanders 1992: 99; MacInnes 1996: 53; Carmines and Layman 1997: 92), and not movement by higher-income whites. Race is often seen as an issue uniformly driving all whites to the Republican Party.

There have been, however, some doubts about the dominance of race. There was clear evidence from surveys that negative attitudes toward blacks were steadily declining (Firebaugh and Davis 1988: 260). In an analysis of results from 1952 to 1972 Beck found little evidence that attitudes about integration were driving partisanship, and suggested that racial issues might decrease in importance in the South (1977: 489–491).

TABLE 5.6   The Rise of Class Divisions: Percent Voting Democratic Within Bottom and Top Third of Income Groups, and Differences, by Decade, All Respondents

	President			House			Senate		
Decade	Low	High	Diff	Low	High	Diff	Low	High	Diff
Entire Nation									
1950s	44	38	6	57	47	10	55	47	8
1960s	54	49	5	60	53	7	55	52	3
1970s	51	35	16	66	52	13	64	51	13
1980s	55	33	22	68	51	17	65	49	16
1990s	64	41	23	66	44	22	64	46	18
Non-South									
1950s	39	37	2	51	43	8	49	43	6
1960s	55	50	5	54	50	4	52	47	5
1970s	50	36	14	59	49	10	60	48	12
1980s	51	35	16	62	50	12	60	47	13
1990s	59	43	16	65	46	19	62	47	15
South									
1950s	58	44	14	80	82	−2	77	79	−2
1960s	52	45	7	75	70	5	61	67	−6
1970s	54	36	18	81	68	13	67	59	8
1980s	64	27	37	81	55	26	71	57	14
1990s	75	37	38	65	32	33	63	43	20

SOURCE: NES Cumulative File 1948–1998.

Later studies found that although race was frequently mentioned as an important issue in surveys in 1964 and 1968, it subsequently declined in prominence (Lawrence 1997: 65–70). By the early 1990s, race attitudes appear to have little relationship to candidate evaluations (Wlezien and Miller 1997: 636). As I will discuss in the next chapter, it may be that race was in large part assumed to be a dominant issue. Systematic studies demonstrating that race was driving lower-income whites away from the Democratic Party were far less common than assertions of the role of race.

The results presented here can by no means answer the question of the ultimate role of race issues in shaping southern political behavior. Much more analysis is necessary to try to disentangle the role of race and class in the South and elsewhere in the nation. It does appear, though, that race issues did not by any means suppress the emergence of class divisions within the South. It may well be that the presumed dominance of race issues in southern politics needs to be reexamined.

Outside the South

The rest of the nation has also experienced considerable change. As noted in Chapter 1, since the 1940s there has been a steady increase in Democratic success in the House and in state legislatures. At the same time there has been considerable discussion about how Democrats have alienated the white working class over social, cultural, and race issues. Is that an accurate statement about what has transpired? The relevant trend involves the less affluent, and that group deserves close attention. Figure 5.8 presents the percent of low-income whites voting for Democratic candidates for the House and the Senate since 1952. It is difficult to see a downward trend in support for Democrats. There have been fluctuations amid the general trend, to be sure, but the trend is clearly upward. The combination of this trend and the essentially flat trend in Democratic support among high-

FIGURE 5.8   Percent Voting for Democratic Congressional Candidates, Nonsouthern Low-Income Voters, Whites Only, 1952–1996

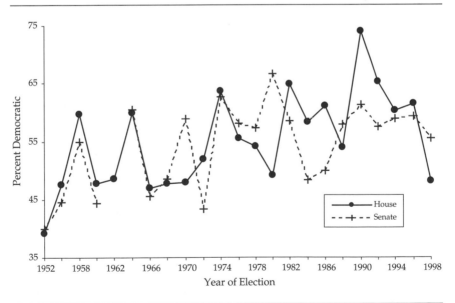

SOURCE: NES Cumulative File 1948–1998.

income whites is that the difference in support for Democrats by class has increased since the 1950s and the 1960s. Tables 5.5 and 5.6 present the decade averages in support for Democratic candidates for lower- and higher-income groups for the nation and by region. Outside the South the pattern is that support for Democrats among higher-income whites and for all respondents has been relatively stable, whereas Democratic support among low-income whites and all respondents has steadily increased. As reported in the tables, the result has been an increase in political divisions by class outside the South.

The evidence appears clear: Class divisions have not declined in American politics. Instead, the trend is a steady increase in class differences in support for Democrats (Petrocik and Steeper 1987: 42). The increases have occurred in the South and outside the South. Figures 5.9 and 5.10 present the differences by income in support for Democratic candidates for the presidency and the House by region since 1952. Again, there are unique factors in specific elections that create fluctuations from election to election. In 1998, for example, reactions to the impeachment suppressed class

FIGURE 5.9   Percent Difference Between Low- and High-Income
             Voter Support for Democratic Candidates for President,
             1952–1996, Whites

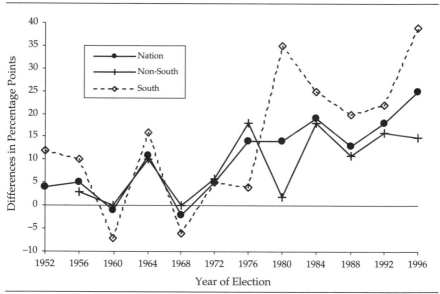

SOURCE: NES Cumulative File 1948–1998.

FIGURE 5.10   Percent Difference Between Low- and High-Income
                Voter Support for Democratic Candidates for House,
                1952–1998, Whites

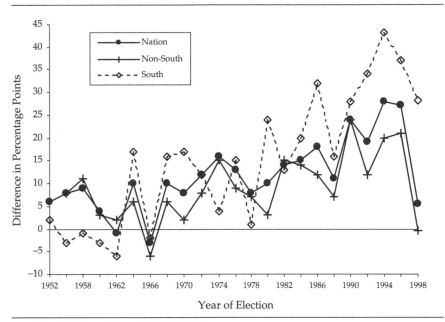

SOURCE: NES Cumulative File 1948–1998.

divisions.[5] The overall trend, however, is clearly toward larger differences.

Finally, consider the issue of whether these divisions have carried over into party identification. Party identification is generally regarded as more enduring than voting in any particular election. Table 5.7 presents the averages by decade of identification with the Democratic Party by income group since the 1950s. The patterns are very similar to those for voting. In the South, the identification of high-income voters with the Democratic Party has steadily declined. Low-income voters in the South are less inclined to identify with the Democratic Party than in the 1950s, but they are currently much more Democratic than high-income voters. Outside the South the identification of low-income voters with the Democratic Party has increased. The results are growing differences by class in party identification.

Party-Line Voting and Split-Ticket Voting

To summarize, the argument here is twofold. First, as reviewed in Chapter 4, the parties experienced considerable turmoil and change in their electoral bases and policy concerns from the 1950s to the 1970s. There were not clear differences between the parties in the 1950s and for part of the 1960s. As the 1980s and 1990s evolved, clear differences in the electoral bases of the parties emerged and their policy concerns diverged. Second, the electorate, with some lag, sorted out their differences and class political divisions have slowly, but steadily, increased in the last several decades.

If the electorate is reacting to broad party images that are becoming more different, and class political divisions are increasing, there should also be some effect on the consistency of partisan voting. It is widely stated that in recent decades electoral dealignment has occurred (less attachment to parties and more of the electorate identifying as independents) (Beck 1984; Mayer 1998: 195–196), split-ticket voting has increased (Burnham 1982: 38–44; Dunham 1991: 78; Luttbeg and Gant 1995: 42; Jacobson 1997: 130; Mayer 1998: 209), and that the political world is candidate-centered (Salmore and Salmore 1989; Aldrich and Niemi 1996).

TABLE 5.7   The Rise of Class Divisions: Percent Identifying with Democratic Party Within Bottom and Top Third of Income Groups, and Differences, by Decade, All Respondents

| | Nation | | | South | | | Non-South | | |
Decade	Low	High	Diff	Low	High	Diff	Low	High	Diff
Whites									
1950s	55	51	3	69	74	−5	49	46	3
1960s	54	51	4	65	61	4	50	48	2
1970s	53	45	8	57	54	4	51	43	8
1980s	53	40	13	56	43	13	51	39	12
1990s	54	40	14	55	31	24	54	42	12
All									
1950s	55	51	3	62	74	−12	51	47	4
1960s	57	52	5	64	63	1	53	49	4
1970s	58	47	11	63	55	8	55	45	10
1980s	59	43	16	63	48	15	56	42	14
1990s	59	42	17	61	37	24	57	44	13

SOURCE: NES Cumulative File 1948–1998.

The argument is that voters vote for candidates and not for parties, resulting in fewer people voting for the same party for different offices. The evidence presented here, however, suggests another possible trend. If parties are acquiring clearer images and diverging in their interests, and class voting has increased, it may also result in more party-line voting and declining split-ticket voting.

The extent of consistency in party voting for different national offices is presented in Table 5.8. The results are presented by party for lower- and higher-income groups because the presumption is that the effects should be different by income group. If class differences are emerging then lower-income groups should vote more consistently for Democrats and higher-income groups should vote more consistently for Republicans. The table presents the percentage of lower-income voters who have voted for Democratic presidential-House candidates, then presidential-Senate candidates, and then House-Senate candidates. The right side of the table then repeats the presentation, but with a focus on the extent to which high-income voters vote consistently for Republican candidates.

The evidence indicates that after an extended period of declining party-line voting, it is now increasing, particularly for lower-income voters. With some exceptions, the general pattern for this group is that the levels of party-line voting in the 1970s and the 1980s were lower than in the 1950s and the 1960s. By the 1990s, they rose to levels higher than in the 1950s and the 1960s. This holds for all pairs of offices. This pattern accords with what would be expected if the parties experienced murky images in the 1960s and 1970s, followed by greater clarity in policy concerns. The relatively high levels of party-line voting during the 1950s may have been a product of the legacy of the higher-class voting that occurred in the 1930s and the 1940s. The party turmoil that developed in the late 1960s and 1970s then surely reduced levels of party-line voting. As the party images solidified over time, the electorate, with some lag, then distinguished the differences between the parties. By the 1990s, low-income voters were voting for Democratic candidates at higher levels, and were voting at higher levels for all Democratic candidates.

For high-income voters, the pattern is one of declines in the 1960s and 1970s from the 1950s, followed by increases in the 1980s and 1990s. The levels of party-line voting in the 1990s do not reach the levels of the 1950s, but there has been a general rise in party-line voting since the 1960s. The more modest increase in this behavior for the more affluent may result from the continuing ambivalence toward the Republican Party that was reviewed in Chapter 4.

If this consistency is increasing, the result should also be a decline in split-ticket voting. Figure 5.11 presents the pattern of split-ticket voting (the percentage voting for different parties for pairs of elections) for all

TABLE 5.8   Party-Line Voting by Income Groups, Presidential Years
             Only, 1952–1996

	Low-Income Voting for Democrats			High-Income Voting for Republicans		
Decade	President-House	President-Senate	House-Senate	President-House	President-Senate	House-Senate
1950s	41.2	40.7	49.9	52.3	53.9	49.7
1960s	48.5	47.0	49.1	42.1	40.1	38.1
1970s	35.8	38.6	48.5	45.3	44.9	36.7
1980s	40.7	43.2	47.8	46.3	48.8	38.7
1990s	56.1	56.3	51.6	46.2	48.3	44.7

SOURCE: NES Cumulative File 1948–1998.

voters since 1952 for years with a presidential election. The results are for
all voters (the results for low- and high-income voters follow the same
pattern). As party electoral bases and concerns began to change during
the 1960s and party images became less clear, the degree of split-ticket
voting steadily increased. As these party images sorted out, the degree of
split-ticket voting began to decline (Aldrich 1999: 23). By 1996 it had returned to the lower levels of the late 1950s and the early 1960s. Since the
1970s class voting has increased, as has party-line voting, whereas split-
ticket voting has declined.

Conclusions

For the last two decades it has become common to argue that the Democratic Party alienated the white working class and that it is virtually im-
possible for the party to raise issues of equality of opportunity because
the electorate sees such arguments as catering to minorities. The argument is that working-class whites have deserted the Democratic Party
and left the party without its most important base. The evidence from the
National Election Studies does not support that argument.

It appears that judgments about the plight of the Democratic Party and
about class divisions were formed during the early 1980s and were not
revisited. The Democratic Party surely had its troubles in the late 1960s
and during the 1970s. The public may well have been troubled by the turmoil associated with the party during the late 1960s because of race issues, Vietnam (MacInnes 1996), and the subsequent presidential candi-
dacy of George McGovern, who was portrayed as very liberal. The party
may also have been hurt by the economic problems of high inflation and
unemployment associated with the administration of Jimmy Carter.

FIGURE 5.11   Split-Ticket Voting in National Elections, Presidential
Years, 1952–1996

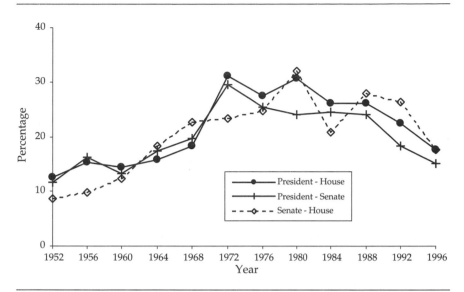

SOURCE: NES Cumulative File 1948–1998.

There is some evidence that support in the public for conservative positions rose during the late 1970s and early 1980s, though that increase did
not persist (Mayer 1992: 108–110). Democrats did lose some blue-collar
voters in the 1980 presidential election, but as noted in Chapter 4, they
lost support among all voters in that election. Whatever short-term losses
Democrats experienced, these changes were too readily seen as enduring
trends. In reality, during the early 1980s, when many analysts assumed
that Democrats were losing blue-collar voters, class political divisions
were beginning to increase. Why those interpretations were accepted is
an interesting, but distinct issue, which the Appendix addresses.

The survival of Democrats and their retention of the less affluent was
also probably helped along by a Republican Party that steadily lost its relatively liberal northern base and developed a more conservative image.
The combination of a Democratic Party that responded to its difficulties
and a Republican Party that shifted its electoral base and policy concerns
in a conservative direction has resulted in lower-income voters comparing the two parties and increasingly gravitating to the Democratic Party,
particularly outside the South. As noted earlier, there is much to learn

about exactly how all this occurred, but it is clear that less-affluent whites have not moved away from the Democratic Party and that class divisions have not declined in American politics.

NOTES

1. The initial distribution of all sample respondents by income categories is used to code individuals into thirds of the income distribution. If whites are then selected for analysis, the original distributions are still used to classify respondents. Since whites on average have higher incomes than nonwhites, this means that among the sample of whites, the percent in the top third is really more than one-third (a higher percent of whites are in this category), and the percent in the lower third is less than a third. Once actual voters are assessed, the top third contains an even higher percentage because high-income respondents vote more. It is recognized that these shifts in composition occur, but the goal of this analysis is to classify respondents by where they fall in the overall distribution of income in American society.

2. The data reported are the Democratic percentage of the three-candidate vote. Voting results are reported by NES in two ways: the percent received by the Democratic Party of the total vote for the two major party candidates, and the percent received by the Democratic Party of the total of all major candidates. The issue of which one to use becomes relevant primarily with presidential election results. In 1968 George Wallace received 11.5 percent of the reported vote. In 1980 John Anderson received 9.8 percent, and in 1992 H. Ross Perot received 18.5 percent of the vote. If the former measure is used, the percentage provides an easily understood comparison with Republicans, but it does not represent the actual percentage of the vote received by Democratic candidates. The decision of what to use here is driven by the focus of the analysis. The concern is how Democrats have fared absolutely among the electorate. Given this focus, the percent of the three-candidate vote is presented.

3. I conducted the same analysis of likes and dislikes for congressional House candidates. Among the less affluent the net likes regarding Democrats is positive, if somewhat erratic across the 1950s through 1990s, ranging from .29 to .75. The major change is that among the less affluent (bottom third) the net likes (likes minus dislikes) for Republican candidates steadily declines from .79 in the 1950s to -.65 in the 1990s. The result is that the less affluent become relatively much more positive toward Democratic candidates. Among the more affluent the reaction toward the Democratic Party becomes negative by the 1990s. The net reaction to the Republican Party is generally positive (though, much as polls indicate, it turns negative during the 1990s).

4. The basis for the conclusion that voters had little coherence to their views is the work of Converse (1966b). Although his analysis is often used as a benchmark, some have argued that his requirements for "coherence" were too demanding, and that if there is allowance for an occasional opinion that does not fit with expectations, the percentage with coherent views is much higher (Brody 1986: 666).

5. The concern of this analysis is trends, not specific elections. Despite that focus, it is difficult not to see the 1998 House results and wonder what happened to virtually eliminate the class divisions that had developed in prior elections. Trying to understand what affect the 1998 results have is important for trying to understand if the same pattern may occur in 2000, or if the pattern of 1994 and 1006 is likely to return.

It appears that reactions to the impeachment issue had a powerful impact on voting for the House in 1998, and those reactions resulted in a significant suppression of whatever class divisions that might have occurred. This came about because of several relationships. First, reactions to the impeachment issue did not vary by class. Within each income group (grouped into thirds), the division of opinion on this issue was roughly the same. Second, differences of opinion about impeachment within each income group had a powerful impact on partisan voting. The effect was the elimination of class as a source of division. Those within the bottom third who supported impeachment efforts voted strongly Republican, and this lowered voting for Democrats from levels that prevailed in prior years. Those in the top third who opposed impeachment efforts (and there were many in this category) voted strongly Democratic, and this raised voting for Democrats from levels that prevailed in prior years. The overall effect was that class divisions were compressed. The following tables present information from the cumulative NES file for 1948–1998 and the 1998 NES survey on these patterns.

The 1994 and 1996 elections produced a significant division by class in support for the Democratic Party. There were significant differences between the low- and high-income groups in their approval of the president, identification with the Democratic Party, and voting for Democratic House candidates. The 1998 elections clearly produced a lesser division. The interesting matter is why that "collapsing" of differences occurred.

It appears that a crucial issue was how reactions to the impeachment issue were distributed and their effect on voting. The following table indicates responses by income group to several impeachment related questions included in the 1998 NES survey. While approval of Clinton and support for the Democratic Party was divided by classs in 1994 and 1996, the reaction to the impeachment issue was relatively uniform across income groups. Disapproval of Congress, opposition to impeachment, and agreement that the issue was a private matter were almost uniform across income groups.

These differences in reactions to the impeachment had a powerful effect on voting Democratic in the House elections. The following tables indicate how those with different reactions to the impeachment issue split their vote between Democrats and Republicans. Those who disapproved of congressional handling of the issue, opposed impeachment, or thought it was a private matter, voted for Democrats by approximately 40 percentage points more than those supportive of Congress and impeachment. The effect was to negate class differences. Within the low income group, a substantial proportion supported impeachment, and those supporting it voted heavily Republican. This reduced voting for Democrats within this group. Within the high income group, a very substantial proportion opposed impeachment, and those opposing it voted heavily Democratic. This increased

TABLE 5.9 Support for Democrats by Income Groups: Approval of Presidential Job Performance, Identification with Democratic Party, and Vote for Democratic Candidates in House Elections, 1994–1998

	Presidential Job Approval			Identify with Democrats			Vote for House Democrats		
Income	1994	1996	1998	1994	1996	1998	1994	1996	1998
Low	55	74	72	55	59	52	59	60	47
Middle	48	65	72	42	52	47	44	46	47
High	41	58	67	33	38	43	32	35	42
Difference	14	16	5	22	21	9	27	25	5

SOURCE: NES Cumulative File 1948–1998.

TABLE 5.10 Responses to NES Questions About Impeachment, by Income Groups, 1998 NES Survey (percentages with indicated responses)

	Approval of Congressional Handling of Clinton Scandal		Should Clinton Be Impeached?		Is the Clinton Matter a Private or a Public Issue?	
Income	Approve	Disapprove	Yes	No	Private	Public
Low	27	72	27	73	66	28
Middle	26	74	31	69	64	31
High	29	71	31	69	58	37

SOURCE: NES Cumulative File 1948–1998.

TABLE 5.11 Voting for Democratic House Candidates by Responses to Impeachment Questions, and by Income Groups, 1998 NES Survey (percentages voting for Democrats and then Republicans)

	Approval of Congressional Handling of Clinton Scandal		Should Clinton Be Impeached?		Is the Clinton Matter a Private or a Public Issue?	
Income	Approve	Disapprove	Yes	No	Private	Public
Low	30–70	58–42	26–74	63–37	68–32	28–72
Middle	23–77	60–40	20–80	66–34	68–32	18–82
High	17–83	55–45	14–86	58–42	63–37	20–80

SOURCE: NES Cumulative File 1948–1998.

voting for Democrats within this group. The net effect was the compressing of class differences in party voting in 1998.

Finally, it is unlikely that impeachment, over as a focus of attention in early 1999, will play much of a role in 2000. It may in selected races, where an opponent seeks to make it an issue, but it will probably have faded as a general issue and will be replaced by new issues. If class issues—tax and budget cuts and their effects by class—become dominant, then class divisions will probably return to levels similar to those that prevailed in 1994 and 1996.

6

Reconsidering Party and Issues in American Politics

The demise of the New Deal coalition has generated considerable commentary and anguish among some scholars. For those troubled about this demise, the concern is that the Democratic Party alienated some of its core constituency and the party is no longer able to play the vital role of articulating concerns about inequality of opportunity, fairness in distribution of income, and related economic issues. As inequalities in the distribution of income and access to education increase, and access to health care and pensions remains unequal, there is concern that these issues are not a part of political debates because the Democratic Party cannot play the role of articulating these concerns. If the Democratic Party fails to play that role, there is no alternative political means to make the case for responding to shifting social conditions. Absent Democratic efforts, the concerns of the less affluent get less attention in the political process.

The view that Democrats once did but no longer carry the argument for the less affluent, however, has several flaws. First, the New Deal coalition in the 1950s and the 1960s did not embody as much class division as is often presumed. The party had a clear advantage among white southerners, Catholics, union members, Jews, and blacks, but class divisions were limited.

> In the 1950s and the 1960s the poorer one-third of the white electorate was no more Democratic than the middle class, and upper-income voters were as likely to be Democrats as Republicans. Income had less to do with party preference than race, religion, union membership or region. (Petrocik and Steeper 1987: 42)

The results presented in prior chapters indicate just how limited political divisions by income were in the 1950s and the 1960s. Although evidence exists that there were significant class divisions during the 1930s and 1940s (Cantril 1951: 588–939; Ladd and Hadley 1975: 69–71; Stonecash 1999b), by the 1950s political divisions by income had declined.

The class division that is often regarded as the defining characteristic of the New Deal coalition was in reality limited in the 1950s.

Not only were class divisions not pronounced, but the Democratic Party and its New Deal coalition did not serve, during the 1950s and the 1960s, as a coherent source of liberal legislation during that era (Smith 1996: 259). The Democratic Party was a complex coalition of liberal activists who developed many new initiatives to have government play a greater role in addressing social and economic problems, and conservative southern Democrats who were reluctant to support such efforts (Sundquist 1968: 385–410, 486–488). From the 1940s through the 1960s, the southern wing of the Democratic Party was a consistent source of opposition to many liberal legislative efforts (Rohde 1991: 45–65; Katznelson, Geiger, and Kryder 1993; Rae 1998: 44–47). Sometimes southern Democrats were overridden by a coalition of northern Republicans and Democrats from outside the South. The Civil Rights Act of 1957 passed with southern Democrats voting against it and northern Democrats voting for it, with northern Republicans providing the votes to pass the legislation (Congressional Quarterly Almanac 1958: 816–817). In 1963 this coalition enacted aid to colleges and students, despite the opposition of southern Democrats (Congressional Quarterly Almanac 1963: 753–754). The Civil Rights Act of 1964 was passed with the same combination of votes (Congressional Quarterly Almanac 1965: 758–760). It was also a relatively common situation for southern Democrats to join with northern Republicans to block liberal legislation. In 1958 this coalition blocked increases in unemployment compensation or federal aid to education (Congressional Quarterly Almanac 1959: 764–765). In 1959 the southern Democrat–northern Republican coalition sought to cut public housing and urban renewal funds (Congressional Quarterly Almanac 1960: 135). In later years the coalition blocked numerous efforts to have the federal government provide aid to local and higher education, to fund mass transit, and to provide aid to urban areas.[1] Not only was the New Deal coalition in the electorate not quite what is often presumed, but the Democratic Party was by no means the primary source of liberal legislation for the 1950s and 1960s. Northern Democrats were often a source of liberal legislation, but the Democratic Party struggled with that role.

Second, class divisions have not declined since then, but they have grown. The argument, therefore, that since the 1950s and the 1960s Democrats have alienated the once-loyal working class and caused the demise of historic class divisions appears to be backwards. Instead, limited class divisions in the 1950s and 1960s have evolved to increasing divisions, at least measured by voting differences by income groups. Much of the commentary about change appears to be based on a less than accurate view of the past.

Since the 1950s, there has been significant change in the electoral bases of the parties, in the concerns they espouse, and in the polarization of parties in Congress. The parties' reliance on particular areas of the country have shifted, with more Republicans seats coming from the South and West. The party in the House now has more seats in relatively affluent districts. Democrats now do better in the North and have more House seats in low-income areas. Party concerns have shifted accordingly, with the Republicans articulating more conservative concerns and the Democrats presenting proposals more liberal than the Republicans. Class divisions in party voting have also steadily increased.

The increase in class political divisions has enormous implications for interpretations of American politics. As noted earlier, many contemporary interpretations argue that cultural and social issues such as civil liberties, abortion, gay rights, prayer in the schools, race, and so forth (Ladd and Hadley 1975: 181–225; Edsall and Edsall 1991b: 137–153; Ginsberg 1996: 9) have become so dominant that class divisions have been displaced. If class has, however, come to play more of a role, those arguments need reconsideration. Other analysts argue that campaigns have become candidate centered, and stress the role of campaign funds and incumbency as factors shaping electoral outcomes (Salmore and Salmore 1989; Jacobson 1997). These interpretations do not explicitly rule out major roles for constituencies and class, but they are certainly relegated to secondary status in such perspectives. A growing relationship between income and party voting, however, suggests that party positions connect with the economic situations of voters more than has been realized. Perhaps the role of candidate attributes and resources—incumbency, staff and office resources, and campaign funds—in driving electoral outcomes need some reconsideration. It may well be that policy debates about equality, party images, and electoral responses are more important than is often presumed.

The Current and Future Debate

Where does all this leave us? The United States now has two parties with electoral bases and policy concerns that are diverging. The Democrats have not alienated the white working class, except perhaps in the long-ago presidential elections of 1968 and 1972. It is also clear that the economic problems during Jimmy Carter's tenure as president did not help Democrats in 1980. But it is also clear that since 1980 the trend has been for lower-income whites to move to the Democratic Party. The Republicans, on the other hand, have not fared as well as many people presume. Their general image has not become more positive in the last decade, and there is evidence it has drifted toward a negative image. Republicans, despite much talk about Reagan Democrats, have not attracted the white working class. Republicans have attracted the white affluent population in the South and retained that portion of the electorate outside the South, resulting in relatively greater support among the more affluent. The result of these shifts is that now differences in party electoral bases exist. The basis for a sustained debate between the parties about the extent of equality of opportunity and what public policies might be adopted to increase opportunity now exists, unlike the 1950s.

This division could persist. The difference in party voting by income groups has emerged among all age cohorts, which makes it more likely that it will be a continuing feature of American politics. Table 6.1 presents differences between the higher and lower income groups in the percentage voting Democratic for the president and for members of the House by age groups by decade since the 1950s. Since the concern is the general pervasiveness of this division in American politics, and since nonwhites

TABLE 6.1   Difference Between Lower and Upper Third in Percentage Voting Democratic, by Decade and Age Groups, 1950s–1990s (all respondents)

	Presidential Elections Age Groups			House Elections Age Groups		
Decade and Groups	*18–34*	*35–59*	*60 plus*	*18–34*	*35–59*	*60 plus*
1950s						
Lower	43	44	43	59	61	53
Higher	42	39	27	49	51	37
Difference	1	5	16	10	10	16
1960s						
Lower	53	66	51	54	70	59
Higher	55	48	45	55	53	52
Difference	−2	18	6	−1	17	7
1970s						
Lower	55	56	46	69	67	64
Higher	49	33	28	55	50	50
Difference	6	23	18	14	17	14
1980s						
Lower	58	58	52	72	69	66
Higher	32	34	34	49	52	48
Difference	26	25	18	23	17	18
1990s						
Lower	60	67	63	67	72	69
Higher	38	44	37	44	45	43
Difference	22	23	26	23	27	26

SOURCE: NES Cumulative File 1948–1998.

are becoming a larger proportion of the electorate, all respondents in NES surveys are included.[2]

If the increase in class divisions is largely among older people, and not among younger people, then this division might be a carryover of political divisions from prior generations and might fade in importance as generational replacement occurs. The results, however, indicate that, comparing the 1950s and 1960s to the 1980s and 1990s, the difference in the percentage voting Democratic increased for all age groups. It is as prevalent among younger voters as it is among older voters. There has been an increase in the percentage of the lower third supporting Democrats in the last two decades across all ages and an increase in the division in class voting across all ages. Again, the electoral basis for a sustained debate about equality of opportunity issues has clearly developed.

Whether that debate will fully emerge depends on trends in the economy and how the parties respond to those trends. The history of inequality in the twentieth century is one of cycles of greater and lesser inequality over time, rather than a continuous trend (Plotnick et al. 1998). As inequality increased from the 1920s through the 1930s, class political divisions correspondingly increased (Stonecash 1999b). In recent decades, despite increases in average incomes there has been a steady increase in inequality, which could make this issue more central to American political divisions. The current trend, however, could reverse itself and inequality could decline. If so, that might reduce the political saliency of the issue.

There is also the crucial issue of how the parties respond and position themselves on public policy issues. As of now the parties seem locked into policy differences that have very different class consequences. Currently Democrats and Republicans differ in what they see as "problems" and what should be done about various concerns. Democrats see many less-affluent people with significant problems in a changing economy and are more supportive of programs to respond to those problems. Republicans see a federal government that is too large and intrusive and want to constrain it or cut it back. During the 1999 budget process, for example, with a significant budget surplus possible in future years, the parties took very different stances on how this surplus should be used. The Republicans proposed a major tax cut and acknowledged that most of the cut would go to the affluent. President Clinton and congressional Democrats argued that the country should use most of the surplus for "problems," such as Social Security, Medicare, and education. Although "class" is rarely part of the language used in debates about such issues, it is clear that the policies proposed by each party will have very different effects by class. Tax cuts will give small monetary benefits to the less affluent but deprive government of resources for programs that could help the less affluent. As noted in Chapter 3, Social Security and Medicare are far more important to less-affluent seniors. Education aid, at least as currently distributed, is also far more important to less affluent than to more affluent school districts. If inequality persists or increases and party policies continue to differ, then class political divisions are likely to be central to American politics.

Political parties, however, are not simplistic entities who ignore their context. Each party contains members who believe the party should moderate its positions and "move to the middle." If either party experiences significant, sustained electoral losses, the argument will intensify about whether the party should moderate its positions. If moderation on class issues does occur for one or both parties, then the electorate is less likely to see differences between the parties and class political divisions would decline somewhat. Moderation may be difficult to achieve, however, if a party loses in moderate districts and is left with its most conservative or most liberal electoral base. Regardless, the point is that future class political divisions are contingent on the economy and the party's response to changes.

The Turnout Issue

The future of political debate also hinges on trends in turnout. The less affluent vote less, and their turnout rate appears to have declined over time, increasing the differential in turnout by class (Burnham 1982: 121–203; Piven and Cloward 1988: 160–166; Rosenstone and Hansen 1993: 234–244; Darmofal 1999). These turnout differences and their increase create significant problems for Democrats. Even if the party appeals to the less affluent, it is unlikely they will vote as much as the more affluent. From this perspective, it may not be wise politically to focus on the less affluent, whether they are a natural constituency for the Democrats. They may not show up at the polls in sufficient numbers to make it wise to appeal to them and rely on them.

Figure 6.1 indicates the turnout rates by those in the lower, middle, and upper thirds of the income distribution since the 1950s. There has been change in the relative rates of voting by income groups. If the 1950s results are considered as a whole, the turnout rate among the less affluent was 64, whereas it was 83 among the more affluent, for a difference of nineteen percentage points. That differential has grown since then. If the 1990s are considered as a whole, the rates were 52 and 77, respectively, for a differential of twenty-five. That differential is important. Even though the less affluent are voting for Democrats at a greater rate, their turnout is gradually declining relative to the more affluent. The Democrats do face a continuing challenge in trying to appeal to the less affluent, and in trying to mobilize them to vote.

FIGURE 6.1   Percent Voting by Income Group, 1952–1996

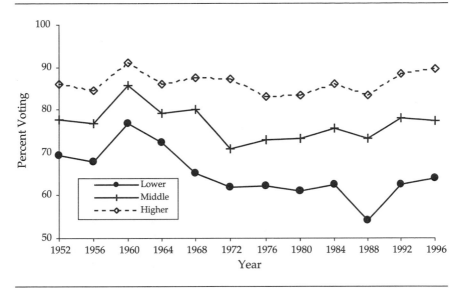

SOURCE: NES Cumulative File 1948–1998.

But the increases in voting differentials do not appear to be so great that the party will not benefit from representing the less affluent. How these differentials affect the party is complicated, and depends on the closeness of elections for the presidency across various states (because of the electoral college rule of winner-take-all outcomes within states) and the closeness of elections for House and Senate districts. If elections are close and the less affluent vote less, then differentials in turnout matter. If elections are not as close then the differentials matter less. Whether and how much this differential harms Democrats can only be assessed by examining specific situations. The party is deriving more support from the less affluent, but generating turnout by these constituents presents a challenge for Democrats. Some things do not change in politics. Mobilizing your electoral base is crucial for generating support and winning elections (Andersen 1979).

The Role of Other Issues

The primary concern of this analysis is the emergence of class voting as a significant political division. If class voting is increasing, it may be taken as implying that class has displaced other sources of political division. A case for the significance of one issue is often taken as a case for the declining significance of other issues, as if one issue displaces others (Weakliem and

Heath 1997: 940–941). This presumption that there is a trade-off between the relative impact of issues is particularly important, given the arguments that other issues have increased in significance in recent years. Carmines and Stimson, for example, argue that race, and issues associated with it, has become a "polarizing" issue (Carmines and Stimson 1980: 80; 1982: 6; 1986: 915). Race issues are often seen as powerful enough to drive much of the white population away from the Democratic Party (Kinder and Sears 1981). Others argue that "value" disputes have become more important as a source of political division (Wattenberg 1995).

This is not the place for a complete analysis of other sources of political division, but an analysis of the role of racial issues may provide an illustrative example of the impact of other issues and how the impact of other issues is related to the impact of class divisions. Race issues, for example, are important in and of themselves, but also because they have been presumed to play a role in reducing the effects of class in American politics (Huckfeldt and Kohfeld 1989: 6–16; Weakliem and Heath 1997: 940–941). As discussed in Chapter 4, some analysts argue that race issues are so important because people with less education are more likely to harbor resentments about efforts to help minorities. Since the Democratic Party is more likely to be seen as sympathetic to minority interests, less educated people, also likely to be less affluent, may be alienated from the Democratic Party because of this resentment. If this occurs, then it should have two very significant effects. It should make less-affluent whites less inclined to support the Democratic Party and it should also reduce the extent of class divisions that would occur, absent the presence of race issues. As Huckfeldt and Kohfeld state: "the decline of class as an organizing principle in contemporary American electoral politics is directly related to the concurrent ascent of race" (1989: 1–2). The rise of race issues could also lead to a general reduction in support for the Democratic Party among whites. This view of the role of race issues, for example, seems to be behind the repeated observation that Democrats have not been able to win a majority of white votes since 1964. The implication is that the party has experienced the erosion of white support since 1964, when race issues became more prominent in American politics. Given the importance of this argument, what, then, has been the impact of race issues? Exploring this question is important to understand the impact of this issue and how other sources of political division are related to class divisions.

As a first step in this analysis, there is the issue of whether white support for Democrats has declined over time. Figures 6.2 and 6.3 present the percentage of whites voting for Democratic candidates for president and the House since 1952. The NES cumulative file for 1952–1998 is used. The

FIGURE 6.2   Percent of Whites Voting for Democratic Presidential
             Candidates, by Region, 1956–1996

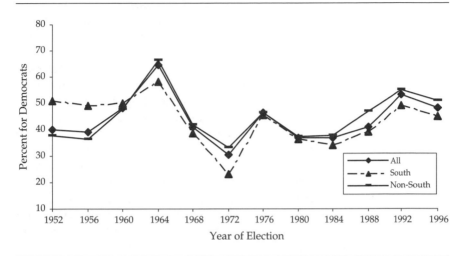

SOURCE: NES Cumulative File 1948–1998.

FIGURE 6.3   Percent of Whites Voting for Democrats, House of
             Representatives, by Region, 1956–1998

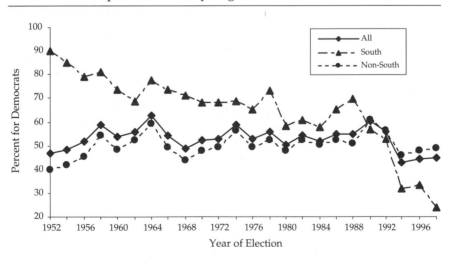

NOTE: Results for 1954 are interpolated; no NES survey that year.
SOURCE: NES Cumulative File 1948–1998.

results present a very different picture of trends than some analysts have suggested. Clearly, the presidential election has seen considerable fluctuation over time, but there is no discernible downward trend over almost fifty years. There was a surge to the Democrats in 1964 and significant movement away from them in 1972, but since then there has been fluctuation, with 54 percent of whites voting Democratic in 1992 and 48 percent in 1996. In House elections, three matters are important to note. The trend in the South has clearly been a decline in white support for Democrats, owing in large part to the affluent moving to the Republican Party. For the rest of the nation, and for the nation, there are fluctuations, but there is also no clear downward trend since the 1960s or the 1970s. Finally, if there has been a significant loss in white support, it did not occur until 1994, and whether that decline will persist is unknown. Evidence does not indicate a trend of declining white support for the Democratic Party.

Does this rough stability of the white vote (except for the South) somehow mean that race issues have not mattered? Given the history of race issues in the nation, such an argument would be difficult for anyone to accept. Race issues do matter. The important matter, however, is how they matter. Specifically, have they become more important over time as a source of partisan cleavage, and have they driven less-affluent whites away from the Democratic Party more than affluent whites, such that class divisions are reduced owing to race issues? The first question involves general trend opinions on race issues; the second involves the effects of opinions on race issues by income groups.

To address the trend issue first, if race issues have played an increasing role in shaping party support, that role could stem from several sources. It could be that people holding negative opinions about race issues have gradually increased as a proportion of the electorate, and people with negative views are likely to support Republicans, who have opposed policies such as affirmative effort on the grounds that they favor one segment of the electorate. Second, it could be that the general level of support for black concerns has changed little, but negative views have become more salient and more significant in shaping party support, as suggested by the work of Carmines and Stimson (1981: 114–117; 1986, 1989). In other words, people with negative views are moved more now than they were thirty years ago.

Table 6.2 summarizes the distribution of responses over time on some crucial race issues and their effect on party support.[3] Whites only are included since the concern is how race issues affect white political behavior. The table presents the percentage of respondents holding differing views over time on three questions involving different and fundamental race issues. The questions are: whether progress on civil rights is occurring "too slowly," at an "okay" pace, or "too fast"; should government

TABLE 6.2 Trends in Opinion on Race Issues

	1960s	*1970s*	*1980s*	*1990s*
Shifting Civil Rights Positions: Percent holding different views				
Civil rights progress?				
Too slow/okay	25.4	49.4	67.1	70.5
Too fast	74.6	50.6	32.9	29.5
Help minorities?				
Government should help		26.2	22.3	18.8
Neutral		25.2	29.8	26.2
Individual responsibility		48.6	47.9	55.0
Fair treatment for minorities?				
Government see to fairness	42.3	48.9	49.7	48.2
Not government responsibility	57.7	51.1	50.3	51.8

SOURCE: NES Cumulative File 1948–1998.

get involved in helping minorities or should they help themselves; and should government intervene to ensure fair treatment for blacks or is that not government's responsibility. The first question inquires about generalized reactions to the civil rights movement. Kinder and Sanders argue that in recent years the crucial divisive racial issue has been resentment about favoritism of blacks (1996: 92–127). The latter two questions, although not the same as those Kinder and Sanders use, surely tap into similar feelings since the focus is whether blacks should benefit from government intervention.

The responses are recoded somewhat from the original scores in the NES file. For the first question "too slow" and "okay" are grouped together (since there are so few too slow responses, and both represent a nonnegative response). For the second question, a seven-point scale is involved. To condense the responses, for both questions those choosing 1–3 (government should get involved) and 5–7 (government should not get involved) are grouped together. These questions have not been asked for all years, and to reduce problems of skipped years and small numbers of cases in some years, the results are grouped by decade so the focus will be on trends across decades.[4] Although this misses the effects of events in particular years, here the emphasis is on the broad trend across decades and the effects of these opinions.

Using these responses as an indicator of opinions on race issues, the results do not suggest that race issues have become more important in the nation. The proportion of people who think progress is occurring too fast has declined significantly since the 1960s. For the other two questions, there is a slight increase over time in the percentage who think government should stay out of this issue, but the increase is small. The responses do not suggest that there has been a general increase in negative opinions about race issues.

Although the percentage holding negative views about race issues has not increased, it may be that these issues are more important to some people, and those holding negative views are now more likely to move away from the Democratic Party. Table 6.3 presents the percentage voting for Democratic presidential and House candidates by responses to these race issues, by decade. The difference in the percentage voting Democratic for

TABLE 6.3   The Effect of Race Issue Opinions on Party Support

	1960s	*1970s*	*1980s*	*1990s*
Race Issue Positions and Democratic Presidential Vote				
Civil rights progress?				
Too slow/okay	60.1	40.6	40.9	45.2
Too fast	46.7	32.6	28.5	34.7
Effect of negative view	−13.7	−8.0	−12.4	−10.5
Help minorities?				
Government should help		47.7	56.4	66.9
Neutral		34.8	37.1	49.0
Individual responsibility		29.2	26.1	34.8
Effect of negative view		−18.5	−30.3	−32.1
Fair treatment?				
Government see to fairness	61.0	39.4	46.4	55.8
Not government responsibility	40.5	23.3	31.9	32.7
Effect of negative view	−20.5	−16.1	−14.5	−23.1
Race Issue Positions and Democratic House Vote				
Civil Rights Progress?				
Too slow/ok	60.0	53.0	54.5	58.7
Too fast	55.0	54.5	49.8	50.9
Effect of negative view	−5.0	+1.5	−4.7	−23.1
Help minorities?				
Government should help		61.9	65.4	68.8
Neutral		53.5	54.8	54.3
Individual responsibility		51.0	46.0	41.3
Effect of negative view		−10.9	−19.6	−27.5
Fair treatment?				
Government see to fairness	62.8	57.9	57.8	61.2
Not government responsibility	51.5	51.6	51.1	42.1
Effect of negative view	−11.3	−6.3	−6.7	−19.1

SOURCE: NES Cumulative File 1948–1998.

the two responses is also presented, and it serves as an indication of the political effect of holding a negative opinion about government intervention on behalf of blacks. The responses indicate that for at least two of the questions, race issues have come to have a more divisive political impact in the 1990s than they had in the 1960s. The two issues that now divide people more are those that Kinder and Sanders focus on (1996: 92–127), whether government should intervene to help blacks. For both of these questions, the pattern is the same over the decades. The effect of a negative opinion is to reduce support for Democrats by approximately fourteen percentage points in the 1960s. The difference dips in the 1970s and then grows in the 1980s and 1990s. It does appear that the impact of this aspect of race issues has grown to a significant level by the 1990s. This suggests that race issues are another source of political division (Weissberg 1991). Expressed in quantitative analysis language, they may be seen as having an additive, independent effect on political divisions.

The crucial matter, however, is how race issues affect class divisions. As noted earlier, it is often suggested that race issues suppress class divisions by driving working-class whites away from the Democratic Party because they are most threatened, and accordingly reduces class divisions. If this occurs, it could come about in two ways. The less affluent might simply be more negative about government intervention on behalf of blacks, so that fewer of them end up supporting Democrats. Or they may have similar opinions to the more affluent, but the issue may be more salient to them so their negative views push them away from Democrats more and thereby lessen class political divisions.

Table 6.4 reports responses to the same three questions by decade, but by income groups. Only the percentage choosing the "negative" response about race issues is reported because this is the opinion that should presumably drive voters away from the Democratic Party. If race issues are suppressing class political divisions, then it should be that antiblack opinions should be higher among less-affluent whites. It is difficult to find any systematic evidence that lower-income whites are more prone to negative views than more affluent whites (Weakliem and Heath 1997: 945–951). For the issue of the progress of civil rights, the less affluent are somewhat more negative by about six percentage points, but there is a significant drop among all income groups by the 1990s, so it is difficult to imagine this issue playing a constant, much less increasing, role in affecting class divisions. For the other two issues, there is no significant difference across income groups in the presence of negative opinions.

Finally, consider the issue of whether negative views might move lessaffluent whites away from the Democratic Party more than they move affluent whites. Table 6.5 presents differences in support for Democratic presidential and House candidates by opinion on race issues and by income.

TABLE 6.4   Negative Opinions on Race Issues, by Decade, and by
Income Groups, Whites Only

	1960s	1970s	1980s	1990s
Percentage holding negative opinions on race issues				
Civil rights progress too fast				
Low income	74.7	52.6	36.3	32.2
Middle income	77.4	52.3	36.7	30.3
Higher income	71.8	46.0	28.4	26.1
Minorities help themselves				
Low income		48.1	46.0	50.0
Middle income		49.1	48.1	55.4
Higher income		48.1	48.6	58.7
Government should not see to fair treatment				
Lower income	55.2	50.2	50.5	49.8
Middle income	59.7	52.1	52.0	52.3
Higher income	57.6	50.9	46.4	51.6

SOURCE: NES Cumulative File 1948–1998.

The crucial matter is the effect of negative views by income group on support for Democrats for each issue. This is the number shown under the column labeled "diff." The level of Democratic support for those with negative views is subtracted from the level of Democratic support for those with positive views. A negative number indicates the negative view reduced Democratic support.

If race issues are suppressing class divisions, then the declines in support for Democrats should be consistently greater among the less affluent compared to other income groups. It should also be the case, if race issues have become more important, that this effect should be greater in the 1980s and 1990s. The results do not indicate any pattern of greater defection from the Democrats by less-affluent whites, or any consistent shift across time.[5] If anything, the interesting matter is that the differences in support for Democrats by income groups grow over time, even as it appears that race issues have a roughly similar effect over time.

Race issues matter, but they do not appear to matter more for lower-income groups than others. They do not create more defections among less-affluent whites than among others. These issues serve as another source of division within the electorate. People who are more affluent are more likely to support Republicans. In addition, the more affluent who oppose government intervention to help minorities are even more supportive of Republicans. Likewise, those who are less affluent and who support government intervention are very supportive of Democrats. To

TABLE 6.5   Race Issues, Income, and Reduced Support for Democrats: Party ID

Decade and Income	Civil Rights Progress			Help Minorities			Fair Treatment		
	Too Slow/Okay	Too Fast	Diff	Govt Should	Individ	Diff	Govt Should	Should Not	Diff
President Votes									
1960s									
Lower	62.1	48.8	−13.3				58.5	44.1	−14.4
Middle	61.5	48.5	−13.0				63.8	42.5	−21.3
Higher	57.6	43.9	−13.7				60.2	36.8	−23.4
1970s									
Lower	43.4	39.4	−4.0	46.0	43.6	−2.4	35.1	32.6	−2.5
Middle	43.2	33.7	−9.5	52.8	35.6	−17.2	39.7	24.8	−14.9
Higher	45.8	37.6	−11.5	43.9	34.4	−12.5	41.2	16.9	−24.3
1980s									
Lower	50.3	40.8	−9.5	67.1	36.0	−31.1	51.6	39.3	−12.3
Middle	44.1	27.8	−16.3	59.1	27.2	−31.9	52.8	31.4	−21.4
Higher	33.8	20.5	−13.3	47.7	19.6	−28.1	39.3	28.0	−11.3
1990s									
Lower	53.5	49.5	−4.0	69.6	56.9	−12.2	64.4	44.7	−19.7
Middle	51.5	33.1	−18.4	68.7	49.2	−19.5	59.8	34.2	−25.6
Higher	37.9	25.6	−12.3	64.1	44.2	−19.9	49.5	24.9	−24.6
House Votes									
1960s									
Lower	68.9	57.8	−11.1				65.9	58.3	−7.6
Middle	59.9	56.8	−3.1				66.2	53.3	−12.9
Higher	54.3	51.4	−2.9				57.3	44.9	−12.4
1970s									
Lower	59.5	63.5	+4.0	69.2	57.0	−12.2	65.9	58.3	−7.6
Middle	55.5	56.2	+.7	61.3	53.6	−7.7	66.2	53.3	−12.9
Higher	48.6	47.6	−1.0	58.7	45.9	−12.8	57.3	44.9	−12.4
1980s									
Lower	62.6	61.1	−1.5	74.0	56.6	−17.4	69.6	56.0	−13.6
Middle	53.6	48.1	−5.5	67.5	46.7	−20.8	54.3	51.3	−3.0
Higher	50.7	44.6	−6.1	59.0	40.5	−18.5	55.8	47.6	−8.2
1990s									
Lower	69.4	63.5	−5.9	71.8	53.4	−18.4	78.7	58.3	−20.4
Middle	63.7	52.7	−11.0	62.6	41.4	−21.2	74.1	40.4	−33.7
Higher	51.2	39.1	−12.1	54.7	36.2	−18.5	58.8	33.4	−25.4

SOURCE: NES Cumulative File 1948–1998.

assess the impacts of these factors, Table 6.6 presents a regression of party identification, and presidential and house voting on income, sex, and the three race issue responses. Those results are presented using standardized regression coefficients that allow comparison of the relative effects of variables. There is a clear and consistent pattern to the results. From the 1970s to the 1990s the effect of income steadily increases such that by the 1990s it has one of the stronger effects of the variables included. Sex has a very erratic effect over time and across elections. Race issues generally have a significant impact by the 1990s, though the specific question that is significant varies by party support indicator.

TABLE 6.6   The Relative Impact of Income, Sex, and Race Issues on Party Support, 1970s–1990s

	1970s	*1980s*	*1990s*
Party Identification			
Income	−.01	−.02	−.13*
Sex	.07	.03	.03
Civil rights progress	.12*	−.01	−.06
Fair treatment	−.03	−.13*	.00
Help minorities	−.05	−.04	−.18*
R²	.02	.03	.06
Presidential Voting			
Income	−.06*	−.07*	−.14*
Sex	.09*	.04	.07*
Civil rights progress	−.06*	−.07	−.07*
Fair treatment	−.12*	−.07*	−.18*
Help minorities	−.16*	−20*	−.18*
R²	.08	.08	.14
House Voting			
Income	−.11*	−.10*	−.15*
Sex	.01	−.04	.05
Civil rights progress	.04	−.00	−.05
Fair treatment	−.06*	−.04	−.10*
Help minorities	−.09*	−.11*	−.08*
R²	.03	.03	.06

* Significant at .10 or greater. All responses within a decade are considered together, without weighting. The coding is as follows. For presidential and House elections, Democrat is coded as 1 and all others are coded as 0. Female is coded 1 and males as 0. For the race issue questions, the position opposing government involvement is coded with the highest value, and the position favoring government involvement is the lowest value. Negative signs for coefficients indicate a decline in support for the Democratic Party as the variable value increases.

SOURCE: NES Cumulative File 1948–1998.

These results confirm the results from the prior tables. Income has a strong effect on political divisions. Other issues also matter. Race issues have an additive effect, further increasing divisions. Presumably the same kind of pattern might occur for cultural issues, involving abortion, gay rights, and other such concerns.

Conclusions

There are many issues that this analysis does not address. The results presented here suggest that the combination of growing inequality and party differences has led to growing class political divisions. To substantiate a clear connection between these matters, one needs to understand how perceptions of equality of opportunity have evolved over time and what role any changes have played. For example, how long must inequality in the distribution of income and wealth increase until it becomes accepted that things are not going to get better and, in a society that values individualism, political actions are seen as an appropriate means to seek responses to the issue? We need to know more about whether inequality of school conditions and inequality in access to higher education are recognized and how much they matter to the public. In general, we need to know whether the less affluent regard inequality as just the way things work or whether they regard it as unfair and illegitimate. In general, we need to know more about perceptions of opportunity and how this becomes an issue people think the political process should address.

We also need to understand the dynamics of party images. How much have presidential contests and congressional battles affected how people see parties? Were particular events or policy battles more prominent and significant than others in shaping public perceptions of parties? We need to know whether there were conversions to the Democratic Party among lower-income whites in the North, or replacement of an elderly cohort by a younger cohort. Likewise, in the South, were there conversions of affluent whites to the Republican Party or did most of the support come from those migrating into the South?

We also will simply have to wait to see if inequality in the distribution of income continues and if the connection between income and class political partisan continues. Thus far, inequality has steadily increased every year since approximately 1970. Although the growth of class political divisions have been erratic, the trend is clearly toward an increase. If these trends continue, partisan politics is likely to grow more divisive because the gulf between income groups is growing and the stakes involved in public policy disputes have increased. Even if political divisions by class cease to increase and stabilize at current levels, we will have a political process in which political parties, with diverging electoral bases, are likely to sharply divide. We should not lack for a sustained debate about equality of opportunity in America. Rather than class divisions fading in relevance, they are likely to be a staple of American politics for some time.

NOTES

1. Congressional Quarterly, in their annual almanac (1957, 1958, 1960, 1961, 1962, 1963, 1964, and 1965), provided a specific assessment of the split in the Democratic Party between southern and northern Democrats, and the relationship of these two wings of the party to Republicans. Those annual reports indicate a continuing division between southern Democrats and the remainder of the party. The specific reports relied on are listed in the References under Congressional Quarterly.

2. For this analysis, all results within a decade are grouped together. The cumulative NES file for 1948–1996 is used.

3. The 1948–1996 cumulative NES file is used.

4. The 1948–1996 cumulative NES file is used.

5. Some of this inconsistency may, of course, be owing to the relatively small sample sizes within the subgroups.

Appendix

The Analysis of Class Divisions in American Politics

As noted throughout the prior analysis, the conventional wisdom is that class divisions in American politics have steadily declined as cultural, social, and racial issues displaced them as sources of political division. The results in Chapter 5 indicate, however, that if income is used as a measure of class, the trend is one of increasing class political divisions. The difference in these findings is not trivial. The results in Chapter 5 suggest that parties play more of a role than is recognized in organizing the electorate along economic lines, and that the reactions by the electorate about issues should be reconsidered. But such reconsiderations will follow only after the emerging class divisions are recognized as "facts" in need of explanation. They do not have that status now, and probably will not for some time, given the predominance of the conventional wisdom.[1]

Given the discrepancy between the predominant conclusion and the findings presented here, there is the important question: How could such a discrepancy emerge? Although this book concerns changes in the electoral bases and concerns of parties, electoral reactions, and the extent to which the parties organize political debate around class issues, the question of how this divergence could occur is worthy of considerable attention. Anyone reading the current literature is likely to be very puzzled about the difference and wonder how it could have developed.

Attempting to answer this question involves answering two major questions. First, the relatively simple empirical question is whether the two indicators—self-identified class and income level—really differ in the extent of political division associated with them. Assuming there is a sig-

An earlier version of this appendix was presented at the 1998 American Political Science Association Meetings, Boston, September 1998.

nificant difference, there is then the larger question of why so many were inclined to accept the conclusion that class was less relevant to American politics. Ultimately, a conventional wisdom developed because that seemed to "make sense." That leads to less inclination to explore the role of class in American politics. Why did the issue of trends in class voting not receive more scrutiny and study? Why was the argument that class was of declining relevance so readily accepted without extensive analyses to make sure that was the case? This Appendix is an attempt to answer the latter question. It is, of course, not possible to definitively explain why such a conclusion might be accepted. It is possible, however, to reconstruct why a conclusion of the declining relevance of the role of class might have seemed plausible.

Indicators and Different Trends

The impact of how class is measured is clear. Figure A.1 indicates political divisions using self-identified class and by income. Results are averaged within each decade. Using self-identified class, divisions are clearly declining in presidential elections and somewhat less in U.S. House elections. In stark contrast, the political divisions by income are steadily increasing for presidential and U.S. House elections.

The growing relationship of income to party support, relative to other indicators of economic situation, can also be seen if a multivariate ap-

FIGURE A.1   Differences in Voting for Democratic Presidential and Congressional Candidates for Self-Identified Class and Income, 1950s–1990s, Whites Only

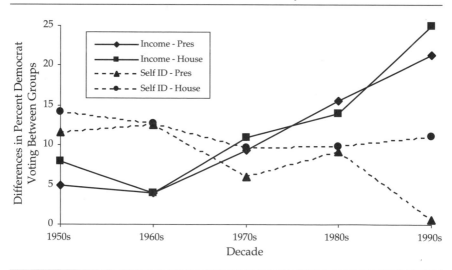

TABLE A.1 Relative Impact of Economic Position and Related
Indicators on Party Voting and ID, 1950s–1990s

			Standardized Regression Coefficients		
Decade	R^2	Income	Self-ID Class	Education	Occupation
Voting for Democratic Presidential Candidates					
1950s	.02	.00	−.10*	−.04	−.09**
1960s	.04	−.01	−.07*	−.15*	−.02
1970s	.01	−.07*	−.01	.02	−.02
1980s	.02	−.11*	−.06*	−.07*	.07*
1990s	.02	−.14*	.06	−.05**	.04
Voting for Democratic House Candidates					
1950s	.02	−.02	−.07*	−.10*	−.01
1960s	.04	−.01	−.09*	−.13*	−.04
1970s	.02	−.05*	−.04*	−.02	−.03
1980s	.02	−.07*	−.07*	−.06*	.04*
1990s	.04	−.16*	−.05**	−.07*	.05**
Party Identification					
1950s	.02	−.01	−.12*	−.05*	.01
1960s	.04	.02	−.10*	−.15*	.00
1970s	.03	−.04*	−.05*	−.12*	−.01
1980s	.03	−.09*	−.09*	−.08*	.02
1990s	.04	−.14*	−.04*	−.11*	.07*

NOTES: Only whites are included. Decades are run as pooled, not averaged, analyses. *Significance levels:* **−.10, *−.05. *Variables:* All are used without any condensing to maximize variation in the independent variables. For presidential (v704) and House (v707) voting, the coefficient is 1 for Democrat and 0 for Other. For Party ID, v301, the variable is recoded so higher numbers in the 7-point scale are Democratic. For all demographic variables, the variables are recoded so higher scores represent higher status. For self-identified status, 1 equals middle and 0 equals working. For occupation, 1 equals farming and 5 equals professional. For education, 1 equals 8th grade or less and 7 equals advanced degrees. All scores of don't know, didn't answer, missing, or not appropriate are coded as missing.

SOURCE: NES Cumulative File 1948–1998.

proach is taken. Table A.1 presents the results of regressing voting for Democratic candidates and party identification on occupation,[2] education, self-identified class,[3] and income since the 1950s. Since the focus in class voting has been on the behavior of whites, only whites are included in the analysis. The table presents the standardized coefficients, to avoid problems stemming from the different scales of the variables, of the regression of measures of partisan support on various economic position indicators. Negative coefficients indicate that since the concern is changes over several decades, and not individual elections, responses are grouped by decade to focus attention on broad changes. Decades are not presumed to be "eras," but just convenient, relatively neutral ways of organizing the results so trends are easier to see.

The relative impact of these indicators on partisan behavior has shifted significantly. Self-identified class, as many analysts have noted, did have a significant impact on political divisions in the 1950s and 1960s. It now has much less of a relationship to partisan attachments. Education and occupation exhibit no trends in their relationships. Income, on the other hand, changed from a limited impact during the 1950s to steady growth since the 1960s. It is now the indicator with the greatest impact on party voting and party identification. The standardized regression coefficient of voting and party identification on income is generally at least twice that for the other indicators.

Income, therefore, in addition to having intuitive validity as an indicator of economic location has emerged with a stronger relationship to partisan behavior than others. Its temporal emergence also follows the pattern that one would expect, given the steady emergence of inequality beginning in the early 1970s. The empirical evidence, then, appears clear that income has emerged as a significant source of partisan divisions.

Neglecting Analyses: Why?

The interesting question, then, given the steady increase in inequality in American society, growing differences between the parties, and the empirical emergence of class divisions, is why the conclusion that class was of diminishing importance emerged largely unchallenged. Sociologists have persisted in their interest in this issue (Clark and Lipset 1991; McNall, Levine, and Fantasia 1991; Goldthorpe and Marshall 1992; Clark, Lipset, and Rempel 1993; Clark 1994; Hout, Brooks, and Manza 1995; Evans 1999; Brooks and Menza 1997a; Brooks and Menza 1997b; Rose, 1998), but within political science the topic has drawn only sporadic interest (Glenn 1972; Hamilton 1972; Schlozman and Verba 1979; Jackman and Jackman 1983; Harrigan 1993a). There were occasional suggestions that class polarization might be returning (Schneider 1983: 2200; Schneider 1984: 2130; Miller and Ferroggiaro 1995), that income has come to play a greater role in dividing people than occupation and education (Petrocik 1987), or that class divisions are increasing in the South (Nadeau and Stanley 1993). None of these suggestions, however, stimulated renewed scrutiny of the issue of class divisions. Indeed, it appears, without counting, that the number of analyses concluding that class was of less relevance and that the New Deal coalition was finished continued to increase. Again, the question is why that development occurred.

Missed Signals and Bad Luck

A stimulus to devote more attention to class divisions might have come from watching political events unfold. Since the early 1980s, as reviewed in Chapters 3 and 4, there has been a steady stream of evidence that inequality has increased and that the parties differ on policies in ways that have clear class implications. As reviewed in Chapter 3, the growing inequality of income has become the focus of books (Levy 1988; Danziger and Gottschalk 1995), newspaper stories[4] and political commentary (Philips 1991, 1993; Samuelson 1997; Kaus 1992). Access to higher education has become more unequal (Mortenson 1995: 1–8). There are continuing problems in access to pensions and health care and people with lower incomes are less likely to have these benefits (Mishel, Bernstein, and Schmitt 1997).

At the same time, Republicans have attacked welfare and other social programs, advocated income tax cuts for the affluent, fought for cuts in the capital gains tax, and sought to cut a broad array of programs that benefit the less affluent (Dionne 1996; Balz and Brownstein 1996; Maraniss and Weisskopf 1996). The parties are clearly articulating differing sets of concerns, which might prompt increasing class divisions (Aldrich 1995: 170–176; Taylor 1996). Bill Clinton's 1998 state of the union address, with his pledge to help various needy groups, and Trent Lott's response, with the message that government assistance and taxes are bad, might prompt concern for how lower- and higher-income groups would react to each message. These differing messages from politicians, however, did not prompt reconsideration of the conclusion that class did not much matter.

It may be that simple bad luck played a role. Analysts may simply have been unlucky enough to gravitate toward relying on an indicator of class divisions that became less relevant. Most analysts have chosen to use self-identified class; that indicator has become less relevant as an indicator of political divisions. It may also be that this result is a product of the discipline's preoccupation, perhaps near fixation, with using presidential results to define all of American politics. Most studies concentrate on presidential election results and give secondary attention to congressional results. If the focus is only on class voting in presidential elections, and if self-identified class is used (see Figure A.1), it would be easy to miss other trends. Bad luck may have played a role in other ways. Some analysts chose to focus on the impact of income, but cross-tabulated income with party identification, excluding leaners, and those analyses give the clear impression that political divisions by income are declining (Carmines and Stanley 1992; Carmines and Layman 1997). If leaners are included, there is no decline.[5]

It may also be that bad timing played a role. Political divisions by income began to increase in the 1980s, just as many analysts were concluding that class divisions were losing their significance in American politics.[6] It may simply be that a consensus emerged just at the time that change developed, and that conclusion was not reexamined such that the change was missed.

Neglecting Class Analyses: The Importance of Other Research

For whatever reasons, detailed analyses of class divisions were not frequent. The argument I present here is that this neglect occurred because academics relied on results from other bodies of research that created doubts about the interests and capabilities of the less affluent. A paradigm about how to assess class divisions emerged and there were no significant doubts about the paradigm because bodies of other, related research provided supporting evidence that the argument of declining class conflict "made sense." With other research indirectly supporting the conclusion, normal science prevailed (Kuhn 1970) and the decline in class division became conventional wisdom.

Specifically, three strands of research provided supporting evidence. First, analyses of social mobility and postmaterialism suggested that the working class was experiencing increasing affluence, and they were less interested in material conflicts. This made the conclusion that class divisions were declining plausible. Another body of research suggested that the working class was not inclined to vote their class interests because they were prone to authoritarianism and intolerance and were driven by other concerns, from cultural issues to racial hostilities. The conclusion that class conflict was declining "made sense" if this research was accepted as valid.

Finally, the argument that economic interests are not central to campaigns was made more plausible by the emergence of a perspective on politics and an accompanying research focus that suggests that campaign outcomes are a product of incumbency resources and money. That perspective is perhaps best embodied by the view proposed by Mayhew (1974a). In brief, he suggested that analysts think of politicians as calculators of how to posture, claim credit, and exploit resources to win re-election. Despite his title of *The Electoral Connection*, his perspective, *whether intended or not*, has led to a general research agenda in which representation and connections to the electoral are deemphasized. Candidate resources, broadly defined, are regarded as primary in driving electoral outcomes, which renders constituencies and their connections to parties less relevant. The combination of the two bodies of supporting research and the framework that focuses on campaign resources directed our attention away from the extent of class divisions in American politics.

The evolution of the study of class and how it has been shaped by other matters is a relatively involved story. This appendix will first review the development of the paradigm about how to research class divisions. The roles of supporting evidence that supported the plausibility and appropriateness of the conclusions about class will then be reviewed.

The Measurement of Class

Class conflict and the issue of how to assign people to different classes has been a matter of contention since the beginning of the nation (Manley 1994; Roth 1998). There have been disputes about whether there are classes, how many classes there should be, and what criteria to use in classifying individuals. Those debates continued throughout the 1800s, with many of the distinctions derived from the perspective that the significant differences are between people owning the means of production, and those working for owners (Burke 1995: 1–21).

The issue moved from the abstract to the empirical world beginning in the 1930s when the first individual-level surveys were conducted. Simplifying, class was discussed and represented in at least four ways. Some analysts discussed it as if it meant status, apparently representing respect, worth, or importance. Others focused on economic position, measured by income. Some emphasized the legacy of the Marxian view and measured economic position by occupation and divided people by whether one was a worker (manual occupation) or was in a nonmanual position (Centers 1949). Others, with more concern for how people see themselves (Eulau 1955: 367–370) or with the sense of solidarity or identification with a class, focused on self-identity (Jackman and Jackman 1983: 13–41). These approaches to class clearly differ in the notion of class involved (Shingles 1989: 936–939), but, as often occurs within the academic community, researchers tended to resolve the problem by choosing the approach they preferred, and the distinctions among them were glossed over.

The empirical issue of what measure to use was first confronted when Gallup polls were conducted, and it was necessary to classify people with some reference to class. It was necessary to decide whether to use occupation, education, income, or some assessment of status. Gallup did not ask about income, but did inquire about occupation and education, and did have interviewers judge the affluence of those interviewed (Ladd and Hadley 1975: 53). From this information, indexes of socioeconomic status were constructed, and political divisions by SES became a regular part of analyses. During the late 1940s the first NES surveys were conducted, and income was added to the questions posed.

Students of class politics argued that it was not enough for individuals to have the same occupations, incomes, or education. It was also necessary that people see themselves as sharing a common situation (Jackman and Jackman 1983: 10–17, 34–41). There had to be some common sense of situation or fate to presume that individuals would vote as a class. Following that logic, the NES surveys added the following question: "There is a lot of discussion about class in American society. Do you regard yourself as middle or working class, or do none of those apply?" If respondents declined to place themselves, they were then "pushed," and asked: "If you had to place yourself, would you choose either middle or working class?" There does not appear to have been any controversy about the issues of why the terms middle and working were chosen (rather than owner of production or worker) or why only two categories were offered, rather than a range, or allowing respondents to volunteer their own designation.[7]

Regardless, by the 1950s, researchers using NES surveys could distinguish people by class on the basis of occupation, education, income, self-identified class, the attributes of parents, or some combination. Although some diversity of approaches to measuring class prevailed, the most common approaches for the next several decades appear to have been to use an SES index, the manual-nonmanual distinction, or the self-identified class measure. Each measure had its merits and limitations.

The SES index involved an attempt to designate the class status of respondents. Since academics were often reluctant to classify people, some verified their designations by asking the public to rank the status of occupations (Jackman and Jackman 1983). The inclusion of education and income, and balancing the three, presumably reduced the bias from any one component. On the other hand, the flaw of the index is that the focus is on societal status and the connection of status to economic position is not always clear. The manual-nonmanual distinction, although perhaps a useful distinction in a society of managers and factory workers, is increasingly suspect in a world in which there are more and more service workers whose manual-nonmanual status is ambiguous. Finally, some argue that there are widespread errors in self-reported occupation, such that relying on these data is questionable (Mellow and Sider 1983; Mathiowetz 1992).

The self-identified class measure was presumably more reflective of the perceived status of respondent, since individuals could place themselves (Jackman 1979). The difficulty is that the connection of self-designated class to objective economic situation, to other measures of status, and to other opinions about class issues has received only limited attention (Heaton 1987: 612–615). In addition, in a society that prizes equality, there are many subtle pressures for people to publicly designate themselves as middle class. How self-identification relates to economic class surely deserves more scrutiny than it has received.

In general, there was little critical research about these measures. A search of the literature, not exhaustive, to be sure, suggests that the two measures of SES and self-identification became relied upon without extensive analysis of their merits. There does not appear to have been extensive debate about the validity of relying on status or self-definition as measures of class, of the possible relationships of the indexes and their components, and whether the relative impact of the measures on party voting was stable over time. These measures became the accepted approaches. They became the tools of "normal science" (Kuhn 1970: 10–51).

With research relying primarily on SES, the manual-nonmanual distinction, and self-identified class, the argument began to emerge as early as the late 1950s that class was of declining significance in American politics. As early as the late 1950s Converse suggested that class political differences might be declining (1958: 391–392). Alford conducted class analyses by calculating the difference in the percentage voting Democratic in presidential elections between manual and nonmanual workers (1963: 79–81) and suggested that class divisions were waning (35–36). Others compared one election to another and also found support for a declining association. A comparison of 1964 with 1974 found the greatest Democratic losses among those of lower SES (Ladd and Hadley 1975: 239). Comparisons of presidential results from 1960 and 1970 (Sundquist 1973: 573) or 1976 and 1980 (Lanouette 1980: 18–32; Pierce and Hagstrom 1980: 18–77) indicated significant shifts to the Republican column among self-identified blue-collar voters, providing support for the idea that class divisions were declining. From 1980 to 1984 Democrats experienced their highest percentage losses among voters with less than a high school education (Sundquist 1983: 11–13).

There was little dissent to these conclusions. A steady stream of studies confirmed the declining relevance of class divisions in American politics (Glenn 1972; Abramson 1974: 102–105; Ladd and Hadley 1975: 73, 233–239; Trilling 1976: 95–130; Abramson 1976: 1070; Ladd 1978a: 98; Sundquist 1983–1984: 583; Stanley, Bianco, and Niemi 1986: 975; Ladd 1991: 31–33; Beck and Sorauf 1992: 166; Keefe 1994: 214; Flanigan and Zingale 1994: 104–105; Abramson, Aldrich, and Rohde 1995: 146, 152–153; Ladd 1996: 204–206; Teixeira 1996; Beck 1997: 145; Lawrence 1997: 40). By the 1990s the self-identified working class did not vote any differently than the self-identified middle class, and identification with the Democratic Party among the bottom third of the income distribution was found to be steadily declining (Carmines and Stanley 1992; Carmines and Layman 1997).

With little counterevidence to slow the momentum, it soon became a presumption of studies, a "fact," that Democrats had alienated the white working class (Black and Black 1987: 246; Huckfeldt and Kohfeld 1989; Edsall and Edsall 1991b: 3–4; Ginsberg 1996: 9; Freedman 1996). With the fact established, the focus shifted to explaining how that loss had occurred. A cottage industry emerged to explain how Democrats had managed to "squander" their electoral majority (Edsall and Edsall 1991; Brown 1991; Greenberg 1996; Radosh 1996). Some focused on the increasingly liberal image of the Democratic Party on race issues (Carmines, Renten, and Stimson 1984; Carmines and Stimson 1989) and how this had alienated the white working class. There was anguish about how race had come to dominate the national agenda, some scholars revealing dismay that white leaders had let blacks make race such a central issue (MacInnes 1996). Others argued that the party became too dominated by liberal intellectuals who pushed the party to support civil liberties issues, gay rights, free speech, and a host of other issues too liberal for the working class. Others emphasized the movement of the working class into the middle class and their declining interest in class politics (Inglehart 1971; Ladd and Hadley 1975: 195–200; Galston 1985: 17).

The few suggestions that class might still be relevant apparently elicited little attention. Petrocik and Steeper noted in the late 1980s that divisions by income were steadily increasing, whereas divisions by the other standard components of SES indexes seemed to be of declining significance (1987: 41–44). Phillips argued that income inequality was increasing and it was sure to have political consequences (1991 and 1993), but that prompted little attention to divisions by income. Edsall observed that class divisions were greater after 1984 than in 1956 (1989: 282–283), but then ignored his own analysis in later work. Textbooks on parties have reported significant divisions by income, but at the same time report that class divisions are declining (Beck and Sorauf 1992: 166; Beck 1997: 145; Miller and Shanks 1996: 532). The consensus that class was of less relevance was so strong that sociologists found themselves proposing complicated methodologies to try to establish that class was still relevant (for example, Brooks and Menza 1997a; Brooks and Menza 1997b). Others were reduced to simply arguing that class matters (Grusky and Sorensen 1998). Rose, for example, almost as a statement of faith, argues ". . . I still think class matters" (1998: 20).

Supporting Evidence:
Real Income and Transforming the Public

The interesting question, given the results presented in Chapter 5, is why this consensus developed with so little opposition. Research results are likely to be accepted when they are compatible with, or reinforced by, other research results. As noted earlier, three strands of research provided supporting evidence for the conclusion that conflict was declining. The first body of supporting research was the argument that the working class is gradually fading away. Long-term economic development raises incomes and education levels, which moves more of the population into the middle class. At the simplest level, the argument is that a more middle-class population will have a smaller percentage of working-class people, and class conflicts and concerns will have less relevance (Lipset 1981: 253; Bell 1962; Wilensky 1966; Nisbet 1959; Bell 1973). From this perspective, the problem confronting the Democrats is that their constituency, the working class, has moved into the middle class, and is more concerned with preserving their newfound status than supporting redistributive policies. A focus on class issues alienates this constituency.

At a more complex level, the argument was that increasing affluence is accompanied by altered values. As education and income increase and concerns about scarcity and materialism slip away, people become more concerned about the quality of life and postmaterial values (Inglehart 1971, 1981, 1985, 1990; Inglehart and Abramson 1994). Class conflict then declines in the United States (Ladd 1976–1977: 577; Inglehart 1977; Ladd 1978b; Ladd and Hadley 1975: 195–200; Ladd 1981: 18) and in Europe (Books and Reynolds 1975; Inglehart 1977: 197–215; Abramson and Inglehart 1986; Abramson and Inglehart 1986: 232; Inglehart 1987: 1298; Inglehart 1997: 260). If the working class is declining, it makes considerable sense that a decline in class conflict would follow.

Despite some plausibility, these analyses are badly flawed. At the most basic level, the analyses make the mistake of conceiving of class as a ratio-level phenomenon. Class membership is presumed to be a function of an individual's absolute position on a scale of education or income. If an individual moves from a low level of real income to a higher level, the individual's class and concerns change. The difficulty is that class has always involved ordinal rankings of individuals, not absolute placements. The positive relationships found between income and responses to survey questions involve comparing relative positions, not absolute positions. It is a considerable leap to then convert that relative relationship to any sort of functional relationship, such that real increases in income will result in increases in adoption of different value positions. There is no necessary dynamic of movement along the path of a relationship as levels of income increase. As an example of this fallacy, the same approach to analysis was utilized by Nie, Powell, and Prewitt (1969a, 1969b). They found a positive relationship between education and participation levels, treated education as an absolute scale, and assumed that as education levels in the United States increased, levels of participation would increase. Obviously there has been a significant discrepancy from that prediction over time.

If class has any meaning, it surely refers to the *relative* economic position that individuals hold in society (Easterlin 1974; Jackman and Jackman 1983: 8–9). Individuals judge their difference from others and form their own judgments as to whether those differences are so significant as to give them a different sense of needs and concerns such that their position would affect the party they support. Absolute levels of income do not shape that judgment.[8]

Equally important, there are serious measurement problems with the postmaterialism analyses (Flanagan 1987; Davis and Davenport 1999). The basic argument is that people are less concerned about material aspects of their lives, and there is less concern about, and less conflict over, material issues. Presumably any assessment of this issue, to be valid, should ask people about conflicts over policies that have material consequences. For example, there should be questions about the importance of equality of opportunity in society, about perceptions of whether opportunity has become more or less equal over time, whether the government should do anything about inequality, and whether government should adopt policies to address specific inequalities in the areas of quality of local schools, access to higher education, housing, health care, and pensions. None of these issues are explored in the surveys that are used to measure postmaterialism. The questions used to measure postmaterialism inquire how important it is to have beautiful cities, or to have economic growth, or to have more say on the job (Inglehart 1997: 351–356). It is very difficult to know just what such questions measure (Davis 1996).[9] What is clear, however, is that anyone trying to discern the extent of conflict about the distribution of wealth, current income, or opportunities would ask a very different set of questions than used to measure "postmaterialism." To ask a series of questions that do not ask about material conflicts, and then use the results to argue that material concerns are declining is surely one of the oddest logics of analysis ever presented in social science.

What is equally puzzling and remarkable is that anyone could write that postmaterialism is emerging at the same time that the inequality in the distribution of wealth and income are rising, that an increasing proportion of children are living in poverty, that a declining proportion have access to health care, and that a declining proportion are covered by pension programs.[10] The argument that material concerns are of less relevance to the electorate is largely a matter of assertion rather than documentation. Studies have not found that the most affluent are the most liberal, as Ladd and Inglehart argue (Himmelstein and McRae 1988: 492–495; Duch and Taylor 1993). Other studies indicate that the younger generation has become more concerned about their material situation in life (Easterlin and Crimmins 1991: 499–500).

Nonetheless, the arguments that some members of the New Deal coalition have experienced upward mobility and the research that increases in income result in a postmaterial concern with cultural issues reinforces the conclusion that class conflict has declined (Inglehart 1997: 255). It becomes plausible that class conflict has declined, and the demands for careful, confirming supporting analyses subside.

Supporting Evidence: Intolerance and Doubts About Class Inclinations

Another body of research raised doubts about the inclination of lower-income individuals to act with a focus on class issues. Three streams of research have combined to suggest that their political intolerance has more significance than class issues as a source of political behavior. First, following in the wake of Hitler and Joe McCarthy, there was considerable concern about the development of the mass media and the possibility of using electronic mediums to manipulate individuals (Kornhauser 1959). Second, evidence was emerging that lower-income individuals were more likely to be uninformed about politics, issues, and candidates. People with less information were also more likely to be influenced by new information (Converse 1966b). With the emergence of television campaign ads, the implications were clear. The less educated and less affluent were easier to "move" during campaigns with ads that manipulated them and distracted them from class issues.

Third, the inclination of the less educated to being swayed by other issues was made more plausible by the evidence that the working class was less "tolerant" (Prothro and Griggs 1960; McClosky 1964; Jackman 1972). As Lipset summarized it, building on the work of Stouffer (1955), in commenting on "working-class authoritarianism":

> The gradual realization that extremist and intolerant movements in modern society are more likely to be based on the lower classes than on the middle and upper classes has posed a tragic dilemma for those intellectuals of the democratic left who once believed the proletariat necessarily to be a force for liberty, racial, and social progress. (1981: 87)

Studies asked about the willingness of Americans to allow free speech and dissent, support for democratic principles, equality for women, abortion rights, and homosexuality. The less educated were regularly found to have lower levels of acceptance of blacks (Lewis and Schneider 1985: 14), diversity of views, or rights than the more educated (Erikson, Luttbeg, and Tedin 1989: 172–173). Together, these three developments—the power of the mass media to manipulate and lower levels of information and tolerance among the working class—created the potential that class divisions in voting would be diminished because lower-class voters would become preoccupied by other issues and other lines of cleavage would drive voting.

The role of intolerance exploded into real political impacts in the 1960s. The "cultural" issues of free speech, civil rights, feminism, and gay rights all became part of the political debate (Edsall and Edsall 1991b). Perhaps the most explosive issue was that of race, involving busing, open housing, access to public and private facilities, voting rights, and eventually affirmative action. To many analysts, the significance of race and its power to divide people was confirmed by the political success of George Wallace. He expressed hostility to the national government and experts and made populist appeals to the "little man" who was being run over by these elites. He also made overt statements of hostility to blacks and garnered far more votes than anyone expected (Edsall and Edsall 1991b: 77–80; Kazin 1995a: 221–242; Carter 1995: 324–370). Goldwater and Nixon capitalized on these concerns and the South soon began its movement to the Republican Party (Black and Black 1992: 141–210).

It was not long before the conventional focus of analyses became how "white southerners" had defected from the party (Ladd and Hadley 1975: 227–231; Brown 1991: 75–150; Black and Black 1992: 141–175; Gillon 1992: 288–289; Sanders 1992: 99; MacInnes 1996: 53; Carmines and Layman 1997: 92). There seemed little doubt that race had become the driving force of American politics. Studies argued that race issues were powerful and were destroying the Democratic Party (Edsall and Edsall 1991b; MacInnes 1996). Race had become the issue central to political beliefs (125–132); it was the great issue "transforming" American politics (Carmines and Stimson 1989: 14). Stanley Greenberg, later to be Bill Clinton's pollster, convened focus groups of whites and reported their intense opposition to continued breaks and preferential treatment for blacks (1986; 1996). V. O. Key's warning that race issues could drive lower-income whites away from focusing on class issues had come true for the South and for the nation (1949: 298–344). As Meyerson noted:

> The American Left has long struggled with what it would term an under-developed level of working-class consciousness and organization, due in large part to the ethnic and racial divisions within that class. (1996a: 87)

The problem was, however, that the analyses purporting to indicate the power of race did not always demonstrate the effect of race issues as much as they presumed it. The literature on the role of race has several problems. There are analysts who have doubts about the validity of intolerance indexes (Hamilton 1972: 399–402; Sullivan, Pierson, and Marcus 1979; Erikson, Luttbeg, and Tedin 1989: 123–128). But the more serious problem has been the absence of studies documenting the suggestion that intolerance actually pulls lower-income voters away from class voting. For example, with race issues, the general approach was to document the significant and persistent differences in opinions between blacks and whites and conclude that these differences drive whites to vote against the Democratic Party, which was seen as supporting minorities. Movement of whites in the South to the Republican Party was consistently presented as "whites," when it was the affluent who were moving Republican (Nadeau and Stanley 1993; Stonecash and Brewer 1999). Votes for George Wallace were quickly assumed to be driven by racism. The populist strain of Wallace was downplayed, as was the possibility that opposition to blacks was driven by resentments of the more affluent (Giles, Gatlin, and Cataldo 1976).

There is not space here to present a full critique of the analyses addressing the impact of cultural and racial opinions on voter behavior. If, however, one is to conclude that social, cultural, or race issues are pulling white working-class voters away from the Democratic Party, then several specific and neglected matters need to be documented. As discussed in the prior chapter, we need to assess the impact of race issues by income levels. We need to determine if "intolerance" is greater among lower-income whites, if this intolerance results in lower-income whites moving away from the Democratic Party more than affluent whites so that the relationship of class to Democratic voting declines. The analysis in Chapter 6 is just one example of how such analyses might be done, and that analysis does not suggest that the presumed patterns exist.

Distracting Frameworks and Agendas, and the Declining Interest in Constituency-Politician Connections

Finally, a broader framework exists that has played a role in drawing attention away from the relationship between class and parties. In general, relationships between class and party voting are likely to be pursued if political research is shaped by a perspective that focuses on constituent-politician relationships or the broad issue of representation. Beginning in the 1970s a concern with representation was gradually displaced by a perspective that is preoccupied with the resources of politicians and their ability to win elections with those resources. Representation questions have been displaced by questions of reelection rates and campaign finance. This line of research contains suggestive implications about the nature of representation in American politics, but there is little actual research on representation. The consequence has been further shifting of attention from how constituency characteristics affect voting, and perhaps more inclination to accept the argument that class conflict has declined.

The 1970s produced two models of research on Congress. One was not adopted and the other was, with very significant consequences for concerns with constituency-party connections among academics. Fenno's

Home Style was concerned with how House members interact with and represent constituents (1978). His much cited analysis was passed over for Mayhew's *The Electoral Connection,* which is concerned with how members get reelected (1974a). Mayhew first asserts that "no theoretical treatment of the United States Congress that posits parties as analytic units will go very far" (1974a: 27). He then postulates that the three activities a member must do to win reelection are advertising, credit claiming, and position taking (1974a: 49–61).

Whether intended or not, this framework makes the activities and resources of candidates the core concern. Although Fenno's work made the connections between candidates and constituents the primary focus, Mayhew's framework makes candidates and their resources the primary focus. A dominant focus soon became incumbency advantages and reelection rates (Cover 1977; Collie 1981), margins of victory of candidates (Mayhew 1974b; Fiorina 1977a, 1977b; Ferejohn 1977; Jacobson 1987), the use of office-related perks (Johannes and McAdams 1981; Cover and Blumberg 1982; Serra 1994), and the effects of campaign spending (Jacobson 1978, 1985, 1990; Thomas 1989; Abramowitz 1989, 1991; Gierzynski and Breaux 1991; Kenny and McBurnett 1992).

Without the argument ever being made explicitly, much of this work implies that connections between constituents, party images, and voting are less important than incumbency, office resources, and campaign funds. If members of Congress can retain office largely through creating high name recognition, by "working" the constituency with benefits, and by spending far more than challengers, the unspoken implication is that members can somehow win reelection without regard to constituency characteristics. The connection between constituents and party outcomes becomes less of a central focus in research. It is revealing, for example, that textbooks on Congress and congressional elections (Jacobson 1997; Herrnson 1998) do not include a table on the relationship between district characteristics and party outcomes or an analysis of how demographic traits are associated with party voting. The evidence indicates that class divisions at the district level have increased since the 1960s (Stonecash and Lindstrom 1999), but this is apparently not a major concern in congressional analyses. Instead, analyses of voters focus on incumbency and name recognition (Jacobson 1997: 85–122).

If candidate resources are deemed most important in explaining outcomes, then a neglect of constituency connections is appropriate. The mass media has a negative image of American politics (Patterson 1994), and much of the research on reelection rates and campaign finance seems to implicitly confirm the notion that campaigns are not about substantive policy disputes. What is interesting is that very few scholars have approached the question of incumbency success and longer stays (Polsby

1968) by asking whether legislators might simply be working harder, spending more time on the job, getting to know their constituents better, doing a better job representing them, and connecting more with their constituents. Perhaps it is just that academics are following the principle of the drunkard's search (look where the numbers are, rather than where the questions are [Kaplan 1964: 11]). There is, to be sure, a part of the discipline that focuses on the dynamics of advocating policies and electoral reactions (for example, Sundquist 1983, Carmines and Stimson 1989), but this perspective does not seem as dominant as that evolved from the Mayhew framework. To the extent that framework is relied upon, it is less likely that the connections between constituents and politicians will be investigated. They are simply not seen as central to what keeps politicians in office.

Consequences

Much academic research has a limited impact on politics. The development of the argument that class divisions have declined have, however, had considerable impact. The argument that Democratic Party positions on cultural, social, and race issues drove away the working class and hurt the party's chances in presidential elections (Edsall and Edsall 1991b; Radosh 1996; Lawrence 1997; Carmines and Layman 1997) has become a fundamental part of interpreting American politics. Much of the evidence about this declining division was accepted because other research provided a basis for concluding that this conclusion made sense. If anything, this review suggests how powerful the impact of academic research can be in creating inclinations to accept particular conclusions and stop examining the evidence.

Notes

1. Some may quite justifiably argue that the thrust of this analysis is just that results vary by the indicator chosen, and that it should not simply be concluded that one measure is the appropriate one and that class divisions have increased. This suggests that the real issue might well be the need to have a methodological debate about appropriate measures. That may well be the case, but the point to be addressed in this chapter is that a methodological debate about class did not occur, and the interesting question is why that debate did not occur.

2. The treatment of the occupation of homemakers presents a problem in how to code them. During the 1950s approximately 35 percent of women classified themselves as homemakers, but by the 1990s this had dwindled to 9 percent. If homemakers were excluded it would eliminate a significant percentage of women. The occupation of spouses is not given in the cumulative file. Rather than estimate the occupation of women as a function of their spouse, homemakers are

excluded. This is not an optimal solution, but I also do not wish to infer the oc-cupation of women. I also ran the analysis recoding women on the basis of fam-ily income and found no significant differences in the results.

3. The relationship of income with self-identified class has not changed over time. The Spearman correlation between income and self-identified class has been very stable over time, within .23 to .29 (middle class = 1, working class = 0, so if the percent identifying as middle class increases with income, the relationship is positive). People who regard themselves as working class are just as likely to be in the bottom third now as in the 1950s. This stability is important. How people see themselves and how that is associated with income has not changed. What has changed is that self-identity has declined in relevance as an indicator of vot-ing, and income has become more relevant.

4. As examples, see the newspaper articles "Even Among the Well-Off, The Richest Get Richer" (Nasar 1992a) and "Fed Gives New Evidence of 80s Gains by Richest" (Nasar 1992b).

5. I cross-tabulated party ID (leaners included) by income, grouped by thirds, for 1952–1996, using the NES cumulative file, and the pattern is that identification with the Democratic Party among the bottom third is essentially flat, with occasional fluc-tuations, over that time period. The issue is whether leaners should be excluded.

6. Wattenberg (1992, 1996), for example, develops a very interesting analysis of reactions to parties, but much, though not all, of his interpretation is built around analyses covering the years 1952–1980. If differences between the parties began to increase in the 1980s, an analysis focusing largely on the 1952–1980 time period would miss the change.

7. NES does include a question that allows more variation, but this question has not always been used, and it did not become used nearly as much as the sim-ple working–middle class distinction did.

8. The limitations of some presumed transition point for moving from working to middle class becomes evident when we take a broader historical perspective. Surely over the last 200 years there have been regular presumptions that eco-nomic development would raise more people out of the working class and make everyone middle class. Yet people making $10,000 a year now do not focus on early pioneers, and conclude that they are better off than those pioneers, and being more affluent, material concerns are of little consequence to them. The post-materialism analyses presume this. They choose some arbitrary point in history, and presume that as people make more income from that point henceforth, peo-ple cease to worry about their relative position. The argument is far too simple and ignores relative situations.

9. Others have accepted the validity of the questions and argued over what variables should be included in analyses to explain the trends found (Duch and Taylor 1993). The crucial issue, however, has to be whether any of these questions really have anything to do with what they purport to measure. On those grounds the questions seem very questionable.

10. It is also odd that it could be asserted that material concerns have declined at the same time that annual surveys of college freshmen indicate that there has been a steady increase in the percentage who indicate that "being well off finan-cially" is "essential" or "very important" (cited in Levy 1998: 85).

References

Abramowitz, Alan I. "Campaign Spending in U.S. Senate Elections." *Legislative Studies Quarterly* 14, No. 4 (November 1989): 487–507.

_____. "Incumbency, Campaign Spending, and the Decline of Competition in U.S. House Elections." *Journal of Politics* 53, No. 1 (February 1991): 34–56.

_____. "Issue Evolution Reconsidered: Racial Attitudes and Partisanship in the U.S. Electorate." *American Journal of Political Science* 38, No. 1 (February 1994): 1–24.

Abramowitz, Alan I., and Kyle L. Saunders. "Ideological Realignments in the U.S. Electorate." *Journal of Politics* 60, No. 3 (August 1998): 634–652.

Abramson, Paul R."Generational Change in American Electoral Behavior." *American Political Science Review* 68, No. 1 (March 1974): 93–105.

_____. *Generational Change in American Politics.* Lexington, Mass.: D. C. Heath, 1976.

Abramson, Paul R., and Ronald Inglehart. "Generational Replacement and Value Change in Six Western European Societies." *American Journal of Political Science* 30, No. 1 (February 1986): 1–25.

Abramson, Paul R., John H. Aldrich, and David W. Rohde. *Change and Continuity in the 1984 Elections.* Washington, D.C.: CQ Press, 1986.

_____. *Change and Continuity in the 1992 Elections.* Washington, D.C.: CQ Press, 1995.

_____. *Change and Continuity in the 1996 Elections.* Washington, D.C.: CQ Press, 1998.

Advisory Commission on Intergovernmental Relations. "Indicators of Federal Growth." In *The Federal Role in the Federal System: A Crisis of Confidence and Competence,* A-77. Washington, D.C.: U.S. Government Printing Office, July 1980.

_____. *The Condition of Contemporary Federalism: Conflicting Theories and Collapsing Constraints.* Washington, D.C.: U.S. Government Printing Office, 1981.

Aistrup, Joseph A. *The Southern Strategy Revisited.* Lexington: University of Kentucky Press, 1996.

Aldrich, John H. *Why Parties?* Chicago: University of Chicago Press, 1995.

_____. "Political Parties in a Critical Era." *American Politics Quarterly* 27, No. 1 (January 1999): 9–32.

Aldrich, John H., and Richard G. Niemi. "The Sixth American Party System: Electoral Change, 1952–1992." In *The Broken Contract: Changing Relationships Between Americans and Their Government,* ed. Stephen Craig, 87–109. Boulder: Westview, 1996.

Alford, Robert R. *Party and Society: The Anglo-American Democracies.* Westport, Conn.: Greenwood Press, 1963.

Allen, Jodie T. "Rich and Poor: Yachts Still Float Higher Than Dinghies." *U.S. News and World Report* (May 24, 1999): 57.

Andersen, Kristi. *The Creation of a Democratic Majority 1928–1936*. Chicago: University of Chicago Press, 1979.

Axelrod, Robert. "Where the Votes Come From: An Analysis of Electoral Coalitions, 1952–1968." *American Political Science Review* 66, No. 1 (March 1972): 11–20.

_____. "Communications." *American Political Science Review* 72, No. 2 (June 1978): 622–625.

_____. "Presidential Election Coalitions in 1984." *American Political Science Review* 80, No. 1 (March 1986): 281–284.

Balz, Dan, and Ronald Brownstein. *Storming the Gates: Protest Politics and the Republican Revival*. Boston: Little, Brown and Co., 1996.

Banfield, Edward C. *The Unheavenly City*. Boston: Little, Brown and Co., 1970.

Barnes, James. "The Democrats' 'Vision Thing.'" *American Enterprise* (March/April 1990).

Barnes, James A., and John C. Weicher. "Urban Blight: The Democrats' Eroding Metropolitan Base." *Public Opinion* (February/March 1985): 49–51.

Baumer, Donald C., and Howard J. Gold. "Party Images and the American Electorate." *American Politics Quarterly* 23, No. 1 (January 1995): 33–61.

Beck, Paul Allen. "Partisan Dealignment in the Postwar South." *American Political Science Review* 71, No. 2 (June 1977): 477–496.

_____. "The Dealignment Era in America." In *Electoral Change in Advanced Industrial Democracies*, edited by Russell J. Dalton, Scott C. Flanagan, and Paul Allen Beck, 240–266. Princeton: Princeton University Press, 1984.

_____. "The Changing American Party Coalitions." Paper presented at the conference on The State of the Parties: 1996 and Beyond, University of Akron, Ray C. Bliss Institute of Applied Politics, Akron, Ohio, October 9 and 10, 1997.

Beck, Paul Allen, and Frank J. Sorauf. *Party Politics in America*. 7th ed. New York: HarperCollins, 1992.

Bell, Daniel. *The End of Ideology*. New York: Collier Books, 1962.

_____. *The Coming of Post-Industrial Society*. New York: Basic Books, 1973.

Bernard, Richard M., and Bradley R. Rice, eds. *Sunbelt Cities: Politics and Growth Since World War II*. Austin: University of Texas Press, 1985.

Black, Earl. "The Militant Segregationist Vote in the Post-*Brown* South: A Comparative Analysis." *Social Science Quarterly* 54, No. 1 (June 1973): 68–84.

_____. *Southern Governors and Civil Rights*. Cambridge: Harvard University Press, 1976.

Black, Earl, and Merle Black. "The Demographic Basis of Wallace Support in Alabama." *American Politics Quarterly* 1, No. 3 (July 1973): 279–304.

_____. *Politics and Society in the South*. Cambridge: Harvard University Press. 1987.

_____. *The Vital South*. Cambridge: Harvard University Press, 1992.

Blakely, Edward J., and Mary Gail Snyder. *Fortress America: Gated Communities in the United States*. Washington, D.C.: Brookings Institution Press, 1997.

Bonafede, Dom. "For the Democratic Party, It's a Time for Rebuilding and Seeking New Ideas." *National Journal* (February 21, 1981): 317–320.

_____. "Democrats Hope Their Midterm Meeting Will Send a Message of Party Unity." *National Journal* (June 19, 1982): 1098.

_____. "Democratic Party Takes Some Strides Down the Long Comeback Trail." *National Journal* (October 8, 1983): 2053–2055.

_____. "Self-Seduction." *National Journal* (January 26, 1985): 216.

Books, John W., and JoAnn B. Reynolds. "A Note on Class Voting in Great Britain and the United States." *Comparative Political Studies* 8, No. 3 (October 1975): 360–376.

Brady, David W., Joseph Cooper, and Patricia Hurley. "The Decline of Party in the U.S. House of Representatives, 1887–1968." *Legislative Studies Quarterly* 4 (1979): 381–407.

Brady, David W., and Charles S. Bullock III. "Coalition Politics in the House of Representatives." In *Congress Reconsidered*, 2d ed., edited by Lawrence C. Dodd and Bruce I. Oppenheimer, 186–203. Washington, D.C.: CQ Press, 1981..

Bragg, Rick. "Disappointment Greets News of Gingrich, Symbol of Independence in His Self-Reliant District." *New York Times* (November 7, 1998): A-8.

Brennan, Mary C. *Turning Right in the Sixties: The Conservative Capture of the GOP.* Chapel Hill: University of North Carolina Press, 1995.

Brinkley, Joel. "Clinton Says No to Any Tax Cut of $500 Billion." *New York Times* (July 26, 1999): A-1.

Brint, Steven, and Jerome Karabel. *The Diverted Dream: Community Colleges and the Promise of Educational Opportunity in America, 1900–1985.* New York: Oxford University Press, 1989.

Broder, David S. "Election '84: A Class Struggle." *Washington Post: National Weekly Edition* (January 16, 1984): 9–10.

Brody, Charles J. "Things Are Rarely Black and White: Admitting Gray into the Converse Model of Attitude Stability." *American Journal of Sociology* 92, No. 3 (November 1986): 657–677.

Brooks, Clem, and Jeff Menza. "Class Politics and Political Change in the United States, 1952–1992." *Social Forces* 76, No. 2 (1997a): 379–408.

_____. "Social Cleavages and Political Alignments: U.S. Presidential Elections, 1960—1992." *American Sociological Review* 62 (1997b): 191–208.

Brown, Peter. *Minority Party: Why Democrats Face Defeat in 1992 and Beyond.* Washington, D.C.: Regnery Gateway, 1991.

Bullock, Charles S., III. "Regional Realignment from an Officeholding Perspective." *Journal of Politics* 50, No. 3 (August 1988): 553–574.

Bullock, Charles S., and Mark J. Rozell. "Southern Politics at Century's End." In *The New Politics of the Old South: An Introduction to Southern Politics*, edited by Charles S. Bullock and Mark J. Rozell, 3–21. Lanham, Maryland: Rowman and Littlefield, 1998.

Burke, Martin. *The Conundrum of Class: Public Discourse on the Social Order in America.* Chicago: University of Chicago Press, 1995.

Burnham, Walter Dean. *Critical Elections and the Mainsprings of American Politics.* New York: W. W. Norton, 1970.

_____. *The Current Crisis in American Politics.* New York: Oxford University Press, 1982.

Campbell, Angus, Philip E. Converse, Warren E. Miller, and Donald E. Stokes. *The American Voter*. New York: John Wiley and Sons, 1960.

Campbell, Bruce A. "Change in the Southern Electorate." *American Journal of Political Science* 21, No. 1 (February 1977): 37–64.

Cantril, Hadley. *Public Opinion*. Princeton: Princeton University Press, 1951.

Carmines, Edward G., and James A. Stimson. "The Two Faces of Issue Voting." *American Political Science Review* 74, No. 1 (March 1980): 78–91.

_____. "Issue Evolution, Population Replacement, and Normal Partisan Change." *American Political Science Review* 75, No. 1 (March 1981): 107–118.

_____. "Racial Attitudes and the Structure of Mass Belief Systems." *Journal of Politics* 44, No. 1 (February 1982): 2–20.

_____. "On the Structure and Sequence of Issue Evolution." *American Political Science Review* 80, No. 3 (September 1986): 901–920.

_____. *Issue Evolution: Race and the Transformation of American Politics*. Princeton, N.J.: Princeton University Press, 1989.

Carmines, Edward G., Steven H. Renten, and James A. Stimson. "Events and Alignments: The Party Image Link." In *Controversies in Voting Behavior*, 2d ed., edited by Richard G. Niemi and Herbert F. Weisberg, 545–560. Washington, D.C.: Congressional Quarterly Press, 1984.

Carmines, Edward G., and Harold W. Stanley. "Ideological Realignment in the Contemporary South: Where Have All the Conservatives Gone?" In *The Disappearing South*, edited by Robert P. Steed, Laurence W. Moreland, and Tod A. Baker, 21–33. Tuscaloosa: University of Alabama Press, 1990.

_____. "The Transformation of the New Deal Party System: Social Groups, Political Ideology, and Changing Partisanship Among Northern Whites, 1972–1988." *Political Behavior* 14 (1992): 213–237.

Carmines, Edward G., and Geoffrey C. Layman. "Issue Evolution in Postwar American Politics: Old Certainties and Fresh Tension." In *Present Discontents*, edited by Byron E. Shafer. Chatham, N.J.: Chatham Publishers, 1997.

Carter, Dan T. *The Politics of Rage: George Wallace, the Origins of the New Conservatism, and the Transformation of American Politics*. New York: Simon and Schuster, 1995.

Cassel, Carol A. "Class Bases of Southern Politics Among Whites, 1952–1972." *Social Science Quarterly* 58, No. 4 (March 1978): 700–707.

Cawley, R. McGreggor. *Federal Land, Western Anger*. Lawrence: University Press of Kansas, 1993.

Centers, Richard. *The Psychology of Social Classes*. Princeton: Princeton University Press, 1949.

Citizens for Tax Justice. *Who Pays: A Distributional Analysis of the Tax Systems in All 50 States*. Washington: Citizens for Tax Justice and Institute on Taxation and Economic Policy, 1996.

Clark, Blair. "Can We Put New Life in the Party?" *Nation* (November 2, 1985): 440–443.

Clark, Terry N. "Race and Class vs. the New Political Culture." In *Urban Innovation: Creative Strategies for Turbulent Times*, edited by Terry N. Clark, 21–78. Thousand Oaks, Calif.: Sage, 1994.

Clark, Terry Nichols, and Seymour Martin Lipset. "Are Social Classes Dying?" *International Sociology* 6, No. 4 (December 1991): 397–410.

Clark, Terry N., Seymour Martin Lipset, and Michael Rempel. "The Declining Political Significance of Class." *International Sociology* 8 (1993): 293–316.

Clinton, William J. "Prepared Text of President Clinton's State of the Union Message." *New York Times* (January 28, 1998): A19–20.

Coleman, John J. "The Resurgence of Party Organization? A Dissent from the New Orthodoxy." In *The State of the Parties*, edited by Daniel Shea and John Green, 311–327. New York: Rowman Littlefield, 1994.

College Board. *Trends in Student Aid*. Washington, D.C.: 1998.

Collie, Melissa P. "Incumbency, Electoral Safety, and Turnover in the House of Representatives, 1972–1976." *American Political Science Review* 75 (1981): 119–131.

Collie, Melissa P., and David W. Brady. "The Decline of Partisan Voting Coalitions in the House of Representatives." In *Congress Reconsidered*, 3d ed., edited by Lawrence C. Dodd and Bruce I. Oppenheimer, 272–287. Washington, D.C: CQ Press, 1985.

Commission on National Investment in Higher Education. *Breaking the Social Contract: The Fiscal Crisis in Higher Education*. New York: Council for Aid to Education, 1996.

_____. "How Big Is the North-South Democratic Split?" *Congressional Quarterly Almanac*, 813–817. Washington, D.C.: Congressional Quarterly, Inc., 1957.

Congressional Quarterly. "Basic Democratic Divisions Examined." *Congressional Quarterly Almanac*, 764–769. Washington, D.C.: Congressional Quarterly, Inc., 1958.

_____. "Extent of North-South Democratic Split Analyzed." *Congressional Quarterly Almanac*, 135–146. Washington, D.C.: Congressional Quarterly, Inc., 1959.

_____. "Extent of North-South Democratic Split Analyzed." *Congressional Quarterly Almanac*, 117–130. Washington, D.C.: Congressional Quarterly, Inc., 1960.

_____. "Extent of North-South Democratic Split Analyzed." *Congressional Quarterly Almanac*, 642–657. Washington, D.C.: Congressional Quarterly, Inc., 1961.

_____. "Extent of North-South Democratic Split Analyzed." *Congressional Quarterly Almanac*, 723–735. Washington, D.C.: Congressional Quarterly, Inc., 1962.

_____. "Extent of North-South Democratic Split Analyzed." *Congressional Quarterly Almanac*, 740–754. Washington, D.C.: Congressional Quarterly, Inc., 1963.

_____. "Democrats from North and South Split on 24% of Votes." *Congressional Quarterly Almanac*, 745–760. Washington, D.C.: Congressional Quarterly, Inc., 1964.

_____. "Democrats Regional Divisions Remain Great in 1965." *Congressional Quarterly Almanac*, 1083–1098. Washington, D.C.: Congressional Quarterly, Inc., 1965.

Conniff, Richard. "Federal Lands." *National Geographic* 185, No. 2 (February 1994): 2–39.

Conover, Pamela Johnston, and Stanley Feldman. "Projection and the Perception of Candidates' Issue Positions." *Western Political Quarterly* 25, No. 2 (June 1982): 228–244.

Converse, Philip E. "The Shifting Role of Class in Political Attitudes and Behavior." In *Readings in Social Psychology*, 3d ed., edited by E. E. Maccoby, T. M. Newcomb, and E. E. Hartley, 388–399. New York: Holt, Rinehart, and Winston, 1958.

_____. "On the Possibility of Major Political Realignment in the South." In *Elections and the Political Order*, edited by Angus Campbell, Philip E. Converse, Warren E. Miller, and Donald E. Stokes, 212–242. New York: John Wiley and Sons, 1966a.

_____. "The Nature of Belief Systems in Mass Publics." In *Ideology and Discontent*, edited by David E. Apter, 227–231. New York: Free Press, 1966b.

Coontz, Stephanie. *The Way We Never Were*. New York: Basic Books, 1992.

Cover, Albert D. "One Good Term Deserves Another: The Advantage of Incumbency in Congressional Elections." *American Journal of Political Science* 21 (1977): 523–542.

Cover, Albert D., and Bruce S. Blumberg. "Baby Books and Ballots: The Impact of Congressional Mail on Constituency Opinion." *American Political Science Review* 76, No. 2 (June 1982).

Covington, Sally. "How Conservative Philanthropies and Think Tanks Transform US Policy." 'http://www.infoasis.com/www/people/stevetwt/Democracy/ConservThinkTanks.html' (winter 1998).

Craig, Stephen C. "The Angry Voter: Politics and Popular Discontent in the 1990s." In *The Broken Contract: Changing Relationships Between Americans and Their Government*, edited by Stephen Craig, 46–66. Boulder: Westview, 1996.

Curme, Michael A., Barry T. Hirsch, and David A. Macpherson. "Union Strength Among the States." *Industrial and Labor Relations Review* 44, No. 1 (October 1990): 22–26.

Danielson, Michael N. *The Politics of Exclusion*. New York: Columbia University Press, 1976.

Danziger, Sheldon, and Daniel H. Weinberg. *Fighting Poverty: What Works and What Doesn't*. Cambridge: Harvard University Press, 1986.

Danziger, Sheldon, and Peter Gottschalk. *America Unequal*. Cambridge: Harvard University Press, 1995.

Dao, James. "$2.3 Billion in Housing Aid is Cut from Spending Bill." *New York Times* (May 2, 1998): B-3.

Darmofal, David. "Socioeconomic Bias in Turnout Decline: Do the Voters Remain the Same?" Paper presented at the 1999 American Political Science Association Meeting, Atlanta, Georgia, September 1999.

Davis, Darren W., and Christian Davenport. "Assessing the Validity of the Postmaterialism Index." *American Political Science Review* 93, No. 3 (September 1999): 649–664.

Davis, James A. "A Review Essay of *Value Change in Global Perspective*." *Public Opinion Quarterly* 60, No. 2 (summer 1996): 322–331.

Deckard, Barbara, and John Stanley. "Party Decomposition and Region: The House of Representatives, 1945–1970." *Western Political Quarterly* 27 (1974): 249–264.

Declercq, Eugene, Thomas L. Hurley, and Norman R. Luttbeg. "Voting in American Presidential Elections, 1956–1972." *American Politics Quarterly* 3, No. 3 (July 1975): 222–246.

DeParle, Jason. "Democrat's Invisible Man Specializes in Making Inequity of the Poor Easy to See." *New York Times* (August 19, 1991): A-12.

_____. "Complexity of a Fiscal Giant: A Primer on Social Security." *New York Times* (February 11, 1993): A-1.

DeSart, Jay A. "'Generational Change' and Party Support in the House of Representatives." Paper presented at the Midwest Political Science Association Meeting, Chicago, Illinois, April 1998.

Dionne, E. J., Jr. *They Only Look Dead.* New York: Touchstone, 1997.

Dole, Robert. "Text of Robert Dole's [acceptance] speech to the Republican National Convention, August 15, 1996, San Diego, California.http://www-CGI.CNN.COM/ALLPOLITICS/1996/conventions/San.Diego/transcripts.

Drew, Elizabeth. *Showdown: The Struggle Between the Gingrich Congress and the Clinton Whitehouse.* New York: Touchstone Books, 1996.

Duch, Raymond M., and Michael A. Taylor. "Postmaterialism and the Economic Condition." *American Journal of Political Science* 37, No. 3 (August 1993): 747–779.

Dunham, Pat. *Electoral Behavior in the United States.* Englewood Cliffs, N.J.: Prentice-Hall, 1991.

Easterlin, Richard A. "Does Economic Growth Improve the Human Lot? Some Empirical Evidence." In *Essays in Honor of Moses Abramovitz,* edited by Paul David and Melvin Reder. New York: Academic Press, 1974.

Easterlin, Richard A., and Eileen M. Crimmins. "Private Materialism, Personal Self-Fulfillment, Family Life, and Public Interest: The Nature, Effects, and Causes of Recent Changes in the Values of American Youth." *Public Opinion Quarterly* 55, No. 4 (winter 1991): 499–533.

Eckholm, Eric. "Double Sword for President." *New York Times* August 23, 1993): A-1.

Edsall, Thomas Byrne. *The New Politics of Inequality.* New York: W. W. Norton, 1984.

_____. "The Changing Shape of Power: A Realignment in Public Policy." In *The Rise and Fall of the New Deal Order,* edited by Steve Fraser and Gary Gerstle, 269–293. Princeton: Princeton University Press, 1989.

_____. "Willie Horton's Message." *New York Review of Books* (February 13, 1992): 7–11.

Edsall, Thomas Byrne, and Mary D. Edsall. "Race." *Atlantic Monthly* (May 1991a): 53–86.

_____. *Chain Reaction: The Impact of Race, Rights, and Taxes on American Politics.* New York: W. W. Norton, 1991b.

Elazar, Daniel J. *American Federalism: A View from the States.* 3d ed. New York: Harper and Row, 1984.

Employee Benefits Research Institute. *The 1997 Retirement Confidence Survey Summary of Findings.* http://www.ebri.org/rcs/1997/97rcs_es.htm (October 16, 1997).

Erikson, Robert S., Thomas D. Lancaster, and David W. Romeo. "Group Components of the Presidential Vote, 1952–1984." *Journal of Politics* 51, No. 2 (May 1989): 337–346.

Erikson, Robert S., Norman R. Luttbeg, and Kent L. Tedin. *American Public Opinion.* 3d ed. New York: Macmillan, 1989.

Erikson, Robert S., Gerald C. Wright, and John P. McIver. *Statehouse Democracy.* New York: Cambridge University Press, 1993.

Erikson, Robert S., and Gerald C. Wright. "Voters, Candidates, and Issues in Congressional Elections." In *Congress Reconsidered,* 6th ed, edited by Lawrence C. Dodd and Bruce I. Oppenheimer. Washington, D.C,: CQ Press, 1997.

Eulau, Heinz. "Perceptions of Class and Party in Voting Behavior: 1952." *American Political Science Review* 49, No. 2 (June 1955): 364–384.

Evans, Geoff, ed. *The End of Class Politics.* Oxford: Oxford University Press, 1999.

Faux, Jeffrey. *The Party's Not Over.* New York: Basic Books, 1996.

Fenno, Richard. *Home Style.* Boston: Little, Brown and Co., 1978.

Ferejohn, John A. "On the Decline of Competition in Congressional Elections." *American Political Science Review* 71 (1977): 166–176.

Ferguson, Thomas, and Joel Rogers."Why Mondale Turned Right."*Nation* (October 6, 1984): 313–315.

_____. "The Myth of America's Turn to the Right." *Atlantic Monthly* (May 1986): 43–53.

Fiorina, Morris. *Congress: Keystone to the Washington Establishment.* New Haven, Conn.: Yale University Press, 1977a.

_____. "The Case of the Vanishing Marginals: The Bureaucracy Did It." *American Political Science Review* 71 (1977b): 177–181.

_____. *Retrospective Voting in American National Elections.* New Haven, Conn.: Yale University Press, 1981.

Firebaugh, Glenn, and Kenneth E. Davis. "Trends in Antiblack Prejudice, 1972–1984: Region and Cohort Effects." *American Journal of Sociology* 94, No. 2 (September 1988): 251–272.

Flanagan, Scott C. "Value Change in Industrial Societies." *American Political Science Review* 81, No. 4 (December 1987): 1303–1318.

Flanigan, William H., and Nancy H. Zingale. *Political Behavior of the American Electorate.* 8th ed. Washington, D.C.: CQ Press, 1994.

_____. *Political Behavior of the American Electorate.* 9th ed. Washington, D.C.: CQ Press, 1998.

Fleisher, Richard, and Jon R. Bond. "Why Has Party Conflict Among Elites Increased if the Electorate is Dealigning?" Paper presented at the Midwest Political Science Association Meeting, Chicago, Illinois, April 1996.

Fossey, Richard. "The Dizzying Growth of the Federal Student Loan Program." In *Condemning Students to Debt: College Loans and Public Policy,* edited by Richard Fosssey and Mark Bateman, 7–18. New York: Teachers College Press, 1998.

Free, Lloyd A., and Hadley Cantril. *The Political Beliefs of Americans: A Study of Public Opinion.* New Brunswick, N.J.: Rutgers University Press, 1967.

Freedman, Samuel G. *The Inheritance: How Three Families and America Moved from Roosevelt to Reagan and Beyond.* New York: Simon and Schuster, 1996.

Friedman, Milton. *Capitalism and Freedom.* Chicago: University of Chicago Press, 1962.

Galston, William. "The Future of the Democratic Party." *Brookings Review* (winter 1985): 16–24.

Galston, William, and Elaine Ciulla Kamarck. "The Politics of Evasion: Democrats and the Presidency." Washington, D.C: Progressive Policy Institute, September 1989.

Gans, Curtis B. "A Crosscurrent, Not a Watershed." *Nation* (December 13, 1980): 630–632.

Gatlin, Douglas S. "Party Identification, Status, and Race in the South: 1952–1972." *Public Opinion Quarterly* 39, No. 1 (spring 1975): 39–51.

Geer, John G. "The Electorate's Partisan Evaluations: Evidence of a Continuing Democratic Edge." *Public Opinion Quarterly* 55, No. 2 (summer 1991): 218–231.

_____. "New Deal Issues and the American Electorate, 1952–1988." *Political Behavior* 14, No. 1 (1992): 45–65.

Gerring, John. *Party Ideologies in America.* Cambridge: Cambridge University Press, 1998.

Gierzynski, Anthony, and David Breaux. "Money and Votes in State Legislative Elections." *Legislative Studies Quarterly* 16, No. 10 (May 1991): 203–218.

Gilder, George F. *Wealth and Poverty.* New York: Basic Books, 1981.

Gilens, Martin. "Racial Attitudes and Opposition to Welfare." *Journal of Politics* 57, No. 4 (November 1995): 994–1014.

_____. "'Race Coding' and White Opposition to Welfare." *Journal of Politics* 90, No. 3 (September 1996): 593–604.

Giles, Michael W., Douglas S. Gatlin, and Everett F. Cataldo. "Racial and Class Prejudice: Their Relative Effects on Protest Against School Desegregation." *American Sociological Review* 41, No. 2 (April 1976): 280–288.

Giles, Michael W., and Kaenan Hertz. "Racial Threat and Partisan Identification." *American Political Science Review* 88, No. 2 (June 1994): 317–326.

Gillon, Steven M. "The Trail of the Democrats: Search for a New Majority." In *Democrats and the American Idea,* edited by Peter B. Kovler, 285–303. Washington, D.C.: Center for the National Policy Press, 1992.

Gimpel, James G. "Selective Migration and Political Change in American Politics." Paper presented at the American Political Science Association Meeting, Atlanta, Georgia, September 1999.

Gingrich, Newt, and Dick Armey. *Contract with America.* New York: Times Books, 1994.

Ginsberg, Benjamin. "The 1994 National Elections: A Debacle for the Democrats." In *Do Elections Matter?.* 3d ed, 5–22. Armonk, N.Y.: M. E. Sharpe, 1996.

Gladieux, Lawrence E. "Federal Student Aid Policy: A History and an Assessment." Paper delivered at the Conference on Financing Postsecondary Education: The Federal Role, Charleston, S.C., October 1995.

Glaser, James M. "Back to the Black Belt: Racial Environment and White Racial Attitudes in the South." *Journal of Politics* 56, No. 1 (February 1994): 21–41.

_____. *Race, Campaign Politics and the Realignment in the South.* New Haven: Yale University Press, 1996.

Glenn, Norvall D. "Class and Party Support in the United States: Recent and Emerging Trends." *Public Opinion Quarterly* 37 (spring 1972): 31–47.

_____. "Class and Party Support in 1972." *Public Opinion Quarterly* 39, No. 1 (spring 1975): 117–122.

Glynn, Carroll J., Susan Herbst, Garrett J. O'Keefe, and Robert Y. Shapiro. *Public Opinion.* Boulder: Westview Press, 1999.

Goldfeld, Michael.*The Color of Politics: Race and the Mainsprings of American Politics.* New York: The New Press, 1997.

Goldthorpe, John W., and Gordon Marshall. "The Promising Future of Class Analysis: A Response to Recent Critiques." *Sociology* 26, No. 3 (August 1992): 381–400.

Gottfried, Paul, and Thomas Fleming. *The Conservative Movement.* Boston: Twayen Publishers, 1988.

Greeley, Andrew M. "How Conservative Are American Catholics?" *Political Science Quarterly* 92, No. 2 (summer 1977): 199–218.

Green, John C., Lyman A. Kellstedt, Corwin E. Smidt, and James L. Guth. "The Soul of the South: Religion and the New Electoral Order." In *The New Politics of the Old South,* edited by Charles S. Bullock III and Mark J. Rozell, 261–276. Boulder: Rowman and Littlefield, 1998.

Greenberg, Stanley. *Report on Democratic Defection.* Washington, D.C.: The Analysis Group, April 15, 1985.

_____. "Plain Speaking: Democrats Speak Their Minds." *Public Opinion* (summer 1986): 44–50.

_____. *Middle Class Dreams.* New York: Times Books, 1996.

Greenhouse, Steven. "Unions Are Battling Drives in 21 States to Curtail Sharply Their Political War Chests." *New York Times* (March 27, 1998): A-10.

Grosclose, Tim, Steven D. Levitt, and James M. Snyder Jr. "Comparing Interest Group Scores Across Time and Chambers: Adjusted ADA Scores for the U.S. Congress." *American Political Science Review* 93, No. 1 (March 1999): 33–50.

Grusky, David B., and Jesper B. Sorensen. "Can Class Analysis be Salvaged?" *American Journal of Sociology* 103, No. 5 (March 1998): 1187–1234.

Hacker, Andrew. "Playing the Racial Card." *New York Review of Books* (October 24, 1991): 14–18.

Hale, Jon F. "The Making of the New Democrats." *Political Science Quarterly* 110, No. 2 (1995): 207–232.

Hamilton, Richard F. *Class and Politics in the United States.* New York: John Wiley, 1972.

"Forum: What's Wrong with the Democrats?" *Harper's* (January 1990): 45–55.

Harrigan, John J. *Empty Dreams, Empty Pockets: Class and Bias in American Politics.* New York: Macmillan, 1993a.

Harrigan, John J. *Political Change in the Metropolis.* 5th ed. New York: Harper-Collins, 1993b.

Harris, Louis. *Is There a Republican Majority?* New York: Harper and Brothers, 1954.

Hartwig, Frederick, William R. Jenkins, and Earl M. Temchin. "Variability in Electoral Behavior: The 1960, 1968, and 1976 Elections." *American Journal of Political Science* 24, No. 3 (August 1980): 553–558.

Hayghe, Howard V. "Developments in Women's Labor Force Participation." *Monthly Labor Review* (September 1997): 41–46.

Hearn, James C. "The Growing Loan Orientation in Federal Aid Policy: A Historical Perspective." In *Condemning Students to Debt: College Loans and Public Policy,* edited by Richard Fossey and Mark Bateman, 47–75. New York: Teachers College Press, 1998.

Heaton, Tim B. "Objective Status and Class Consciousness." *Social Science Quarterly* 68, No. 3 (1987): 611–620.

Herrnson, Paul S. *Congressional Elections: Campaigning at Home and in Washington.* Washington, D.C.: CQ Press, 1998.

Himmelstein, Jerome L., and James A. McRae Jr. "Social Issues and Socioeconomic Status." *Public Opinion Quarterly* 52, No. 4 (winter 1988): 492–512.

Hirsch, Herbert. "Suburban Voting and National Trends." *Western Political Quarterly* 21, No. 3 (September 1968): 508–514.

Hochschild, Jennifer L. *Facing Up to the American Dream: Race, Class, and the Soul of the Nation.* Princeton: Princeton University Press, 1995.

Hodgson, Godfrey. *The World Turned Right Side Up.* Boston: Mariner Books, 1996.

Holmes, Steven A. "House Republicans Plan to Keep a Tight Rein on 2000 Census." *New York Times* (February 9, 1998a): A-11.

_____. "Republicans Resisting Census Plan to Correct Undercounting." *New York Times* (February 9, 1998b): A-11.

Hout, Michael, Clem Brooks, and Jeff Manza. "The Democratic Class Struggle in the United States, 1948–1992." *American Sociological Review* 60 (December 1995): 805–828.

Huckfeldt, Robert, and Carol W. Kohfeld. *Race and the Decline of Class in American Politics.* Urbana: University of Illinois Press, 1989.

Huntington, Samuel P. "Postindustrial Politics: How Benign Will it Be?" *Comparative Politics* 6, No. 2 (January 1974): 163–191.

Inglehart, Ronald. "The Silent Revolution in Europe." *American Political Science Review* 65, No. 4 (December 1971): 991–1017.

_____. *Silent Revolution.* Princeton: Princeton University Press, 1977.

_____. "Post-Materialism in an Environment of Insecurity." *American Political Science Review* 75, No. 4 (December 1981): 880–900.

_____. "Aggregate Stability and Individual-Level Flux in Mass Belief Systems: The Level of Analysis Paradox." *American Political Science Review* 79, No. 1 (March 1985): 97–116.

_____. "Value Change in Industrial Societies." *American Political Science Review* 81, No. 4 (December 1987): 1289–1303.

_____. *Culture Shift in Advanced Industrial Society.* Princeton: Princeton University Press, 1990.

_____. *Modernization and Postmodernization.* Princeton: Princeton University Press, 1997.

Inglehart, Ronald, and Paul R. Abramson. "Economic Security and Value Change." *American Political Science Review* 88, No. 2 (June 1994): 336–354.

Jackman, Mary R. "The Subjective Meaning of Social Class Identification in the United States." *Public Opinion Quarterly* 43, No. 4 (winter 1979): 443–462.

Jackman, Mary, and Robert Jackman. *Class Awareness in the United States.* Berkeley: University of California Press, 1983.

Jackman, Robert. "Political Elites, Mass Publics, and Support for Democratic Principles." *Journal of Politics* 54 (August 1972): 753–773.

Jackson, John E. "Issues, Party Choices, and Presidential Votes." *American Journal of Political Science* 19, No. 2 (May 1975): 161–185.

Jackson, Kenneth T. *Crabgrass Frontier: The Suburbanization of the United States.* New York: Oxford University Press, 1985.

Jacobson, Gary C. "The Effects of Campaign Spending in Congressional Elections." *American Political Science Review* 72 (1978): 469–491.

_____. "Money and Votes Reconsidered: Congressional Elections, 1972–1982." *Public Choice* 47 (1985): 7–62.

_____. "The Marginals Never Vanished: Incumbency and Competition in Elections to the U.S. House of Representatives, 1952–1982." *American Journal of Political Science* 31: 126–141.

_____. "The Effects of Campaign Spending in House Elections: New Evidence for Old Argument." *American Journal of Political Science* 34 (1990): 334–362.

_____. "The 1994 House Elections in Perspective." *Political Science Quarterly* 111, No. 2 (1996): 203–223.

_____. *The Politics of Congressional Elections*, 4th ed. New Haven: Yale University, 1997.

Jargowsky, Paul A. "Take the Money and Run: Economic Segregation in U.S. Metropolian Areas." *American Sociological Review* 61 (December 1996): 984–998.

Johannes, John R., and John C. McAdams. "The Congressional Incumbency Effect: Is it Casework, Policy Compatibility, or Something Else?" *American Journal of Political Science* 25 (1981): 512–542.

Johnson, Nicholas, and Iris J. Lav. "Are State Taxes Becoming More Regressive?" Center on Budget and Policy Priorities. http://www.cbpp.org/930sttax.htm. September 30, 1997.

Johnston, David Cay. "'97 Middle Class Tax Relief Benefits Wealthy First." *New York Times* (April 3, 1998): 22.

_____. "Gap Between Rich and Poor Found Substantially Wider." *New York Times* (September 5, 1999): 16.

Judd, Dennis R., and Todd Swanstrom. *City Politics: Private Power and Public Policy*. 2d ed. New York: Longman, 1998.

Kaplan, Abraham. *The Conduct of Inquiry*. Scranton, Pa.: Chandler, 1964.

Katz, Jeffrey L. "Welfare Issue Finds Home on the Campaign Trail." *Congressional Quarterly* (October 15, 1994): 2956–2958.

Katznelson, Ira, Kim Geiger, and Daniel Kryder. "Limiting Liberalism: The Southern Veto in Congress, 1933–1950." *Political Science Quarterly* 108 (summer 1993): 283–306.

Kaus, Mickey. *The End of Equality*. New York: Basic Books, 1992.

Kazin, Michael. *The Populist Persuasion*. New York: Basic Books, 1995a.

_____. "The Worker's Party?" *New York Times* (October 19, 1995b): A-25.

Keefe, William J. *Parties, Politics, and Public Policy in America*. Washington, D.C.: CQ Press, 1994.

Kenski, Henry C., and Lee Sigelman. "Where the Votes Come From: Group Components of the 1988 Senate Vote." *Legislative Studies Quarterly* 18, No. 3 (August 1993): 367–390.

Kelley, Stanley, Jr. "Democracy and the New Deal Party System." In *Democracy and the Welfare State*, edited by Amy Gutman, 185–205. Princeton: Princeton University Press, 1988.

Kenny, Christopher, and Michael McBurnett. "A Dynamic Model of the Effect of Campaign Spending on Congressional Vote Choice." *American Journal of Political Science* 36, No. 4 (November 1992): 923–937.

Key, V. O., Jr. *Southern Politics in State and Nation*. New York: Knopf, 1949.

_____. "A Theory of Critical Elections." *Journal of Politics* 17, No. 1 (February 1955): 3–18.

_____. "Secular Realignment and the Party System." *Journal of Politics* 21, No. 2 (May 1959): 198–210.

Kinder, Donald R., and David O. Sears. "Prejudice and Politics: Symbolic Racism Versus Racial Threat to the Good Life." *Journal of Personality and Social Psychology* 40, No. 3 (1981): 414–431.

Kinder, Donald R., and Lynn M. Sanders. *Divided by Color*. Chicago: University of Chicago Press, 1996.

King, David C. "Party Competition and Polarization in American Politics." Paper presented at the American Political Science Association Meeting, Boston, September 1998.

King, Jacqueline. "Student Aid: Who Benefits Now?" *Educational Record* (winter 1996): 21–26.

Kirkpatrick, Samuel A. "Issue Orientation and Voter Choice in 1964." *Social Science Quarterly* 49, No. 1 (June 1968): 87–102.

Kirkpatrick, Samuel A., and Melvin E. Jones. "Vote Direction and Issue Cleavage in 1968." *Social Science Quarterly* 51, No. 3 (December 1970): 689–705.

Knoke, David. *Change and Continuity in American Politics: The Social Bases of Political Parties*. Baltimore: Johns Hopkins University Press, 1976.

Knoke, David, and Michael Hout. "Social and Demographic Factors in American Political Party Affiliations." *American Sociological Review* 39, No. 5 (October 1974): 700–713.

Knoke, David, and Natalie Kyriazis. "The Persistence of the Black-Belt Vote: A Test of Key's Hypothesis." *Social Science Quarterly* 57, No. 4 (March 1977): 899–906.

Kohlbert, Elizabeth, and Adam Clymer. "The Politics of Layoffs: In Search of a Message." *New York Times* (March 6, 1996): A-1, A-22–23.

Kopkind, Andrew, and Alexander Cockburn. "The Left, the Democrats and the Future." *Nation* (July 21–28, 1984): 42–45.

Kornhauser, William. *The Politics of Mass Society*. Glencoe, Ill.: Free Press, 1959.

Kozol, Jonathan. *Savage Inequalities*. New York: Crown, 1991.

Kreps, Juanita M., and R. John Leaper. "Home Work, Market Work, and the Allocation of Time." In *Women and the American Economy: A Look to the 1980s*, edited by Juanita M. Kreps, 61–81. Englewood Cliffs, N.J.: Prentice-Hall, 1976.

Krugman, Paul. *Peddling Prosperity: Economic Sense and Nonsense in the Age of Diminished Expectations*. New York: W. W. Norton, 1994.

Kuhn, Thomas S. *The Structure of Scientific Revolutions*. 2d ed., enlarged. Chicago: University of Chicago Press, 1970.

Kuklinski, James H., Michael D. Cobb, and Martin Gilens. "Racial Attitudes and the 'New South,'" *Journal of Politics* 59, No. 2 (May 1997): 323–349.

Kuttner, Robert. *The Life of the Party: Democratic Prospects in 1988 and Beyond*. New York: Penguin Books, 1988.

Ladd, Everett Carll, Jr. "Liberalism Turned Upside Down: The Inversion of the New Deal Order." *Political Science Quarterly* 91, No. 4 (winter 1976–1977): 577–600.

_____. "The Shifting Party Coalitions—1932–1976." In *Emerging Coalitions in American Politics*, edited by Seymour Martin Lipset, 81–102. San Francisco: Institute for Contemporary Studies, 1978a.

_____. "The New Lines are Drawn: Class and Ideology in America." *Public Opinion* 1, No. 3 (July/August 1978b): 48–53.

_____. "The Brittle Mandate: Electoral Dealignment and the 1980 Presidential Election." *Political Science Quarterly* 96, No. 1 (spring 1981): 1–25.

_____. "Is Election '84 Really a Class Struggle?" *Public Opinion* (April/May 1984): 41–51.

_____. "As the Realignment Turns: A Drama in Many Acts." *Public Opinion* (December/January): 3–7.

_____. "Like Waiting for Godot." In *The End of Realignment*, edited by Byron E. Shafer, 24–36. Madison: University of Wisconsin, 1991.

_____. "Political Parties and Presidential Elections in the Postindustrial Era." In *American Presidential Elections*, edited by Harvey L. Schantz, 189–210. Albany: SUNY Press, 1996.

_____. "1996 Vote: The No Majority Realignment Continues." *Political Science Quarterl* 112, No. 1 (1997): 1–28.

_____. "Nobody's Buying." *The New Democrat*. (January/February 1998): 10–12.

Ladd, Everett Carll, Jr., Charles Hadley, and Lauriston King. "A New Political Realignment?" *Public Interest* 23 (spring 1971): 46–63.

Ladd, Everett Carll, Jr., and Charles Hadley. *Transformations of the American Party System*. New York: W. W. Norton, 1975.

Lanouette, William. "Turning Out the Vote: Reagan Seeking Larger Share of Blue-Collar Vote." *National Journal* (November 1, 1980): 1832–1835.

Larson, Edward J. *Summer for the Gods*. Cambridge: Harvard University Press, 1997.

Lawrence, David G. "The Collapse of the Democratic Majority: Economics and Vote Choice Since 1952." *Western Political Quarterly* 44, No. 4 (December 1991): 797–820.

_____. *The Collapse of the Democratic Presidential Majority*. Boulder: Westview Press, 1997.

Layman, Geoffrey C. "'Cultural Wars' in the American Party System." *American Politics Quarterly* 27, No. 1 (January 1999): 89–121.

Lemann, Nicholas. *The Promised Land*. New York: Knopf, 1991.

_____. "The New American Consensus." *New York Times Magazine* (November 1, 1998): 37–72.

Levine, Jeffrey, Edward G. Carmines, and Robert Huckfeldt. "The Rise of Ideology in the Post-New Deal Party System, 1972–1992." *American Politics Quarterly* 25, No. 1 (January 1997): 19–34.

Levitan, Sar A. *Programs in Aid of the Poor*. Baltimore: Johns Hopkins University Press, 1990.

Levy, Frank. *Dollars and Dreams: The Changing American Income Distribution*. New York: W. W. Norton, 1988.

_____. *The New Dollars and Dreams: American Incomes and Economic Change*. New York: Russell Sage Foundation, 1998.

Lewis, I. A., and William Schneider. "Black Voting, Bloc Voting, and the Democrats." *Public Opinion* (October/November 1985): 12–16.

Lipset, Seymour Martin. *Political Man*. Expanded edition. Baltimore: Johns Hopkins University Press, 1981.

Lott, Trent. "Prepared Text of Response of Trent Lott." *New York Times* (January 28, 1998): A-21.

Luttbeg, Norman R., and Michael M. Gant. *American Electoral Behavior 1952–1992*. Itasca, Ill.: F. E. Peacock, 1995.

MacInnes, Gordon. *Wrong, for all the Right Reasons: How White Liberals Have Been Undone by Race*. New York: New York University Press, 1996.

Magnet, Myron. *The Dream and the Nightmare: The Sixties Legacy to the Underclass*. New York: William Morrow, 1993.

Manley, John F. "The Significance of Class in American History and Politics." In *New Perspectives on American Politics*, edited by Lawrence C. Dodd and Calvin Jillson. Washington, D.C.: CQ Press, 1994.

Maraniss, David, and Michael Weisskopf. *Tell Newt to Shut Up*. New York: Touchstone, 1996.

Massey, Douglas S., and Nancy Denton. *American Apartheid: Segregation and the Making of the Underclass*. Cambridge: Harvard University Press, 1993.

Mathiowetz, Nancy A. "Errors in Reports of Occupation." *Public Opinion Quarterly* 56, No. 3 (fall 1992): 352–355.

Mayer, William G. *The Changing American Mind: How and Why American Public Opinion Changed Between 1960 and 1988*. Ann Arbor: University of Michigan Press, 1992.

_____. "Mass Partisanship, 1946–1996." In *Partisan Approcahes to Postwar American Politics*, edited by Byron E. Shafer, 186–219. Chatham, N.J.: Chatham House Publishers, 1998.

Mayhew, David R. *The Electoral Connection*. New Haven: Yale University Press, 1974a.

_____. "Congressional Elections: The Case of the Vanishing Marginals." *Polity* 6 (1974b): 295–317.

_____. *Divided We Govern*. New Haven: Yale University Press, 1991.

McClosky, Herbert. "Consensus and Ideology in American Politics." *American Political Science Review* 58. 361–382.

McNall, Scott, Rhonda Levine, and Rick Fantasia, eds. *Bringing Class Back In: Contemporary and Historical Perspective Perspectives*. Boulder: Westview Press, 1991.

McWilliams, Wilson C. "The Meaning of the Election." in *The Election of 1996: Reports and Interpretations*, edited by Gerald M. Pomper et al., 241–272. Chatham, N.J.: Chatham House, 1997.

Mellow, Wesley, and Hal Sider. "Accuracy of Labor Market Surveys: Evidence and Implications." *Journal of Labor Economics* 1, No. 4 (1983): 331–344.

Meyerson, Harold. "Wither the Democrats?" *American Prospect* (March–April 1996a): 79–88.

_____. "Clinton and the Democrats: The Party of Reluctant Retreat." *Dissent* (fall 1996b): 35–39.

Miller, Arthur H., Anne Hildreth, Kevin M. Leyden, and Christopher Wlezien. "Judging by the Company Candidates Keep." *Public Opinion* (July/August 1988): 14–16.

Miller, S. M., and Karen Marie Ferroggiaro. "Class Dismissed?" *American Prospect* 21 (spring 1995): 100–104.

Miller, Warren E., and J. Merrill Shanks. *The New American Voter*. Cambridge: Harvard University Press, 1996.

Miringoff, Marc, and Marque-Luisa Miringoff. *The Social Health of the Nation: How America is Really Doing*. New York: Oxford University Press, 1999.

Mishel, Lawrence, Jared Bernstein, and John Schmitt. *The State of Working America, 1996–97*. Armonk, N.Y.: M. E. Sharpe, 1997.

Mitchell, Alison. "G.O.P. Lawmaker Unveils Proposal For A Big Tax Cut." *New York Times* (June 10, 1997a): A-1.

_____. "Leaders of G.O.P. Seek to Overhaul Federal Tax Code." *New York Times* (September 28, 1997b): A-1.

_____. "Senior Republican Signals Big Battle for Large Tax Cuts." *New York Times* (April 29, 1998): A-20.

_____. "Two Parties Seek to Exploit a Relentless Suburban Boom." *New York Times* (May 4, 1999a): A-1.

_____. "Democrats Again Face Voter Doubt Over Values." *New York Times* (August 20, 1999b): A-18.

Moore, David W., Lydia Saad, Leslie McAneny, and Frank Newport. "Contract with America." *Gallup Poll Monthly* (November 1994): 20–21.

Mortenson, Thomas G. "Educational Attainment by Family Income 1970 to 1994." *Postsecondary Education Opportunity* 41 (November, 1995): 1–8.

Murray, Charles. *Losing Ground*. New York: Basic Books, 1984.

Nadeau, Richard, and Harold W. Stanley. "Class Polarization in Partisanship Among Native Southern Whites, 1952–1990." *American Journal of Political Science* 37, No. 3 (August 1993): 900–919.

Nardulli, Peter F., Jon K. Dalanger, and Donald E. Greco. "Voter Turnout in U.S. Presidential Elections: An Historical View and Some Speculation." *P.S.* 29, No. 3 (September 1996): 480–490.

Nasar, Sylvia. "Even Among the Well-Off, the Richest Get Richer." *New York Times* (March 5, 1992a): A-1.

_____. "Fed Gives New Evidence of 80s Gains by Richest." *New York Times* (April 21, 1992b): A-1.

New York Times. Editorial. "Does Race Doom the Democrats?" (November 20, 1988): A-32.

New York Times. "The Growth of Suburbs" (September 11, 1990): A-20.

Nie, Norman H., and Kristi Anderson. "Mass Belief Systems Revisited: Political Change and Attitude Structure." *Journal of Politics* 36, No. 3 (August 1974): 540–591.

Nie, Norman H., G. Bingham Powell Jr., and Kenneth Prewitt. "Social Structure and Political Participation: Developmental Relationships, I." *The American Political Science Review* 63, No. 2 (June 1969a): 316–378.

_____. "Social Structure and Political Participation: Developmental Relationships, II." *American Political Science Review* 63, No. 3 (September 1969b): 808–832.

Nie, Norman H., Sidney Verba, and John R. Petrocik. *The Changing American Voter*. Cambridge: Harvard University Press, 1976.

Nisbet, Robert A. "The Decline and Fall of Social Class." *Pacific Sociological Review* 2, No. 1 (spring 1959): 11–17.

Oreskes, Michael. "In Racial Politics, Democrats Losing More than Elections." *New York Times* (November 20, 1988): sec. 4, p. 1.

Orfield, Gary. *The Closing Door.* Chicago: University of Chicago Press, 1991.

Orfield, Gary, and John T. Yun. "Resegregation in American Schools." Civil Rights Project, Harvard University, Cambridge, Massachusetts, June 1999.

Page, Benjamin I., and Robert Y. Shapiro. *The Rational Public: Fifty Years of Trends in Americans' Policy Preferences.* Chicago: University of Chicago Press, 1992.

Palmer, John L., and Isabel V. Sawhill, eds. *The Reagan Experiment.* Washington, D.C.: The Urban Institute Press, 1982.

———. *The Reagan Record.* Cambridge: Ballinger Publishing, 1984.

Patterson, Thomas E. *Out of Order.* New York: Vintage, 1994.

Pear, Robert. "Government Lags in Steps to Widen Health Coverage." *New York Times* (August 9, 1998): A-1.

Penn, Mark J. "The New Democratic Electorate." *New Democrat* (January/February 1998): 6–9.

Petrocik, John R. *Party Coalitions: Realignments and the Decline of the New Deal Party System.* Chicago: University of Chicago Press, 1981.

———. "Realignment: New Party Coalitions and the Nationalization of the South." *Journal of Politics* 49, No. 2 (May 1987): 347–375.

———. "Reformulating the Party Coalitions: The 'Christian Democratic' Republicans." Paper presented at the American Political Science Association Meetings, Boston, August 1998.

Petrocik, John R., and Frederick T. Steeper. "The Political Landscape in 1988." *Public Opinion* (September/October 1987): 41–44.

Phillips, Kevin. *The Emerging Republican Majority.* New York: Anchor, 1969.

———. *The Politics of Rich and Poor: Wealth and the American Electorate in the Reagan Aftermath.* New York: Random House, 1991.

———. *Boiling Point: Republicans, Democrats and the Decline of Middle-Class Prosperity.* New York: HarperPerennial, 1993.

Pierce, John C. "Party Identification and the Changing Role of Ideology in American Politics." *Midwest Journal of Political Science* 14 (February 1970): 25–42.

Pierce, John C., and Paul R. Hagner. "Conceptualization and Party Identification: 1956–1976." *American Journal of Political Science* 26, No. 2 (May 1982): 377–387.

Pierce, Neal R., and Jerry Hagstrom. The Voters Send Carter a Message: Time for a Change—to Reagan." *National Journal* (November 8, 1980): 1876–1878.

Piven, Frances Fox, and Richard A. Cloward. *Why Americans Don't Vote.* New York: Pantheon Books, 1988.

———. *The Breaking of the American Social Compact.* New York: The New Press, 1997.

Plotnick, Robert D., Eugene Smolensky, Eirik Evenhouse, and Siobhan Reilly. "The Twentieth Century Record of Inequality and Poverty in the United States." Institute for Research on Poverty, Discussion Paper no. 1166–98. http://www.ssc.wisc.edu/irp/ (July 1998).

Polsby, Nelson. "The Institutionalization of the House of Representatives." *American Political Science Review* 62, No. 1 (March 1968): 144–168.

———. *Consequences of Party Reform.* New York: Oxford University Press, 1983.

Polsky, Andrew J. "The 1996 Elections and the Logic of Regime Politics." *Polity* 30, No. 1 (fall 1997): 153–166.

Pomper, Gerald M. "Toward a More Responsible Two-Party System? What, Again?" *Journal of Politics* 33, No. 4 (November 1971): 916–940.

_____. "From Confusion to Clarity: Issues and American Voters, 1956–1968." *American Political Science Review* 66, No. 2 (June 1972): 415–428.

Popkin, Samuel L. *The Reasoning Voter: Communication and Persuasion in Presidential Elections*. Chicago: University of Chicago Press, 1994.

Prothro, James W., and Charles W. Griggs. "Fundamental Principles of Democracy: Bases of Agreement and Disagreement." *Journal of Politics* 22 (1960): 276–294.

Purdum, Todd S. "California G.O.P. Faces a Crisis as Hispanic Voters Turn Away." *New York Times* (December 9, 1997): A-1.

Radosh, Ronald. *Divided They Fell: The Demise of the Democratic Party, 1964–1996*. New York: Free Press, 1996.

Rae, Nicol C. *The Decline and Fall of the Liberal Republicans from 1952 to the Present*. New York: Oxford University Press, 1989.

_____. "Class and Culture: American Political Cleavages in the Twentieth Century." *Western Political Quarterly* 45, No. 3 (September 1992): 629–650.

_____. "Party Factionalism, 1946–1996." In *Partisan Approaches to Postwar American Politics*, edited by Byron E. Shafer, 41–74. Chatham, N.J.: Chatham House Publishers, 1998.

Reddy, Patrick. "Democrats and Demographics." *American Enterprise* (March/April 1991): 65–67.

Reed, Adolph. "Race and the Disruption of the New Deal Coalition." *Urban Affairs Quarterly* 27 (1991): 326-333.

Reeher, Grant, and Joseph Cammarano. "In Search of the Angry White Male: Gender, Race, and Issues in the 1994 Elections." In *Midterm: The Elections in 1994 in Context*, edited by Philip A. Klinkner, 125–136.Boulder: Westview Press, 1996.

Reynolds, Farley. "Recent Trends in Births to Unmarried Women." Testimony presented to the U.S. Senate Committee on Finance, Washington, D.C., October 19, 1993.

Ricci, David. *The Transformation of American Politics: The New Washington and the Rise of Think Tanks*. New Haven, Conn.: Yale University Press, 1993.

Rieder, Jonathan. "The Rise of the 'Silent Majority.'" In *The Rise and Fall of the New Deal Order*, edited by Steve Fraser and Gary Gerstle, 243–268. Princeton: Princeton University Press, 1989.

Robinson, John. "The Ups and Downs and Ins and Outs of Ideology." *Public Opinion* (February/March 1984): 12–15.

Rohde, David W. *Parties and Leaders in the Postreform House*. Chicago: University of Chicago Press, 1991.

Rose, Sonya O. "Resuscitating Class." *Social Science History* 22, No. 1 (spring 1998): 19–27.

Rosenbaum, David E. "Leaders of the G.O.P. Begin to Assemble a Budget Framework of Their Own." *New York Times* (February 4, 1998): A-18.

Rosenstone, Steven J., and John Mark Hansen. *Mobilization, Participation, and Democracy in America.* New York: Macmillan, 1993.

Roth, Randolph. "Did Class Matter in American Politics?" *Historical Methods* 31, No. 1 (winter 1998).

Rothenberg, Stuart. "The No-Growth Party." *American Enterprise* (November/December 1991): 16–21.

Rusk, David. *Cities Without Suburbs.* 2d ed. Washington, D.C.: The Woodrow Wilson Center Press, 1995.

Ryscavage, Paul. *Income Inequality in America.* Armonk, N.Y.: M. E. Sharpe. 1999.

Sack, Kevin. "G.O.P. Moderates Meet to Frown Before an Unflattering Mirror." *New York Times* (February 15, 1999): A-1.

Sale, Kirkpatrick. *Power Shift.* New York: Random House, 1975.

Salmore, Stephen A., and Barbara G. Salmore. *Candidates, Parties, and Campaigns.* 2d ed. Washington: Congressional Quarterly Press, 1989.

Samuelson, Robert J. "A Schizophrenic Party." *National Journal* (August 23, 1980): 1408.

_____. *The Good Life and Its Discontents.* New York: Vintage Books, 1997.

Sanders, Arthur. "The Meaning of Party Images." *Western Political Quarterly* 41, No. 3 (September 1988): 583–599.

_____. *Victory.* Armonk, N.Y.: M. E. Sharpe, 1992.

Sass, Steven A. *The Promise of Private Pensions: The First Hundred Years.* Cambridge: Harvard University Press, 1997.

Saunders, Jennifer L. "Party Unity Voting in the U.S. House of Representatives: A Look at the Moderates." Paper presented at the Midwest Political Science Association Meeting, Chicago, Illinois, April 1998.

Scammon, Richard M., and Ben J. Wattenberg. *The Real Majority.* New York: Coward-McCann, 1970.

Schlozman, Kay Lehman, and Sidney Verba. *Injury to Insult: Unemployment, Class and Political Response.* Cambridge: Harvard University Press, 1979.

Schneider, William. "The Divided Electorate." *National Journal* (October 29, 1983): 2200–2210.

_____. "An Uncertain Consensus." *National Journal* (November 10, 1984): 2130–2132.

_____. "The New Shape of American Politics." *Atlantic Monthly* (January 1987): 39–54.

_____. "An Insider's View of the Election." *Atlantic Monthly* (July 1988): 29–57.

_____. "JFK's Children: The Class of 1974." *Atlantic Monthly* (March 1989): 35–58.

_____. "The Suburban Century Begins." *Atlantic Monthly* (July 1992): 33–44.

Schoenberger, Robert A., and David R. Segal. "The Ecology of Dissent: The Southern Wallace Vote in 1968." *Midwest Journal of Political Science* 15, No. 3 (August 1971): 583–586.

Schulman, Mark A., and Gerald M. Pomper. "Variability in Electoral Behavior: Longitudinal Perspectives from Causal Modeling." *American Journal of Political Science* 19, 1 (February 1975): 1–18.

Schwarz, John E. *America's Hidden Success.* Rev. ed. New York: W. W. Norton, 1988.

_____. *Illusions of Opportunity: The American Dream in Question.* New York: W. W. Norton, 1997.

Schwartz, Tony. "The Test Under Stress." *New York Times Magazine* (January 10, 1999): 30–35 and passim.

Scicchitano, Michael J., and Richard K. Scher. "Florida: Political Change, 1950–1996." In *The New Politics of the Old South*, edited by Charles S. Bullock and Mark J. Rozell, 227–244. Lanham, Md.: Rowman and Littlefield, 1998.

Sears, David O., Richard Rlau., Tom R. Tyler, and Harris M. Allen Jr. "Self-Interest vs. Symbolic Politics in Policy Attitudes and Presidential Voting." *American Political Science Review* 74, No. 3 (September 1980): 670–684.

Serra, George. "What's in it for Me: The Impact of Congressional Casework on Incumbent Evaluation." *American Politics Quarterly* 22 (1994): 403–420.

Shafer, Byron E. "The Democratic Party Salvation Industry." *Public Opinion* (June/July 1985): 45–49.

Shafer, Byron E., ed. *The End of Realignment.* Madison, Wisc.: University of Wisconsin Press, 1991.

Shapiro, Isaac, and Robert Greenstein. "The Widening Income Gap." Washington, D.C.: Center on Budget and Policy Priorities, September 4, 1999.

Shea, Daniel M. "The Passing of Realignment and the Advent of the 'Base-Less' Party System." *American Politics Quarterly* 27, No. 1 (January 1999): 33–57.

Shingles, Richard D. "Class, Status, and Support for Government Aid to Disadvantaged Groups." *Journal of Politics* 51, No. 4 (November 1989): 933–962.

Shively, W. Phillips. "A Reinterpretation of the New Deal Realignment." *Public Opinion Quarterly* 35 (winter 1971): 621–624.

Smith, Robert C. *We Have No Leaders.* Albany: SUNY Press, 1996.

Speel, Robert W. *Changing Patterns of Voting in the Northern United States: Electoral Realignment 1952–1996.* University Park: Pennsylvania State University, 1998.

Stanley, Harold W. "Southern Partisan Changes: Dealignment, Realignment, or Both?" *Journal of Politics* 50, No. 1 (February 1988): 64–88.

Stanley, Harold W., William T. Bianco, and Richard G. Niemi. "Partisanship and Group Support Over Time: A Multivariate Analysis." *American Political Science Review* 80, No. 3 (September 1986): 969–976.

Stanley, Harold W., and David S. Castle. "Partisan Changes in the South: Making Sense of Scholarly Dissonance." In *The South's New Politics*, edited by Robert H. Swansbrough and David M. Brodsky, 238–252. Columbia: University of South Carolina Press, 1988.

Stanley, Harold W., and Richard G. Niemi. "Partisanship and Group Support, 1952–1988." *American Politics Quarterly* 19, No. 2 (April 1991): 189–210.

––––––. "The Demise of the New Deal Coalition: Partisanship and Group Support, 1952–1992." In *Democracy's Feast: Elections in America*, edited by Herbert F. Weisberg, 220–240. Chatham, N.J.: Chatham House, 1995.

Stefancic, Jean, and Richard Delgado. *No Mercy: How Conservative Think Tanks and Foundations Changed America's Social Agenda.* Philadelphia: Temple University Press, 1997.

Stevenson, Richard W. "Seeking Common Ground on Federal Tax Cut." *New York Times* (July 25, 1999): 18.

Stevenson, Richard W., and Michael R. Kagay. "Republicans' Image Eroding Fast, Poll Shows." *New York Times* (December 19, 1998): A-1.

Stone, Walter J., Ronald B. Rapoport, and Alan I. Abramowitz. "The Reagan Revolution and Party Polarization in the 1980s." In *The Parties Respond*, edited by Sandy Maisel, 67–93. Boulder: Westview Press, 1990.

Stonecash, Jeffrey M. "Fiscal Centralization in the American States: Increasing Similarity and Persisting Diversity." *Publius* 13, No. 4 (fall 1983): 123–137.

_____. "Fiscal Centralization in the American States: Findings from Another Perspective." *Public Budgeting and Finance* 8, No. 4 (winter 1988): 81–89.

_____. "Political Cleavage in Gubernatorial and Legislative Elections: The Nature of Inter-Party Competition in New York Elections, 1970–1982." *Western Political Quarterly* 42, No. 1 (March 1989): 69–81.

_____. "'Split' Constituencies and the Impact of Party Control." *Social Science History* 16, No. 3 (fall 1992): 455–477.

_____. "The Politics of State–Local Fiscal Relations." In Russell L. Hanson, ed., *Governing Partners*, 75–91. Boulder: Westview Press, 1998.

_____. "Class and American Politics: The Case of the Missing Analysis." Paper presented at the American Political Science Association Meeting, Boston, September 1998.

_____. "Affluence, Inequality and Political Division in American Politics, 1936–1998." Paper presented at the American Political Science Association Meeting, Atlanta, Georgia, September 1999.

_____. "The Declining Significance of Self-Identified Class for Class Divisions in American Politics." Paper presented at the New England Political Science Association Meeting, Providence, Rhode Island, April 1999.

_____. "Political Cleavage in State Legislative Houses." *Legislative Studies Quarterly* 24, No. 2 (May 1999d): 281–302.

Stonecash, Jeffrey M., and Anna Agathangelou. "Trends in the Partisan Composition of State Legislatures: A Response to Fiorina." *American Political Science Review* 91, No. 1 (March 1997): 148–155.

Stonecash, Jeffrey M., and Mark D. Brewer. "Race, Class, and Political Change in the South." Paper presented at the Midwest Political Science Association Meeting, Chicago, Illinois, April 1999.

Stonecash, Jeffrey M., and Nicole R. Lindstrom. "Emerging Party Cleavages in the U.S. House of Representatives." *American Politics Quarterly* 27, No. 1 (January 1999): 58–88.

Stonecash, Jeffrey M., and Mack D. Mariani. "Republican Gains in the House in the 1994 House Elections: Class Polarization in American Politics." *Political Science Quarterly* (forthcoming 2000).

Stonecash, Jeffrey M., Mark D. Brewer, Mary P. McGuire, R. Eric Petersen, and Lori Beth Way. "Class and Party: Secular Realignment and the Survival of Democrats Outside the South." *Political Research Quarterly* (forthcoming 2000).

Stouffer, Samuel. *Communism, Conformity, and Civil Liberties*. New York: Doubleday, 1955.

Strahan, Randall W. "Partisan Officeholders, 1946–1996." In *Partisan Approcahes to Postwar American Politics*, edited by Byron E. Shafer, 5–40. Chatham, N.J.: Chatham House, 1998.

Sullivan, John L., James Pierson, and George E. Marcus. "An Alternative Conceptualization of Political Tolerance: Illusory Increases 1950s–1970s." *American Political Science Review* 73, No. 3 (September 1979): 781–794.

Sundquist, James L. *Politics and Policy: The Eisenhower, Kennedy, and Johnson Years*. Washington, D.C.: Brookings Institution, 1968.

_____."Whither the American Party System?" *Political Science Quarterly* 88, No. 4 (winter 1973): 559–581.

_____. *Dynamics of the Party System: Alignment and Realignment of Political Parties in the United States*. Rev. ed. Washington, D.C.: Brookings Institution, 1983.

_____. "Whither the American Party System?—Revisited?" *Political Science Quarterly* 98, No. 4 (winter 1983–1984): 573–593.

_____. "The 1984 Election: How Much Realignment: How Much Realignment?" *Brookings Review* (winter 1985): 8–15.

Taylor, Andrew J. "The Ideological Development of the Parties in Washington, 1947–1994." *Polity* 29, No. 2 (winter 1996): 273–292.

Teixeira, Ruy A. "Economic Change and the Middle-Class Revolt Against the Democratic Party." In *The Broken Contract: Changing Relationships Between Americans and Their Government, edited by Stephen Craig, 67–84*. Boulder: Westview, 1996.

_____. "Finding the Real Center." *Dissent* (spring 1997): 51–59.

Teixeira, Ruy A., and Joel Rogers. "Volatile Voters: Declining Living Standards and Non-College Educated Whites." Economic Policy Institute, Working Paper No. 116, August 8, 1996.

Thomas, Scott J. "Do Incumbent Campaign Expenditures Matter?" *Journal of Politics* 51, No. 4 (November 1989): 965–976.

Tolchin, Susan J. *The Angry American: How Voter Rage Is Changing the Nation*. Boulder: Westview Press, 1996.

Trilling, Richard J. *Party Image and Electoral Behavior*. New York: John Wiley, 1976.

Turner, John A., and Daniel J. Beller, eds. *Trends in Pensions 1992*. Washington, D.C.: U.S. Department of Labor, Pension and Welfare Benefits Administration, 1992.

Uchitelle, Louis. "The American Middle: Just Getting By." *New York Times* (August 1, 1999): sec. 3, 1.

U.S. Bureau of the Census, *Congressional District Data Book*. (Districts of the 88th Congress)—A Statistical Abstract Supplement. U.S. Government Printing Office, Washington, D.C., 1963.

U.S. Bureau of the Census, *Statistical Abstract of the United States*. U.S. Government Printing Office, Washington, D.C., 1956.

U.S. Bureau of the Census, *Statistical Abstract of the United States*. U.S. Government Printing Office, Washington, D.C., 1965.

U.S. Bureau of the Census, *Statistical Abstract of the United States*. U.S. Government Printing Office, Washington, D.C., 1975.

U.S. Bureau of the Census, *Statistical Abstract of the United States*. U.S. Government Printing Office, Washington, D.C., 1994.

U.S. Immigration and Naturalization Service. *Statistical Yearbook of the Immigration and Naturalization Service, 1996*. Washington, D.C: U.S. Government Printing Office, 1997.

Wattenberg, Ben J. *Values Matter Most*. Washington, D.C.: Regnery, 1995.

Wattenberg, Martin P. *The Decline of American Political Parties, 1952–1992*. Cambridge: Harvard University Press, 1992.

_____. *The Decline of American Political Parties, 1952–1994*. Cambridge: Harvard University Press, 1996.

Weakliem, David, and Anthony Heath. "Race versus Class: Racial Composition and Class Voting, 1936–1992." *Social Forces* 75 (1997): 939–956.

Weisberg, Herbert F., Audrey A. Haynes, and Jon A. Krosnick. "Social Group Polarization in 1992." In *Democracy's Feast: Elections in America*, edited by Herbert F. Weisberg, 241–259. Chatham, N.J.: Chatham House, 1995.

Weissberg, Robert. "The Democratic Party and the Conflict over Racial Policy." In *Do Elections Matter*, 2d ed., edited by Benjamin Ginsberg and Alan Stone, 150–170. Armonk, N.Y.: M. E. Sharpe, 1991.

Wells, Robert M. "Sharp Ideological Divisions Mark Student Loan Battle." *Congressional Quarterly Weekly* (December 9, 1995): 3740–3741.

Wiebe, Robert H. *The Search for Order 1877–1920*. New York: Hill and Wang, 1967.

Wilensky, Harold L. "Class, Class Consciousness, and American Workers." In *Labor in a Changing America*, edited by William Haber, 12–28. New York: Basic Books, 1966.

Wills, Gary. "What Happened to the Revolution?" *New York Review of Books* (June 6, 1996): 11–16.

_____. "The Would-Be Progressive." *New York Review of Books* (1997): 13–16.

Wilson, James Q. "Realignment at the Top, Dealignment at the Bottom." In *The American Elections of 1984*, edited by Austin Ranney, 297–311. Washington, D.C: American Enterprise Institute, published by Duke University Press, 1985.

Wlezien, Carol, and Arthur H. Miller. "Social Groups and Political Judgments." *Social Science Quarterly* 78, No. 3 (September 1997): 625–640.

Wright, Gerald C., Jr. "Community Structure and Voting in the South." *Public Opinion Quarterly* 42, No. 2 (summer 1976): 200–215.

Index